MEMBERS
OF TWO WORLDS

To Danilo Dolci
and his collaborators —
in gratitude

MEMBERS
OF TWO WORLDS

A Development Study
of Three Villages in Western Sicily

By

Johan Galtung

1971

Columbia University Press

New York and London

ISBN: 0–231–03418–0

Library of Congress Catalog Card Number: 70–114258

PUBLISHED IN OSLO, NORWAY,
FOR SCANDINAVIAN UNIVERSITY BOOKS
FOR THE SERIES PRIO MONOGRAPHS FROM
THE INTERNATIONAL PEACE RESEARCH INSTITUTE,
OSLO, BY UNIVERSITETSFORLAGET

PUBLISHED IN
THE UNITED STATES OF AMERICA AND CANADA BY
COLUMBIA UNIVERSITY PRESS, NEW YORK

Printed in Norway by Aktietrykkeriet i Trondhjem

Preface

This book is an outsider's effort to explore local conditions using some of the tools of social science, and to present a report on what he has found. It is not primarily a study of Western Sicily, but an elaboration of some theories of development using three villages in Western Sicily as an empirical basis to guide us in our explorations. Thus, it should be emphasized right from the beginning that we do not claim the same kind of knowledge and insight into Western Sicily that only the real experts on the region can claim — with varying degrees of justification — and the reader will search in vain for passages in the present book that will make local colors come alive. The scope of this book is limited by its method — we do not try to imitate what others with a different approach would do much better, but rather try to develop a line of reasoning that can be explored with the kind of data we have at our disposal. As such it is intended as a contribution to the literature on the theory of development in general, and on Sicily in particular.

Why Sicily? Because I have visited it many times from 1956 onwards, and have been struck, amazed, almost awed by the resistance to change in that pocket of European underdevelopment known as Western Sicily. My guide from the first was Danilo Dolci, whom I met in the slums of Palermo and the streets of misery in Partinico back in January 1957. Dolci, himself in some ways an outsider but with a more intimate acquaintance with Sicily than anyone else I could find, had dedicated himself to its people with all of his rich personality and encouraged me to return and make a sociological study on the structure, the social basis of this traditionalism. There were several returns, plans and small pilot projects until the present data were finally collected during the fall of 1960, with the gratefully acknowledged assistance of Dolci himself, the *Centro*

Studi e Iniziative per la piena occupazione, created by him and his wonderful collaborators of whom I would particularly like to thank Franco Alasia and the late Teresio Bonini. Teresio was not only the infallible link between the local scene and the outsider, and a provider of data, but also a source of insights and good ideas, of conscientious work in the phases of data collection and data analysis. Without him, the team of interviewers provided by the Centro and the seminars and conferences during which ideas were developed, would not have materialized. His premature death was a terrible blow.

The study was one of the first projects to be undertaken by the emerging peace research institute in Oslo, at that time organized as the Section for Research on Conflict and Peace at the Institute for Social Research, Oslo. It was included in the program of research because of the hunch, which today looks utterly trivial, that the problems listed under 'development' and the problems listed under 'peace' overlap so much that they can be seen as two sides of the same coin or perhaps rather die, since there are indeed also other sides.

For those who believe that projects have to be expensive the budget of the data collection can be stated: $500. This money was made available partly by the Centro in Partinico and partly by the Norwegian Danilo Dolci Committee, 'Danilo Dolcis norske venner', who also contributed to the study by inviting Teresio Bonini to Oslo. To all of them, and to the Institute for Social Research for all kinds of assistance with data prosessing and administration, and to Arvid Amundsen, Wenche Nergård, Siri P. Hole, Marit Halle and Mari H. Ruge for assistance with the preparation of data for analysis, my most sincere thanks.

I have been living with this manuscript for a long time and been chasing the heroes and the villains of the story — the reader will get to know them as the *sensates*, the *movers* and the *familists* — on all kinds of cards and machines and tables in many countries on several continents. Not that so much time has been spent altogether on the analysis, it is rather that I have felt I needed contact with these personages over a longer time span to acquaint myself better with them. And not that I now feel I really know them either. I have benefited greatly from the opportunity to meet them over and over again at other places, and have watched them blend and mix and penetrate into personalities here and there all around the world — not only in these three villages in Western Sicily. They are abstractions, needless to say, but I nevertheless hope that the book will show that they are useful abstractions. That leads me to my expression of gratitude to P. Sorokin, D. Lerner and E. Banfield,

who introduced me to these characters through their inspiring books —
and with the hope that they will not feel I have profaned their works,
for which I have the highest esteem.

And finally, to Ingrid Eide, my good colleague and friend for her
ever perceptive and stimulating comments and criticism, for her compassion with the people this work is about and for her companionship
and keen observations in many countries in different parts of the world.

Johan Galtung

Contents

1. The old world and the new

1.1. Introduction

It is impossible not to feel attached to that island of human endeavor called Sicily, and that is not said at the beginning of this study to pay homage to the region and its inhabitants in the traditional social scientist's effort to be forgiven all he may have to say in the course of this analysis that may look less flattering. It is simply one of these facts so many people experience and that not even the trickiest and least talented effort to catch tourists will be quite able to eliminate. Lampedusa, who no doubt will leave his imprint on many books that deal with Sicily for decades to come, has said about 'the real Sicily' that it is

> ... aridly undulating to the horizon in hillock after hillock, comfortless and irrational, with no lines that the mind could grasp, conceived apparently in a delirious moment of creation; a sea suddenly petrified at the instant when a change of wind had flung waves into frenzy.[1]

Maybe this is 'the real Sicily'. Or maybe the real Sicily is in the square pattern of Messina or in the plains of Catania or even in the distant look at the Capo de Spartivento from the Taormina town terrace; in the mafia of Mussomeli or hidden under the mosaics showing those unlikely swimming beauties in bikinis at the Piazzo Armerina or in the squalor of the Cortile Cascino in Palermo — or maybe it has already left by train to the North and works as a mechanic or scientist in Torino or a vendor of oranges at the Piazza del Duomo in Milano — no attempt will be made here to define the 'real' Sicily. But those sad hills so obviously created for eternity can give to the Northerner a sense of identity with the history of the Western world, for good and for bad, a sense of belonging that is turned into a sense of gratefulness. The hills

1

may be scorched by the *soleone* — the sun lion — they may be bathing in the clearest moonlight or drenched in a moment's rain (never long in duration, however wicked in its frenzy) — they look equally unperturbed and irritatingly worldly-wise as if contemplating with compassion these five million human beings whose lot it is to try to extract from them anything edible or otherwise useful.

All efforts to catch the truth about Sicily in a single formula are doomed; they will never suffice to cover an island and a people about which everything and anything can be said with some grain of truth. To quote Lampedusa again, just to illustrate this point:

> In Sicily it doesn't matter whether things are done well or done badly; the sin which we Sicilians never forgive is simply that of 'doing' at all.[2]

This has no doubt been as great fun to write as it is to read — and yet, is it the truth? Take Enna early in the morning: the sun rising, myriads of people moving from their houses to their places of work, some with mules and donkeys, some with the briefcases of the *uomini degl' affari*, some to buy their daily bread and some to make it; no loafers they! Or the quarries of Central Sicily, with monotonous knocking rhythms shaking the landscape — or the women of the most arid and desolate villages of the interior, constantly striving to make ends meet, carrying water, spreading tomato juice in the sun for drying — or their husbands winnowing in the hottest sunshine, breathing the dust of the grain — or the smallest children in the slums of Palermo, constantly watching for a chance to do some business, usually not the most perfect by moral standards elsewhere, but lazy? *No.* True, most things they do are old things, but they are carried out, from four-thirty in the morning when the train of mules and cattle leaves the shelters in the mountain village till late, late at night when the boats do their fishing for what little catch generations of Phoenicians, Greeks and Romans have left behind.

But, it may object, what about rows and rows of people sitting in the *piazza*? What about stopping in a car with foreign license plates, and immediately being surrounded by scores of seemingly non-working locals, with inquiring, somewhat intense eyes, with a brownish red complexion, short of stature — always dressed in something blue, in dungarees of different kinds and qualities and in different stages of their life cycles from the shining new to the mosaically patched: Are these people really 'doing' anything at all? *Yes.* They are not like teenagers of the North, lying on the beach enjoying themselves and each other.

2

Rather, sitting at the *piazza* is a form of existence that may have its parallel in newspaper reading, in lunch-hour conversations, in long family evenings discussing budgets and plans for tomorrow — but certainly not in completely purposeless relaxation. Men from the North who do not like to be observed during their hours of leisure and who like to give an impression of constant activity and vigilance may not easily understand men from the South with the opposite standards. But if one looks at just one of the numerous shops, figures out how many hours a week the shopkeeper is at work and compares it to the shopkeeper in the North, surrounded and protected by rules and regulations concerning his opening and closing hours, then one may perhaps judge who works harder, certainly not at the same level of exchange of goods and money, but in terms of putting forth considerably more effort.

One may visit the island year after year until it becomes like a passion to see Sicily again, to smell its infinite variety of odors, foul and delicate — to see the undulating hills hailed by Lampedusa, to walk in moonlight over the plateaus of the interior and wonder whether glittering lights are stars or fires from distant villages — not to mention talking with them, the people who seem to be some centuries behind or perhaps ahead of others as judged by the wisdom of their reflections, although the reflections have a tendency rarely to translate into real action. Or one can arrive early in the morning with one of those white ships from Napoli and see the entire Conca d'Oro, with Monte Pellegrino painted in dry, dry brownish color as Palermo becomes visible — or by plane from Reggio Calabria, crossing over completely dry riverbeds, large as valleys with the Sicilian landscape with all these incredible, elaborate wrinkles (so marvelously fit for banditry, so maladapted to any large-scale agriculture or industry) — or one can come late at night by train to Taormina and wake up to see Etna painted a glowing red in the morning sun, and the placid sea glittering below — whatever one does will certainly give more than anyone can give back.

And yet, all these elements of charm and splendor, past and present, are only elements in an existence which for the majority of the people is essentially one of 'backwardness'. There is no need to spell out that word or its synonym in any detail here: the elements of underdevelopment are well known and are all present in Sicily for everybody to see and feel. But nobody can feel them like the Sicilians living with them, having 'backwardness' and 'dominance' not as categories but as their lives. Lampedusa applied his literary genius to the uppermost layer of a decaying feudal order; through his magnifying glass the reader is invited to witness patterns of dissolution in a social order and in a system of belief, a creed, a social credo. But he did not direct his instrument lower down in society, to the layers on which the whole Gattopardo existence was based, if anything but firmly. Lampedusa did not tell the reader how human dignity and self-respect and self-reliance easily disappear or never develop fully in people deprived of anything but the shadow of power and knowledge. But no author can ever do full justice to any theme, since his very effort only serves to make more clear, by contrast, the elements he has left out. Others have been the literary spokesmen of the Sicilian underdogs, brilliant, lucid and artistic — but also with their limitations.

The present work certainly does not have pretensions in the direction of being literary or complete in any sense. It is always presumptuous to write about foreign peoples and countries, especially when the object — unlike the illiterate, remote, isolated societies so often chosen by social anthropologists — is highly articulate and to some extent protecting itself against intrusion. But this is not one more book about Sicily or Western Sicily, it is one more book in the literature on the greatest human drama of our time, *the great transition*, often characterized by a multitude of word pairs, such as 'traditional-modern', 'agricultural-industrial', 'poor-rich', 'undeveloped-underdeveloped-developing-developed', 'dominated-autonomous', etc., using data collected in three villages in Western Sicily as a basis for some explorations in the theory of development. Every bit of understanding in this field will always be in demand by practitioners and theoreticians, and if one feels related to both, there is no need to explain further the motives in making this investigation.

Nor is it necessary to add to what has already been said to explain why Sicily was chosen as the site for the study. We were attracted by

> ... this landscape which knows no mean between sensuous slackness and hellish drought; which is never petty, never ordinary, never relaxed, as a country made for rational beings to live in should be; this country of ours in which the inferno around Randazzo is a few miles from the loveliness of Taormina Bay; this climate which inflicts us with feverish months at a temperature of a hundred and four — and then these rains, which are always tempestuous and set dry river beds to frenzy, drown beasts and men on the very spot where two weeks before both had been dying of thirst.[3]

We wanted this background for a study of some aspects of *the great transition*. But have we chosen the 'inferno around Randazzo' rather than the 'loveliness of Taormina Bay' to blacken Sicily, as Danilo Dolci is so often accused of? No, both could be done, and studies comparing communities that 'develop' and communites that 'stagnate' will always be of value. But we wanted the vantage point of the stable, traditional and old precisely because it represented the contrast to the developing societies of Northern Italy and Northern Europe, to understand better why the villages did not develop further. The villages are representative of 'backwardness', but they are not for that reason representative of all of Sicily, or Southern Italy, or 'the underdeveloped world'. Yet, similar as they are, they are still different enough to provide us with the necessary differentiation for a study of factors preventing the transition. The three villages, thus, are our *stage*, but the transition is our *theme*.

And by these words of introduction, we now turn to the study, and start with a general effort to develop a perspective on socio-economic development.[4]

1.2. *Socio-economic development: a bird's eye view*

To study socio-economic *change* in general and socio-economic *development* in particular, some kind of perspective on these giant processes is, if not indispensable, at least useful to direct research and to develop a focus. At the same time all efforts to extract from the bewildering complexity of these processes some kind of simple focus, an arrow so to speak, are doomed to be unsatisfactory for some, perhaps for most students in the field. This is not only due to the complexity of the phenomenon, but also to the myopia students of the field of development usually develop, partly due to their disciplinary background and corresponding conceptual provincialism, partly due to the principle that perspectives once gained are hard to lose. Finally, there is the danger of committing a sin known as 'evolutionism'.[1] Nevertheless, let us make an effort.

First of all, we must distinguish between 'socio-economic development' on the one hand and some competitive terms from economics and sociology, more particularly the terms 'economic growth' and 'social change' on the other. By 'economic growth' we shall mean the rate of increase in something of which GNP per capita is *one* indicator.[2] This 'something', then, can be referred to as *economic development*, or the average amount of economic value at the disposal of the individual members of the society or social system we are studying. *Economic growth*, thus, is a question of having increments in wealth per capita, of how much more there is to distribute between the members of the social order (whether and how it is distributed is another matter). With a clear definition of wealth, and a simple counting of the number of heads, this is a uni-dimensional variable, relatively easily measured as Δ GNP per capita/Δ t (where Δ t usually is one year).

By 'social change' we shall mean any change in the social structure, where 'structure' is taken to mean a set of social systems, 'system' being defined as a set of statuses in interaction, with 'status' in turn being a set of roles and a 'role', finally, being a set of norms.[3] The change can be in any direction, toward more or less complexity, more or less balance or whatever dimension one might choose to use — it is simply a change, a difference over time. Thus, it is different from 'development', which is a term that should only be used for particular types of changes. And it differs from 'mobility', which merely means that the same positions in the same structure are filled with new people, with no changes in the structure.

More particularly, there are three requirements that should be fulfilled before the term 'development' is used:

1) It should be possible to describe the change in *uni-dimensional* terms — directly or by using index formation.
2) The dimension should be *ordinal*, i.e. there should be a clear ordering of states of the system from 'less developed' to 'more developed'.
3) There should be a *general, overall trend in world history* from the 'less developed' to the 'more developed' along the dimension.

By this we do not mean to imply that there is an evaluation involved in the sense that the 'more developed' is necessarily 'better' in any or all senses. Rather, the idea is only that development is a movement over time along some dimension for at least a class of systems or societies — admitting relapses and stationary states so that the statement will at most be true in a general, statistical sense.[4]

In this sense the economic change found in most contemporary societies is development, economic development — but we are interested in exploring other types of socio-economic development, richer in content and implications. These other types are often seen as *conditions* or *consequences* of economic growth, but we shall be less interested in that perspective and more interested in studying them in their own right.

To arrive at what we consider a fruitful definition of development, we shall start by using the nature-culture dichotomy, and the old image of man as a culture-bearing animal. Nature is what *is* when we remove

6

man; culture is something man adds to it; it is form, structure, patterns of evaluation, but above all it is symbolic.[5] Man stands between the two; he cannot subsist without a link with nature to feed, clothe and shelter him, nor can he help developing culture; thus it has always been and thus it will always remain.

But — and that is the point — the proportion of time spent by the individual human being extracting and processing (at a low level) from nature what he needs, and the time spent in other pursuits (such as high-level processing), which we may then try to identify with culture, may vary. To study this, time-budgets for representative samples of human beings in space and time would be needed — and those would be rather difficult to obtain.[6] Instead one might use another indicator that corresponds much better to the way census data are collected and presented: the proportion of people having as their predominant occupation the extraction of raw materials from nature and/or the subsequent processing of them, and the proportion of people in other occupations. Whereas the time-budget measure would give us some idea as to where the *individual* stands between nature and culture, the second measure would suggest to us where the *society* or social system is standing; and if one is mainly interested in the development of societies and the comparison of them, the second approach would be better (in comparing individuals the first approach would be appropriate). However, it presupposes that one accepts the assumption that all human beings count equally much when such comparisons are made — and we see no important reason why this cannot be accepted here.[7]

The usage of the terms above immediately suggests that we are leaning heavily on Colin Clark, his predecessors and successors,[8] and this is certainly true. Extraction from nature is usually identified as the *primary* sector of the economy, processing as the *secondary* sector, and the *tertiary* sector is all the rest. However, there are well-known difficulties with this distinction, just as we get into troubles when we try to bring in the even more diffuse nature-culture distinction. Some of these difficulties will now be commented upon.

First of all, since the tertiary category is a residual category one would expect to find very different types of human pursuits and occupations in it — and this is indeed the case. Moreover, since the general world trend, indeed, is in the direction of increasing proportions in the tertiary sector one would expect even more differentiations to take place in that sector so that the spectrum becomes even wider. Today one might distinguish between such sub-sectors as trade and commerce, transportation (of goods/passengers), communication (of messages), administration, production of cultural goods, professions and leisure.[9] But all these have in common that there is neither extraction nor is there processing; there is distribution, administration and some other, completely different things.

Secondly, the primary category is often identified with hunting, gathering, lumbering, fishing, agriculture, etc. However, this is dangerous for it overlooks the rapid changes these fields are undergoing. Modern 'industrial farming' and 'industrial fishing' have more in common with a car factory than with hunting-gathering, where degree of processing is concerned, and should, consequently, rather be classified as secondary occupations. 'Nature' as such is barely touched directly, and with further development of the technology may not even be seen: a cow is seen as a machine whose input is grass, etc. and whose output is milk and meat; a fish is another machine whose input is plankton and whose output is protein — and the question is whether they are still the most efficient and economical machines or whether they could suitably be replaced by something 'artificial', man-made, with a better incremental capital/output ratio. In short, the borderline between the primary and the secondary sectors goes between low and high degrees of processing, not between countryside and city[10] for instance.

Thirdly, there is the basic question of what this has to do with the nature-culture distinction. One may accept that a society where the overwhelming majority is occupied with hunting-gathering is predominantly in the primary sector and close to 'nature', whereas a society where automation of various kinds has brought the percentages in the primary and in the secondary sectors down to 5 % in each, leaving 90 % in the tertiary sector,[11] is close to 'culture'. In these two societies man has liberated himself from nature to highly different degrees, not in the sense of being independent of nature — he will never be that — but in the sense of domesticating and dominating nature. Whether he is dominating or dominated by others is another question, whether his life is rich still another one.

And there are difficult problems in between. The artisan who gives form to a piece of wood or a piece of metal, is he closer to 'nature' or 'culture'? And the industrial worker or workers, doing essentially the same? In short, what about the entire secondary sector? We could say that they are precisely in between, that *processing consists of imprinting culture on nature*. Of course, the scientist, the artist, the priest, the politician, etc. are even further removed from nature in the sense that nature comes to them in a highly processed or highly symbolic form. The sacrificial lamb is a symbol to the priest and to the 'primitive' hunter-gatherer, yet meat to the butcher and to the ordinary consumer. But what about the tradesman, especially him who deals in goods with a very low degree of processing? Is he closer to culture or to nature?

This may be hairsplitting, but we would claim the former, for the tradesman, whether he works in a barter, money or credit economy, is dealing with value rather than with the concrete goods. He operates at a higher level of symbolism since he has abstracted from the concrete piece of goods at hand its *value*, and acts by comparing values. He does not merely subsist on what he has extracted. One might, however, draw the distinction (related to the distinction between a barter and a money economy) between him who performs only one kind of exchange, with the goods he has himself extracted and for whom exchange is not a generalized operation but a very concrete act, and him who works at a higher level of abstraction with exchange as such, regardless of what and how many kinds of goods. Only the latter works in the tertiary sector proper; the former has only added some particular exchange activity to his predominantly primary sector type of work. However, a time-budget analysis would here bring out the details more clearly.

With these comments, and fully aware of the many difficulties one encounters when one really tries to operationalize all this, we feel we have given some reasons why one can use the distinctions made in the Clark school as at least indicators of what we are thinking of when we talk about development as 'transition from nature to culture', as the gradual mastery of nature and the cultural embroidery of man's existence. Thus, socio-economic development is that kind of social change that leads in the direction of the liberation of man from direct contact with nature in the production process and permits him to pursue other interests. And if one should use one simple indicator currently used in statistical yearbooks, etc., it would be the percentage of the working population *not* working in the primary sector. The rate of increase in this variable would, then, be socio-economic *growth*.

Let us now return to economic development. Clearly, the definition of (horizontal) socio-economic development given above does not presuppose that the societies are 'rich' in the usual sense of having high GNP per capita. Essentially we get a four-fold situation as in Table 1.2.1. (p. 10)

The main diagonal in this Table is filled with well-known entries, indicating that the population in the poor countries is by and large working in the primary sector, whereas the population in the rich coun-

Table 1.2.1. *The relation between socio-economic development and economic development*

		Economic development	
		Poor societies	*Rich societies*
Socio-economic	*Low*	'Developing' countries	
development	*High*		'Developed' countries

tries has a much higher loading in the secondary and tertiary sectors. Although nobody would argue that this correlation[12] is perfect, the general trend is certainly in that direction — so much so that it does not seem far-fetched to build a theory of economic growth around this correlation (particularly since it holds both synchronically and diachronically).

But this makes the remaining cells only more interesting, as deviant cases. 'Poor societies, high in development', would be societies on a low level of wealth but nevertheless with a high proportion of the population engaged in symbolic activity. One might think of ancient Greece if it had not been for its slavery basis; so certain monastic communities, whether of the Buddhist or Christian variety, where the monks eke out a subsistence level living from the surrounding nature (or through begging from the surrounding society) and devote themselves primarily to spiritual pursuits, would be better examples.

The other combination, 'rich societies, low in development' would perhaps bring to the mind countries that have become rich on oil, such as countries on or close to the Arabian peninsula or Libya or Venezuela. There are also countries like Denmark that depend heavily on intensive agriculture.[13] This indicates that there are ways of becoming rich that do not presuppose growth in what is usually considered the secondary or tertiary sector or both, at least not in the short run. In such countries wealth may pile up at heavily concentrated places in the social structure with a large fraction being used for consumption — or for investment in the same essentially extractive industry.[14]

From what we have said so far it may appear as if we believe that man is necessarily driven by two motives, *to become rich* (economic development) and *to liberate himself from nature* (socio-economic development). But there is no such axiomatic belief. First of all there is no assumption that all men or societies are change oriented at all, and even if they were the changes would not necessarily be in these two directions; they could be in one of them without the other as our examples have indicated, or in neither. Nor is there any assumption to the effect that motives lead to changes or that changes presuppose motivations. All we say is that we define as *horizontal development* those changes that permit the liberation

Table 1.2.2. Stages of socio-economic development

	Primitive	Traditional	Modern	Neo-modern
Term for the stage:	Primitive	Traditional	Modern	Neo-modern
Structure of the stage:	Primary (High / Low)	Pri-mary — Ter-tiary (High / Low)	Pri-mary — Secon-dary — Ter-tiary (High / Middle / Low)	Tertiary — Post-tertiary education / Tertiary education / Secondary education / Primary education
Term for the transition:	Urban revolution	Industrial revolution	Automation revolution	
Population profiles:				
primary sector:	100 ; 90	80 ; 75	50 ; 20	5 ; 0
secondary sector:	0 ; 5	5 ; 10	20 ; 30	5 ; 0
tertiary sector:	0 ; 5	15 ; 25	30 ; 50	90 ; 100
Agricultural productivity:	1:1 and less	1:1.25 ; 1:1.33	1.2 ; 1:5	1:20 and higher
GNP per capita:	up to $50	$50–$600	$600–$4,000	$4,000 and above
Economic system:	subsistence economy	barter economy	money economy	credit economy
Communication:				
goods, persons:	walking, running, rowing	animals, wheels, sailing	steam engine, combustion engine	jet rockets
information:	eye and ear	dispatches	post, telegraph, telephone	tele-satellite
Domain:	group, clan, tribe	village, city-state	nation-state	region, world-state
Magnitude:	10^0–10^2	10^2–10^5	10^5–10^8	10^8–10^{10}
Allocation principles:	'like father, like son', in principle	'like father, like son', in principle	'like talent, like position', in principle	'like talent, like position', in principle

11

of people from the primary (and to some extent also from the secondary) sector as a basis for their living, whether this is accompanied by a high level of economic growth — as it usually is — by a low level of economic growth or even by stagnation or regression. In the latter case large portions may still, theoretically, be 'liberated' in the sense mentioned, but the general pattern is that a primary sector dominated economy with low output per man-hour is only able to maintain a low proportion in the tertiary sector. The exception would be extremely ascetic, ideational communities, probably of a rather limited size.[15]

On the other hand, again, the two motivational assumptions above would not be too far-fetched and would, in fact, serve as an axiomatic basis to explain much of the strivings of individuals and nations today. But this is because they form parts of a particular *ethos* that is currently *en vogue*, diffused from man to man and nation to nation, with a multiplier effect due to mass media. Whether this ethos enters as a cause or as an effect of development is a matter for discussion and empirically based analysis, but it certainly seems to accompany it.

Against this background, let us now sketch very briefly four stages in socio-economic development — with the obvious understanding that the four stages are neither exhaustive nor mutually exclusive, and that they only define extremely broad classes of societies. We shall call the four stages 'primitive', 'traditional', 'modern' and 'neo-modern', trying to use these terms in a way that is consistent with common usage.

They are defined in Table 1.2.2. These categories or four stages mix both in space and in time. One can find segments of all four within the same nation (for instance Brazil), often with very limited contact surfaces (due to their mutual heterology); and the same society may also show important overlaps.[16] Moreover, there is no assumption that a society cannot make 'jumps', that *natura non facit saltus*. What Margaret Mead calls the jump from the stone age to the electronic age[17] is in these terms the transition from the primitive to the neo-modern society. All our knowledge about the plasticity of human infants — that they can, essentially, be socialized to any one culture — would contradict an intra-personal theory about the *necessity* of successive stages.[18] All we are saying is that the general trend we know of is in the direction of the arrow, admitting for standstills and occasional relapses.[19]

This transition is measured, essentially, in the steady decline of the primary sector and the equally steady rise of the tertiary sector, with an intermittent rise and fall of a secondary sector.[20] We have given some such figures as an illustration in the Table. *Human history, in this per-*

spective, is the history of the transition from the pattern 100–0–0 to 0–0–100 via many intermediary stages. In this transition the secondary sector has appeared as a necessity, as a factor helping or pushing a society into an economic takeoff that would permit further steps into societal forms with more of the population in the tertiary and less in the primary sector. However, we are not convinced that a highly developed secondary sector was or is a necessary factor, even if it has been a sufficient one — it has proved effective to combat poverty, but it may also have hampered rather than engendered a rapid growth into the tertiary sector. Thus, it would be interesting to explore more fully models of development that skip the industrialization phase, particularly if the society is a closed system so that it does not merely exchange primary (foodstuffs and raw materials) and tertiary (services) products with manufactured goods from the external world,[21] usually in a way that makes them satellites of the developed metropolis.

The basic factor underlying the decrease of the percentage employed in the primary sector is, of course, the increased productivity in this sector. We have put down some ratios that serve as illustrations, ranging from 1:1 ratio of the neolithic age when one family employed in agriculture, etc. could support one family — itself — to the neo-modern age with industrial, even automated, farming, where one family can support 20, 30, 100 families.[22] In the first case, nearly 100 % were employed in the primary sector, in the second case 5 %, 3 %, 1 % — even less in times to come. Of course, the extreme cases with 100 % and 0 % are for illustration only. There was probably always some element of division of labor giving to some members of the group more symbolic activities than to others (e.g. the administration of ritual). And there will probably always remain somebody in the countryside doing farming, even when the whole food industry has been automated and run by computers, with no use of animals or foodstuffs as inputs and no use of human beings for other purposes than to program and run the computers — and eventually to consume the output.[23]

It should also be emphasized that we have deliberately omitted a major distinction among primitive societies, the distinction between *hunting-gathering* societies living by catching and collecting and the *food-producing* societies characterized by 'actively cooperating with nature — to increase the supplies of food available by cultivating plants and often also by breeding domestic animals'.[24] The transition between the two, between what Morgan used to call 'savagery' and 'barbarism'[25] (rather strange terms today) and what the archeologists called the 'paleolithic'

13

and 'neolithic' periods,[26] was as much of a revolution economically as the urban, industrial and automation revolutions we have focused on. But the distinction does not differentiate in terms of our basic variable, the percentage distribution on the three sectors of the economy. The primary category is too crude to make these important distinctions, just as the tertiary category does not reflect important discriminations to be made in the most developed societies today.

Increase in agricultural productivity took place all the time, but gained real momentum only recently, during the last hundred years or so — linked as it was to scientific discoveries (fertilizers, new seeds, animal husbandry, etc.) together with important changes in social structure. This increase is neither a necessary, nor a sufficient condition for urbanization, although both are often claimed — but certainly heavily correlated with urbanization.

First of all, even if the yield in the primary sector is 1:1 or even less (undernourishment), a sector of the population can be 'liberated' for tertiary sector activity simply forcing the rest of the population to consume less than it produces (and needs) and to hand the surplus over to the tertiary sector (of priests, rulers, military, etc.). This extraction of surplus can be done by means of *normative* power under sacred or secular ideologies, by means of *contractual* power, in exchange for services in the tertiary sector or by means of simple, straightforward, *coercive* power.

And secondly, it is not sufficient either, because surplus production has to be transported, so a city of any size can only emerge when a sufficient amount of agricultural surplus can be transported to it. If the yield is constant, the transportation radius has to be extended for the city to grow; if the means of communication are constant, the yield has to increase — unless imbalances are permitted to develop. Thus, a good place to locate a city or village would be on a crossroads or even better on a river bank, *downstream*, using gravity — which is cheap — to do the job (assuming that the goods to be received in exchange are less bulky, such as symbolic services or 'protection' rendered in the tertiary sector). By doing this the subsistence economy acquired an element of barter economy — and the primitive became a peasant.[27]

Thus, we postulate *productivity* and *communication* (including transportation) as major elements in the technological base permitting this socio-economic development. But this is a two-way proposition:

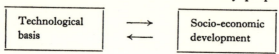

14

The technological basis includes both conditions and is conditioned by the stage of socio-economic development — but how this circular process is set in motion is another question to which many answers have been given, most of them probably correct under some (usually insufficiently specified) conditions.

The next step in productivity, as commonly analyzed, is the industrial revolution. However, we do not think that it started at the end of the eighteenth century. Not that one should belittle the role of the spinning jenny or the steam engine, whether by Newcome or Watt — those heroes of school history textbooks — but the idea of manufacturing and even of mass production is much older. Refined agricultural products, whether from crops or cattle, and artisan products like pottery and textiles have been produced in ways not that different from the forms of production that emerged in the Midlands in the beginning of the last century.[28] But that it increased productivity in the sense of output per man-hour drastically and created a correspondingly drastic increase in the secondary sector of society is obvious. However, the interesting thing about the secondary sector is exactly that it has inside itself the seeds of its own destruction: it creates the very machinery that makes white-collar workers out of blue-collar workers, putting, as it were, more and more hardware between man and nature, leaving for man symbolic activity.[29]

But the industrial revolution also produced and is producing a communication revolution. We have mentioned the function of transportation of goods and markets for the growth of villages into cities via the market-mechanism, and the gradual generalization of the market-mechanisms by means of the transition from barter to money economies. Just as important is the function of information for control and hence for the formation and the extension of political communities. The distance from center to periphery of a political community is as long as the distance of effective control, which is a question of feedback as a reaction to deviance, which again is a question of speed of communication.[30] The time needed for the message about a deviant act in the periphery to reach the center of the community and for adequate responses to reach the periphery must be less than the time needed for the deviant act to start a chain reaction ultimately leading to rebellion and secession. If it is not less, but more, then the periphery will detach itself and acquire some kind of autonomy. But if it less, the political community will often try to expand since it possesses an under-utilized control potential. Again, the point is not that one empirically only finds balance, but rather that imbalance is consequential: the center may have too much or too little con-

15

trol relative to some kind of optimum point. At any rate, the geographical location of the political capitals of most nations bears out this point — they are usually found in relatively central positions in terms of communication[31] (which does not mean that they are all like Madrid or Paris; they are often located on the coast in order to be easily controlled by some dominant metropolitan power, but rarely up in a 'corner'). Thus, just as communication limits the economic hinterland of a city and hence the city itself, it also limits the political hinterland of a capital and hence the nation itself.

For our purposes, the point is that a concomitant of the growth of cities was the potential growth of the political system, in numerical size, both in terms of area and population. But this also implied more resources available within the political unit, natural as well as human ones. The natural ones were available to the extent that they could be *extracted* and *transported*, the human ones to the extent that the social structure permitted their horizontal (from sector to sector) and vertical (from low to middle to high) *mobility* within a reasonable amount of time. *Thus the mobilization of natural and human resources became the crucial problems*, the second one considerably more difficult to solve than the first one.

And here *scale* is important. One type of human talent needed for development and growth is pure intelligence; for if we define intelligence as the ability to handle abstract symbols, then intelligence seems to have considerable survival value and even to be a necessary condition for the emergence of a strong tertiary sector (or at least for many segments within the tertiary sector). But the point is that many of the sub-sectors in the tertiary sector do not need a staffing that is proportionate to increases in the population at large. One may need a corresponding increase of physicians and teachers, but not necessarily of broadcasting staff, journalists, central administrators, inventors, creative scientists. Thus, some tertiary segments are *extensive* or *elastic* in the sense that they vary concomitantly with population if the social order is to remain the same, whereas others would be *intensive* or *inelastic* even to the point of being completely insensitive to population growth (as the number of heads of state).[32] The point is then that a growing population will permit a broader basis for recruitment into these intensive segments, and hence potentially add to their quality and in addition leave a surplus that may develop other tertiary segments.

How difficult this mobilization of talent was and is can best be seen by filling in the cells in the diagram for traditional and modern societies with some representative occupational terms (Table 1.2.3).

16

Table 1.2.3. *The distribution of occupations in traditional and modern societies*

			Traditional		
		Primary			*Tertiary*
					Administrators
					Mercants
	High	Landowners			Professionals
	Low	Farm-hands			Servants

			Modern		
		Primary	*Secondary*	*Tertiary*	
High		Landowners	Capitalists	Professionals	
Middle		Farmers	Skilled workers	White-collar	
Low		Farm-hands	Unskilled workers	Servants	

Typically, these societies permit a lot of horizontal mobility, particularly from generation to generation. The sons of landowners study law and become administrators, the sons of owners of factories become professionals; and lower down: sons of farm-hands and unskilled workers drift to the cities, the citadels of the tertiary sector and later also of the secondary sector,[33] and enter the tertiary category at the lowest level. Thus, there are general horizontal trends of mobility at all levels into the tertiary sector. But the vertical trends, needed to bring talent from below into the daylight, so to speak, were always less pronounced, particularly since the lowest echelons in all three sectors were at some time even filled with slaves with limited chances of manumission, not to mention mobility[34] — or generally with members from other racial or ethnic groups. Moreover, tertiary high positions have often been filled from some *particular* low group, especially in the 'oriental despotisms', since the ruler needed people committed to himself only. In a steep power pyramid mobility may be high seen from above, low seen from below.

To describe this phenomenon, let us contrast two models for the *allocation* of personnel, born into the society, to the various cells in the social structure:

Model I (traditional):   *like father, like son*
Model II (modern):   *like talent, like position*

According to the first model the son is given roughly the same position as the father — in the class society the same stratification *level* ('station' in life, 'estate') and in the caste society also the same economic *sector*

17

and even occupational sub-sector. Thus, in class society some horizontal mobility is possible since the position is only determined up to the class; whereas in caste society not even horizontal mobility would be possible (except by joint group efforts to move the caste as such). At this point it should be added that the general principle of homogamy in choice of marriage partner[35] ensures the choice of a marital partner from the same cell(s) in the social structure: in class society from the same class, in caste society from the same caste. This means that the father-in-law can be used as a vehicle for horizontal mobility in class society, but not in caste society. Homogamy may be protected by more or less strictly enforced norms, but it also seems to have some kind of more deeply rooted basis of a psychological nature.

The point is now that the two models are not contradictory, but may be quite compatible — depending on the kind of talent required *and* to what extent that talent is transferred effectively from one generation to the next by the mechanisms of *genetic* transmission and/or *cultural* transmission (socialization) in the family. A society based on Model I, which certainly has been the dominant model both in time and in space, and particularly in primitive and traditional society, may be able to land the talent where it is needed, at the top of society, simply by virtue of these mechanisms. Thus, if what is needed is a certain elite (gentlemanly) style, a way of talking, a way of behaving, knowledge of particular games and sports, of languages and rituals, then the socialization mechanisms may take care of all this and bring about an allocation pattern in accordance with both models. Of course, one would not expect the fit to be perfect, but the discrepancies (i.e. high talent placed too low and low talent placed too high) may be statistically infrequent, easily concealed or explained away, or suppressed by means of dispersion and/or coercion.

It becomes more difficult when talent is defined in terms of intelligence or one of its many correlates (or, for instance, in terms of McClelland's n-achievement); and this is to a large extent the definition in tertiary sector dominated societies as we know them today. Even granted that:

1) Homogamy will tend to make spouses not too discriminating as to intelligence;[36]
2) Much of the IQ variance is accounted for by the IQ of the parents,[37]
   a) partly by genetic transmission,
   b) partly by cultural transmission,

there is no guarantee that those high up are so high in IQ in the first place, nor is the correlation perfect. The misfits are there for everybody to see: when top positions can no longer be handled adequately by people who rank low in ability to manipulate abstract symbols, then those who have too *high* positions for their *low* IQs (and correlates) will have their legitimacy effectively challenged by those who have too *low* positions for their *high* IQs.[38]

Thus another system of allocation, more in accordance with Model II, will emerge, slowly fighting its way into societies dominated by Model I. One concrete mechanism for doing so is, of course, universal schooling systems, where the *primary* level of education is used for low-level training and for talent-scouting for the *secondary* level of education, which in turn is used for middle-level training and for talent-scouting for the *tertiary* (university, 'high school' in the European sense) level of education where the 'experts' are formed. This is where the elite is bred, but one can also talk of a *post-tertiary* level where the top elite, the creative scientists, the high-level rulers are made, particularly for the neo-modern society. Ideally, the system works on the principle that the *best talent* shall get the *best training*, shall get the *highest position* (in terms of prestige, salary and power) regardless of the position of the parents — just as one can describe the ideal type of the Model I system of allocation as based on the idea that the best placed fathers shall get their sons in the best positions regardless of the talents of the sons. But today that is considered unjust, and it is in the name of *justice* that Model II is substituted for Model I. This adds a third element to our short list of basic motivations, and the application of the general principle of justice to allocation is only one specification among many.

This, then, lays the basis for what we have called the *neo-modern* society — a society not yet completely realized, but rapidly emerging. It is characterized by a very high, close to 100%, loading on the tertiary sector, based on extremely high levels of productivity in the primary and secondary sectors so that few people have to work in those sectors, and those who do the work perform essentially tertiary sector type jobs handling symbols. The transportation and communication systems are so effective that both goods/persons and information can be available anywhere within a very short span of time. The speed of information is, in fact, so quick, that simultaneous coexistence of everybody with everybody is a possibility (by means of two-way, closed, long-distance audio-visual tele-communication via satellite-videophones).[39] This means, in turn, that space tends to disappear as a category for human organization and some kind of universal political system, a world state, is bound to emerge sooner or later. At any rate the communication and information system is quite capable of handling considerable magnitudes of human beings — some such orders of magnitude are indicated in Table 1.2.2. More parenthetically, the economic system also becomes based much less on money and much more on other symbols (checks, drafts, credit cards) — which eventually also will have worldwide validity.[40]

Thus, we have pictured human history as a haphazard, off-and-on struggle for *wealth* (or at least easy satisfaction of immediate needs), *development* (sustained growth of the tertiary sector) and *justice* ('correct' allocation) with the many caveats mentioned above. This can only be justified if we can also at least indicate that a society of that kind has existed in the myths, the utopias, the mental images of the future of mankind, even for a long time. Without going into any details, we feel that this may be the case, although we know of no comparative study of the structure of the transcendental afterlife societies believed in by the different religions. The Christian paradise and indeed the Christian hell have both been the objects of colorful and detailed description.[41] Nevertheless, neither agriculture nor industry seems to be too developed in paradise, so life is probably focused on the tertiary sector, with a heavy loading of music (harps, bassoons) and other arts — not to mention just mere *existence*, a kind of blissful nirvana, which may be seen as an extrapolation from leisure in mundane existence. Thus, paradise seems to be heavily *developed* according to our definition — but probably not *rich* (more like the monastery in Table 1.2.1 in that respect). Economic growth is not a transcendental concern; development is — and justice, but probably in the sense of egalitarianism more than in the sense of adequate allocation of intelligence. Similar features are found in the descriptions of marxist utopias.[42] Thus, we do not think it is too far-fetched to assume a certain correlation between some myths and the general trend of development, but it should also be emphasized that many utopias have looked much more like neolithic, primitive societies — isolated and agricultural.[43]

Today another kind of data would be at the disposal of the social scientist and corroborate further the idea that man, all over the world it seems, wants to get into the tertiary sector, and the sooner and the higher, the better. Questions of the 'What would you like your son to become' type almost invariably elicit responses belonging to that niche of the social structure, particularly in the professions.[44] Education, however modest, is seen as a vehicle leading to that particular cell in Table 1.2.3, moving to the city likewise. Parents lay out strategies for the adequate placement of their children and the strategies seem to be basically

20

sound: *this is the sector of the future*, and even if your son starts low in the tertiary sector, *his* son may make it because the starting point is a good one — close to schools, close to the centers of power, located where things happen. The net result is, of course, a demand on positions in that sector that by far exceeds the social supply of such positions, with the well-known consequences in terms of frustrated ambitions, urban slums, intellectual proletariats, underemployment, people having three or four small jobs but doing none of them well and so on — as seen so clearly in Latin America and some Asian countries.[45]

We shall stop at this point and elaborate the contradictions and possible future changes of the neo-modern society and speculations on what might follow in its wake elsewhere.[46] The point we are making here is only the rather obvious — but easily forgotten — idea that human history does not stop with what terms itself the 'modern' society, just as little as it stopped at what we call the 'traditional' society, just as little as it will stop with the 'neo-modern' society. The terms 'poor-rich' and 'un-developed-underdeveloped-developing-developed'[47] should be regarded as relative terms that may be used to indicate distance anywhere on the primitive-neo-modern axis. It is only a sign of our myopia in space and time that we seem to reserve the term 'development' for that particular transition from traditional to modern that is so much in focus today; it could just as well be used for the other two transitions indicated in Table 1.2.2. *For all these transitions are problematic;* all of them are 'great transitions', 'turning points in history' or whatever one might choose to call them.

* * *

If we now look more closely at Table 1.2.2, a striking feature built into the Table is a certain vertical and horizontal consistency. The different items in the same vertical column feed into each other and it is easily seen how these elements mutually support each other. At the same time there is a certain trend horizontally, an axis of development — all of them closely related to the basic axis having to do with the composition of the working population (which again is based on agricultural productivity and communication). Needless to say, if we had picked some other dimensions of development, for instance how the society extracts and uses the *surplus* (in the marxist sense) from its productive activities we would have arrived at a different picture; but this is the imagery we have felt most attracted by for the purpose of the present study.

The point is now, of course, that the Table is too neat. For these categories are abstract categories, and the Table conceals the basic fact that a given empirical entity — a person, a set of persons, a nation, a set of nations — may be cut across by these categories in any number of ways. The categories are consistent but the empirical entities are not necessarily consistent; they are exposed to lags and leads in development and to all the vagaries of social reality. And this leads to 'social friction', to use an understatement.

Social friction, then, can be found at all levels of social organization:

Intra-personally : As personal conflicts for individuals living at the same time in systems belonging to different stages (e.g. a neo-modern educational establishment, a modern production system and a traditional family system).

Inter-personally : As conflicts between persons rooted in different systems — for instance over power;

Intra-nationally : As conflicts between districts in different stages of development, and, hence, with different values;

Inter-nationally : As conflicts between nations in different stages of development.

By this we are in no sense implying that there are necessarily more frequent or more serious conflicts between units in *different* stages than between units at the *same* stage of development — for similarity and homology will easily foster conflicts over the same scarce values since similar systems by definition are pursuing the same goals.[48] But there are particular types of conflicts that emerge between units, or parts of units, in different stages of development.

Generally speaking, the pattern is as follows: those at a higher level of development will, usually, be able to subdue, exploit or otherwise benefit from those at a lower level of development. Thus, traditional societies made members of primitive societies their *slaves;* modern societies made traditional societies (and their primitive segments) their *colonies* — i.e. they took the whole society and treated them much like the members of traditional societies had treated the slave members of primitive societies[49] — with cruelty and oppression, *and* with paternalism and sometimes benevolent education leading toward 'freedom' and 'independence'. But freedom was followed in both cases by a pattern of continued exploitation of the underdog group. Similarly, neo-modern society, where and when it really emerges, will probably serve as a nucleus for the absorption of the others by virtue of its communication and control potentials (*le défi américain!*) into a world state — just as modern society proved capable of absorbing traditional and primitive segments into a nation state. How?

To discuss this more thoroughly, let us make use of what we have referred to in Table 1.2.2 as *domain* and *magnitude*.[50] So far we have seen these variables in the light of communication of passengers, goods and messages; but there is more to it than that. In general, it is a question of how widely and to how many the net of role partners is thrown, in other words a question of the extension and size of the social network a person is involved in. Neolithic man, with his agriculture based on the simple 1:1 formula, could survive in basically the same way if he were isolated from everything but his own family. This is no longer the case for man in traditional society: a 'peasant' is meaningless without an urban segment, however rudimentary — not to mention how meaningless the merchant is without the rural sector; he could not even survive. And this holds *a fortiori* in modern society: dependence on cheap labor force, on raw materials, etc. throws the web of affiliations quite widely. In neo-modern society there is in principle no limit. Man is much less bound by the production process, much more free to pursue any kind of interest — such as science. Typically, scientific activities do not know national borders except when they are made to serve the specific interests of the nation state. The physicist, sociologist and historian alike will be concerned with the formulation of hypotheses and theories that should extend in space and time. In physics this is a well-known principle of long standing; in sociology it has recently become one, and it will also emerge in history — for sciences seem gradually to give birth to more nomothetic, generalizing efforts to understand our world, and *generalizing science does not know national borders*. Thus, local history corresponds to traditional society, national history to modern society and world history to a world community. But more significantly: the interest in comparisons and generalizations will also increase along this continuum so that there is a development from highly ideographic, local history to a highly nomothetic world history or sociology — the two will probably merge in the not too distant future.[51]

We know of no systematic research in this field, but the methodology is obvious: *For any given social unit, how much of the environment does one have to include, or can one exclude, so that the unit is maintained, basically the same?*[52] The obvious contention is that by this definition of the social system or social network, development implies a constant growth in domain and magnitude. At various periods there have been efforts to draw a circle around the family (farm), the clan, the tribe, the village, the city (state), the nation state — and declare the units as self-sufficient, even hedging around this imposed self-sufficiency by means of implicit or explicit, informally or formally controlled norms,[53] by means of customs barriers, immigration laws, border patrols and whatnot. But the logic of the socio-economic basis of the society will not in the long run respect artificial borderlines around social systems, but will lead to growth in the magnitude and domain of the circle of 'significant others'.

In our chart of development we have posited, and we think by and large correctly, that *the nation state is commensurate with what we have called the 'modern' stage in socio-economic development.* But this has two very important consequences: that people still living in primitive and traditional segments of a nation have not yet 'grown into' the nation state, and that people living in neo-modern segments, correspondingly, have 'grown out' of the ubiquitous nation state. Thus, if we define nationalism as the identification with the nation state, one would hypothesize decreasing nationalism in the most developed societies because of the many people living in a web of cross-, supra- and trans-national affilations. And, one would hypothesize decreasing nationalism in the least developed countries, because their net of affiliations will gradually encompass the nation state in which they live. But at the same time they, and the nation states characterized as 'modern', will be caught in the much richer and wider net thrown from vantage points in neo-modern societies — and this will be the major mechanism of absorption. The nature of this process is social — but its basis is technological.[54]

After this brief excursion into the general theory of development, the crucial problem now facing the social scientist is to get some kind of order in the bewildering number of theories as to necessary and suffcient conditions of development. We shall try to penetrate at least a short distance into the jungle by making three distinctions.

First of all, one should try, at least, to distinguish between *definitions* of development, *conditions* of development and *consequences* of development. Thus, the Colin Clark thesis about the decline of the primary sector, the rise and fall of the secondary sector and the rise of the tertiary sector in our system is neither a condition, nor a consequence of development — it *is* (horizontal, socio-economic) development since we have defined it that way (possibly with the exception of the non-trivial statement about the secondary sector). Increased productivity and improved means of communication will probably enter on the condition side in most theories, but as we have indicated above they could also be put on the consequence side. Since social phenomena are usually linked by (positive or negative) feedback relations and not by uni-directional causal connections we would have to be prepared to accept a mixed, 'both condition and consequence' category. Thus, that would probably have to be the status of the relationship between economic growth and socio-economic development according to our definitions.

Secondly, a distinction should be made between *theories of social change in general*, *theories of development in general* and *theories of one particular type of development*, i.e. of one particular transition in Table 1.2.2. Thus, one may be able to locate and isolate a factor generating social *change*, in general; but whether this potential for social transformation leads in the direction of more or less *development* is another matter. It often happens, however, that by means of specification a theory of social change can be made into a theory of development, and that by means of still further specification it can be made into a theory for a particular type of development, say, from traditional to modern societies.

And finally, as to the theories themselves, some kind of classification system is needed. Usually the theories have a simple form:

$$C \rightarrow D$$

where D is 'development' and C is any kind of factor held to be a condition of development.[55] Most theories are theory atoms, so to speak, in the sense that the author puts forward his favorite condition, C, and claims that this is a necessary or sufficient condition or even both. These theories can then be classified according to the nature of C, and we suggest as a point of departure the very simple system of classification shown in Table 1.2.4, page 26.

The scheme is exhaustive insofar as it refers to all possible categories, and it is also mutually exclusive. Nevertheless, the categories may sometimes be too vague to point to one and only one class for the classification of a given theory. But, to indicate some examples:

Theories relating to non-human resources, geographical location (particularly relating to transportation facilities), climatic factors would be placed in *Class 1*.

Theories relating to biological aspects of man, whether they refer to groups (race theories), to families (heredity theories) or to non-genetic factors such as the effect of malnutrition and chronic diseases, or to the size of the population as well as the shape of the population pyramid, would be placed in *Class 2*.

Theories about value orientations and personality characteristics of the population, seen individually or as groups, would be placed in *Class 3*. We have made two sub-classes of Class 3, regarding 'personality characteristics' as 'deeply inter-

Table 1.2.4. *A classification of development theories*

Class 1:	Non-human environment theories	*Anorganic level*
Class 2:	Biological theories	*Organic level*
Class 3:	Intra-personal theories	
	a) value theories	
	b) personality theories	*Social micro-level*
Class 4:	Inter-personal theories	
	Intra-group theories	
Class 5:	Intra-national theories	
	Inter-group theories	
	a) social structure	
	b) economic structure	*Social macro-leve*
	c) political structure	
Class 6:	Inter-national theories	
Class 7:	Supra-national theories	

nalized values' so that class b is in a sense an extrapolation of class a. They are both theories about properties of individuals that are meaningful also when the individual is isolated — he may still be high on McClelland's n-achievement or on Weber's protestant ethic, but he cannot constitute a 'cyclical interaction network' or be 'rank disequilibrated' in isolation since these are only meaningful in a social context (and hence to be placed in *Class 4* or *Class 5*).

Theories relating to social structure at the *micro-level*, inside the family, the small peer group, the educational or production organization, the smaller territorial units (such as villages), the associations, will be referred to *Class 4*.

Theories relating to social structure at the *macro-level* will be referred to *Class 5*. We have divided them into theories of social structure properly speaking, theories for the generation and distribution of economic value (economic structure) and theories for the distribution of political power (political structure). Social 'structure' will here easily become a very comprehensive residual category. Thus, it will include theories relating to the educational level and the distribution of education in the structure, just as 'economic structure' would refer both to amount and distribution of economic value. Above all, this where is theories of intra-national domination and exploitation enter.

Theories relating to the relations in the international system of nations, whether in terms of social, economic or political structure, will be placed in *Class 6*. Most important would be the theories of inter-national domination and dependence.

Theories relating to other factors at the international level, particularly to international, government organizations (but also to international non-governmental organizations), will be placed in *Class 7*. The dependence-autonomy perspective will play a major role here also.

An effort to classify and systematize such theories will be done elsewhere. The point to be made here is only that any serious effort to account for socio-economic development will have to take into account a spectrum of such factors. It may well be that some time in the future new conceptualizations may make formulations of theories of development in terms of one factor ('single factor theories') more valid than today's, but that day is not here yet.[56] We are still necessarily doing interdisciplinary work when we are working in the field of development theory, and this has one major implication: a good theory of development today should not only be of the multi-factor variety, *but the several factors should preferably be taken from different classes*. Of course, within-class dispersion is also much preferable to a single factor theory, but still better are efforts to span the spectrum of factors over different classes. And by this is not meant simply a listing with one chapter dealing with a theory from Class 1, the next chapter with a theory from Class 2 and so on — this would merely amount to what one could call 'parallel single factor theories'. *The crucial point is to show how the factors interact in facilitating or impeding development, not only to list them.*

In doing this the classification system in Table 1.2.4 may perhaps be simplified, and one way of doing this would be to use the following trichotomy of theories (Table 1.2.5).

Table 1.2.5. *A simplified classification of development theories*

Class of theories	Typical disciplines
I. *Resources (Classes* 1, 2)	Economics, geography, demography
II. *Values (Class* 3, a, b)	Psychology, sociology, anthropology
III. *Structure (Classes* 4, 5, 6, 7)	Anthroplogy, sociology, economics, political science, international relations

Thus, one good rule would be to try to combine two factors from two different classes in this highly simplified system; and still better, one theory from each class. Only by doing this will it be possible to arrive at a sufficiently realistic understanding of factors conditioning development, because of the number of aspects it deals with, to serve as a guide for policy choices. But in order to arrive at this, much more work should be done with a view to collecting and systematizing already existing single factor theories. And this type of task would ideally call for the joint efforts of specialists in all fields concerned with socio-economic development, in other words, from all of the social sciences.[57]

* * *

In the present study we shall try to give one example, however imperfect, of this program for development research. How this will be done will be outlined in more detail in section 1.6 below. But before any plan for multi-factor research can be outlined the single factors or theories to be drawn upon have to be outlined themselves.

Facing the apparent stagnation, even retrogression of Western Sicily in the 1950s, what would be the most appropriate theories to use? Since so much work had already been done using the *resource approach*, and since we did not intend to compare Western Sicily with any other socio-economic unit, we decided against any resource theory or rather: we took the background in those terms for granted and wanted to know more about the sources of development potential in terms of other factors. That Western Sicily was poor in resources without being destitute has been stated by so many authors that we felt no necessity to reiterate that.

That left us with theories about *value* and *structure*. To start with the former: we wanted good theories about *value orientations* as a basis for the research, and for that purpose selected from the enormous literature in the field three works that in our minds were outstanding, both in terms of importance for general theory and in terms of relevance for our study. They are Sorokin's *Social and Cultural Dynamics*, Lerner's *The Passing of Traditional Society* and Banfield's *The Moral Basis of a Backward Society*. We did not select Weber's classic in the field for the reason that it is of less immediate relevance, but we shall have occasion to comment on it. And McClelland's *The Achieving Society* and Hagen's *On the Theory of Social Change* were not published in time to influence the design of the study — but we shall also to some extent draw on these authors and on several others.

The three works are all about the great transition. Sorokin describes and classifies it in the most universal terms with claims for validity unlimited by time and space; Lerner describes the transition of our time with data from the Middle and Near East, and Banfield analyzes the transition that did not take place, in Southern Italy. All three works are of high quality within their respective fields; all three works are worthy of a closer scrutiny, even of criticism and polemics. We shall start with the broadest in scope, Sorokin's, in section 1.3, and narrow it down via Lerner's work (section 1.4) to Banfield's (section 1.5). Actually, we would have liked to have a fourth study at our disposal, dealing with Western Sicily, but there was no modern sociological study in existence that could match the three works mentioned.

28

What then about *structure*? Here we shall proceed in a different manner. The theories in the field are numerous, indeed, but we shall not select two or three of them and expose them to a similar scrutiny. Rather, we shall elaborate the structural theoretical basis ourselves, in connection with the presentation of the data and in line with the vision of 'development' in this section. 'Structure' is then interpreted in two senses: as a *set of social categories*, what the statistically-oriented sociologist often would refer to as the 'values' of his 'background variables', and as the *pattern of interaction between these categories*. Certain categories and combinations of categories are more productive of social change and even of development than others; certain patterns of interaction may faciliate development more than others. But such structural theories have a tendency to become very general, so they have to be tempered by specification or introduction of value orientations.

For the basic social fact that makes such a combined analysis possible at all is the circumstance that the single individual is at the same time a bearer of value *and* a holder of a structural position where he fills structural categories and participates in interaction. This means that the individual can be seen as the tie connecting value and structure. They both meet in him, which again means that if we are in the possession of both kinds of information for a number of individuals, then possibilities exist for a combined analysis. But this will be elaborated further in 1.6.

Finally, it should be added that most most of what we have said so far is biased in the direction of *horizontal* development. Both the definitions of economic development in terms of GNP per capita and of socio-economic development in terms of percentage in the non-primary sectors are *averages*. There is no mention of *dispersions*, of the distribution of income to the individual members of society or the distribution of the non-primary sectors over the districts in the county. Development has been conceived of as *horizontal* development, as *increasing averages*, not as *vertical* development with *decreasing dispersions* leading to a more egalitarian, more just society. We conceive of that bias as a shortcoming, but the data from Sicily do not render themselves so easily to that type of analysis since data almost everywhere are geared to analysis of horizontal, not of vertical development. But what is true for data analysis does not necessarily have to be true for theory formation, so in our effort to bring in social structure the vertical dimension will of course be a major dimension. In other words, efforts must and will be made to discuss even horizontal development in terms of the *internal* structure of dominance. But of at least equal importance is the *external* structure of dominance, the whole network tying these villages to towns that are tied to provincial capitals that are tied to continental centers that are tied to a world metropolis — making the villages political, economic, cultural and social satellites of force far above and beyond their control. This structure of dependence would take in the whole macro-level of analysis (Classes 5, 6 and 7), and our analysis will have to be focused on the micro-level (Classes 3 and 4). However, one basic perspective here will be how the structure of internal dominance at the micro-level ties in with the external dominance at the macro-level. When this and other aspects are not developed further it is not because they are considered insignificant or less significant, but simply because some selection has to be made.

A fuller analysis of development would certainly not stop at the point we stop. It would deal symmetrically with horizontal *and* vertical development, with internal *and* external dominance (dominance at the micro-*and* the macro-levels) at the level of theory formation *and* data collection. But we shall defer that type of effort to a case study that renders itself more easily to this: the study of a whole nation, of Japan, instead of three villages in Western Sicily.[58]

1.3. *Sorokin's theory: the role of cultural mentality*

The famous Polish sociologist Florian Znaniecki has written about Sorokin's *magnum opus* that it is

> ... the only thorough and consistent effort to integrate *all* special cultural science into a general theory of culture. It is cerainly superior to all philosophies of culture developed by his predecessors, including Hegel, Comte, Spencer, Pareto, Toynbee and others.

An evaluation of this kind lies outside our interest, except for one dimension: Sorokin's alleged superiority ('theory' as opposed to 'philosophies') in terms of *testability* of his theories, if not always directly, at least indirectly, by testing some of their consequences. This does not mean that we feel Sorokin himself has tested so many consequences of his theory, nor that the empirical indicators have always been well chosen where it is done, nor that where they have been well chosen the results are necessarily a verification of his theory — only that testing is possible and that the work itself is a gold mine of hypotheses that can keep generations of sociologists busy specifying, elaborating, testing, modifying. Characteristically, however, Sorokin is among the least quoted of the theorists in grand style, and even of the contemporary sociologists of standing, among whom he belongs. One reason for this is that his works are outside the mainstream of sociological endeavor, focusing more on the social macrocosm than the microcosm. He breaks all implicit rules about division of labor between nomothetic and ideographic, diachronic and synchronic social science — he plays on them all. Further, in most academic circles a social scientist can calculate on support for statements to the effect that theorizing about whole cultures is 'impossible', that speculations about 'lines in history', covering centuries not to mention millennia are bound to yield more speculations than lines, etc. Many would therefore feel that the days of academic works like Sorokin's are gone — but it seems that the reason why he is neglected is not so much that he has been tried and found wanting, but rather that he has not yet been discovered. Hence one may predict that there will be a renaissance for Sorokin; that the next generation of sociologists may catch up with him in much the same way that Marx has been rediscovered.

It should be mentioned that the four volumes of the original edition of *Dynamics*[1] have purely physical dimensions that will bar most people from efforts to read them thoroughly. The documentation is extremely extensive, but what is even more difficult is a peculiarity in Sorokin's style. Like his successor at Harvard University, Talcott Parsons, he has a tendency to indulge in tautologies. But unlike Parsons', Sorokin's tautologies are quite plainly expressed: 'After each peak the wave of disturbances subsides and remains low till the next peak.' But this is like Toynbee's 'neither too much, nor too little' principle in connection with challenges: not very helpful. For what else is the meaning of a peak? For these and other reasons we shall limit ourselves to a scrutiny of the one volume edition of *Dynamics*, which will probably have better chances of being widely read.[2]

Most theorists have one fundamental dimension (or several) which they use as levers for their analytical work, usually a dichotomy. Sorokin's major dimension will here be referred to as the *ideational-sensate dimension*. As dimensions are used to classify, even in terms of measurement if the conditions for measurement are met, the first question to be asked may properly be: *What* is classified by means of this dimension? The answer turns out to be anything that is of or with culture: whole civilizations; aspects of civilizations; periods in human history; 'periods' in space, i.e. societies; human groups and individuals, particularly power holders, artists, scientists, etc. — all people who form culture. The objection is immediate: Would not this be like measuring pig iron bars and human beings on the same dimension, e.g. mass, claiming that both measures are equally valid and interesting? The answer is, of course, that it depends on the purpose — for the purpose of air transport weight is an appropriate dimension for both, for the purpose of heavy industry it is not. Sorokin's major concern is always that of *fluctuation*, not development or evolution (he rejects such terms as evaluational and linear) nor change (a term which also fails to connote that linearity is never assumed). And for the purpose of a study of fluctuation this dimension may be appropriate on so many levels, from the inter-national and even down to the intra-personal (which Sorokin does consider explicitly, when he deals with the inner conflicts of people torn between cultural mentalities). For in a study of fluctuations, units of the same kind are compared over time, so the difficulty is avoided by means of essentially diachronic analyses. But we shall see that the scheme also permits considerable flexibility in synchronic analyses.

There are many values on this dimension in Sorokin's scheme, but to get at its *fundamental divisions* we shall only consider the extremes, called *ascetic ideational* and *active sensate*, respectively. Sorokin also has an 'active ideational' type, a 'passive sensate' and a 'cynical sensate' and two 'mixed types': the *idealistic* (which is said to be 'integrated') and the *pseudo-ideational*.[3] All the others can, however, be seen in the light of the extreme types and also be analyzed as more or less integrated mixtures. What Sorokin does in order to define these types is actually exactly the same as Cooley did originally[4] and most other sociologists today would do to define such concepts as, for instance, 'primary' and 'secondary' relations: take a number of important dimensions, dichotomize them and use one set as the definition of 'primary' and the other as the definition of 'secondary'. There are a number of problems connected with this procedure: If n dichotomies are used, what about the $2^n - 2$ combinations that are not elevated into the dignified positions of being basic analytical tools; to what extent are the dichotomies really dichotomies; and how *many* dichotomies should be used for the conceptualization to be scientifically *fruitful?* If only one or two are used no new terminology is really necessary; if many more are made use of the number of non-ideal ('non-scale') types becomes very high, and one also risks losing propositions: too much of interest is already built into the definition. These are questions of scientific strategy, and will have to be considered.

With this in mind, let us present Sorokin's tool *par excellence*, and in his own words:

... the portraiture of the Ideational, Sensate and Mixed types of culture begins properly with the delineation of the major premises of their mentality. As a starting point let us assume that these major premises concern the following four items: (1) *the nature of reality*; (2) *the nature of the needs and ends to be satisfied*; (3) *the extent to which these needs and ends are to be satisfied*; (4) *the methods of satisfaction*.[5]

In slightly different terms: the essence of a culture is supposed to be known when we know its basic answer to the *ontological question*, its supreme *autotelic value* and some major categories concerning the means, the *heterotelic values*. The third category in the quotation does not differentiate between the two extreme types of ideational and sensate, however. The answer to the question about the extent of satisfaction is always 'maximum' — this is actually implicit in the idea of the 'extreme' and pure type. All the remaining five types quoted are described as prescribing less than maximum satisfaction.[6]

Without doing too much injustice to Sorokin's presentation, some of

Table 1.3.1. *Sorokin's ideational-sensate distinction*

	Ideational	Sensate
Nature of reality	*transcendental*, God non-empirical	*mundane*, man empirical
	sensate reality seen as an illusion	ideational reality seen as an illusion
	reality can be grasped through inner experience, revelation, intuition — truth is objective	reality can be grasped through the senses, empirical science — truth is inter-subjective
	reality is being; stability is essential, change accidental	*reality is becoming; change is essential, stability accidental*
Supreme goal, salvation	to become godlike, highest *transcendental* existence, spiritual values	to become ideal-man-like, highest *sensate* existence, sensual values
Nature of means	*introvert, internal change*, self-modification through self-control, knowledge and control of transcendental reality	*extrovert, external change*, modification of the external milieu, knowledge and control of sensate reality

the categories he calls 'logical satellites'[7] can be presented schematically to clarify the description of the 'main elements.' (Table 1.3.1).[8]

Read vertically, these two cultural prototypes or ideal types[9] stand out of history and geography, out of time and space, perhaps with too much clarity. The distinctions are well known; Sorokin has only assembled together some essential dimensions known from the history of ideas and given names to the pure combinations. In so doing a perspective is thrown on cultural, social and personal styles, blurring some distinctions, presumably clarifying others. First some brief comments, concerning the three problems outlined in connection with this general procedure of making concepts by combining dichotomies.

If we imagine that verbal formulas can be found so that it looks as if only three dimensions have been used in Table 1.3.1, eight cultures can in principle be constructed. What about the other six that are not defined as 'ideational' or 'sensate'? Sorokin argues relatively convincingly that these are the only two *logico-meaningfully integrated types* — that the other six would contain inconsistencies that would make them unsustainable.[10] On the other hand, the five less-than-pure types mentioned above do to some extent take care of this problem of the residual categories. They also, to some degree, take care of the second question: Are the dichotomies really dichotomies? This question must be specified as to level of discourse: A dichotomy is a set of two categories that are exhaustive and mutually exclusive, but on what levels should these two properties apply? Clearly, no person *must* choose sides between the two cultural extremes. At the risk of looking inconsistent to extremists and purists, he may well stand with one leg in either camp, engaging in efforts to change external nature and believing in a transcendental existence *post mortem* as well. He may even participate in the transformation of the economic exchange system for the glory of God,[11] or the transformation of the scientific belief system for the glory of God.[12] Of course, such belief systems may be religious, but they are no longer purely ideational in Sorokin's sense. They serve the tremendously important function of *bridge-building* between the ideal type extremes, smoothing out apparently discontinuous ideological jumps.

Thus, *intra*-personally speaking, these are not dichotomies. They may tend to become dichotomies *inter*-personally, however, particularly within a society because of the polarization that may result from a conflict between groups institutionally committed to either side — and this will probably lead to intra-personal polarization as well: everything sensate becomes 'bad'; everything ideational becomes 'good', or vice

34

versa. Logically, all kinds of combinations are possible *between* the dichotomies, even though they will not be called *integrated*; and all combinations *within* the dichotomies are also possible, even though they may not be called *consistent* (they are not excluded by the logical 'principle of contradiction' ($\sim (p \ \& \sim p)$ for instance).[13] To the extent that there are constraints on combinations between and within dichotomies, these are of a psychological nature (in the personal system) and of a social nature (in the social system), not of a logical nature. This does not make the constraints less real, but they will have to be established through empirical exploration rather than through logical analysis.

We are now left with the third question: *What follows from this?* Needless to say, the categories already mentioned cover a tremendous variety of important sub-categories, such as the category of 'sensate salvation', just to mention one. It is defined as the 'highest sensate existence', but this covers, for instance, the alternatives shown in Table 1.3.2.

Table 1.3.2. *A typology of 'sensate salvation'*

	Immediate gratification	Postponed gratification	
	Now	Later	Post mortem
For the individual	carpe diem	gracious living in early retirement	in the success of the children
For a collectivity of which he is a member	'après nous le déluge'	work for usual political goals	'die orgiastische Chiliasmus', millenarism

But why not? These are all sensate alternatives; they are forms of salvation in *this* world — some of them by identification and even by projection into the future — but they do not imply ideas about a transcendental existence. But whether it is *fruitful* to collapse such logically adjacent categories can only be decided on an empirical basis.

After the general elaboration of the central dimension, Sorokin proceeds to more specific considerations. He chooses a cultural realm, say art, and asks: What kind of artistic forms would we expect to follow from the cultural premises given above?

They should be as profoundly different as are the other values ... in the Ideational mentality it is symbolic, its physical exemplars being merely the visible signs of the invisible world and inner values. But in the sensate culture art must be sensate in form; 'naturalistic', in the sense that its intention is to reproduce objects in a shape which imitates closely that in which they appear to our organs of sense. . . . In general, Sensate art deals with those materials which serve and help to increase the sensate happiness of man; Ideational art is the handmaid of religion, absolutistic ethics, eternal values.[14]

Thus, whereas Part One of Sorokin's work deals with the general definitions of the cultural forms, Part Two is devoted to testing his hypotheses about *art* in the different cultures, Part Three, similarly, to *systems of truth and knowledge*, Part Four to *forms of ethical and juridical culture mentality*, Part Five to *systems of social relationships*, Part Six to *war in inter-group relationships*, Part Seven to *internal disturbances in intra-group relationships* and Part Eight to *personality and conduct*. Finally, Part Nine deals with the *why and how of socio-cultural change*. Actually, there are two axes of organization of the material in the different parts: first, to show how forms of art, knowledge systems, etc. are related to the basic cultural mentalities as they are defined in Table 1.3.1, and secondly, to show the dynamics, the fluctuations in time. Evidently, Parts Two through Four deal more with cultural dynamics and Parts Five through Eight more with social dynamics. Since Parts Six and Seven

Table 1.3.3. *Sorokin's main types of social relationships*

Modality	Familistic	Contractual	Compulsory
1. *Conditioning* (mutual or one-sided)	(mutual)	(mutual)	one-sided
2. *Extensity* (specified or complete)	complete	specified	specified
3. *Intensity* (low or high)	high	low (but may be high in the specified sector)	low (but may also be high)
4. *Duration* (limited or durable)	durable	limited (by contract)	both
5. *Direction* (solidary or antagonistic)	solidary	solidary (within sector)	antagonistic
6. *Organization* (organized or unorganized)	(unorganized)	(organized)	(organized)

deal with conflict only, Parts Five and Eight are most valuable from our point of view: finding the concomitants of the two cultural prototypes in the social field.

Sorokin's scientific strategy is to use all his cultural indicators to categorize periods in history as predominantly ideational or predominantly sensate and then to proceed to the fields of *social relations* and *personality*. With suitable indicators, fluctuations may be found in these fields as well — and the test of the theory, then, lies in showing that these fluctuations are 'meaningfully' related to the fluctuations in cultural mentality. Let us examine more closely how this is done.

Sorokin uses his own system of categories to describe social relations, as many sociologists have done before and after him. It is based on a system of dichotomies, where the horns of dilemmas are distributed between his *three* main forms of social relations (Table 1.3.3).[15]

The scheme, as here presented, differs a little bit from Sorokin's own, but we have preferred to present it this way, which seems to us to be completely in line with the way in which he uses the terms. The Table calls for comments concerning the nature of the modalities[16] and the nature of the types of interaction,[17] but we have preferred to give these comments in extensive footnotes in order not to deviate too much from the main line of reasoning.

Imagine a transition where a society undergoes a change from an ideational to a sensate orientation. According to Sorokin, the likely development where the three main types of interaction are concerned is as shown in Diagram 1.3.1.[18]

By and large the idea is that the familistic type will decrease with a transition to sensate culture, the contractual type will increase and the compulsory type will be found in both types:

> Ideational culture has an affinity with the familistic type of social bonds first of all because it inhibits the sensual, carnal desires of its members; thus it makes them less egoistic and less prone to exploit their fellow men, or to bargain with another to obtain as much as possible for as little as possible. ... The Ideational mentality is such that it does not value as highly as that of the sensatist the empirical values of this world.[19]

The ideational culture, in a sense, needs a kind of *incest taboo* to keep going, to use the terms of the familistic system. Or in religious terms: 'A kind of *corpus mysticum* is the only true reality.'[20] This inclusiveness is also the explanation of the 'considerable development of the compulsory form', simply because the 'psychological fusion of the individual "selves"

37

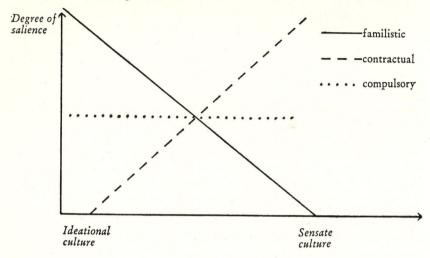

Diagram 1.3.1. *The relation between cultural mentality and types of social relationships, according to Sorokin*

Degree of salience

———familistic

— — —contractual

· · · · · compulsory

Ideational culture

Sensate culture

into one real "we" is limited to the participants of the Ideational culture'.[21] Hence the harsh treatment of outsiders, outcasts, etc. They are regarded as 'a mere empirical instrumentality which can be used as any instrumentality'[22] — but in the sensate culture, compulsion is used because there are no inherent inhibitions against using force as the *ultima ratio* of expediency. 'No *corpus mysticum* is hurt because no such corpus exists.'[23]

Further, since the value is on external change and exploitation of the empirical world, familism will decrease because of the competition for all these scarce values; and contractualism will serve the function of establishing some solidarity that may be beneficial to both parties, but not necessarily of any duration. The sensate values provide *everybody* who wants it with all the bargainable commodities and services necessary to make up a contract. It remains only to mention that to Sorokin the big 'isms' of our century are 'groping and looking for these forms',[24] for familism and contractualism, in an effort to avoid compulsion, but with little success.

Finally, Sorokin shows that cultural mentality is linked to *personal style* in a way that may seem tautologous: 'there are indeed Ideational, Sensate, Idealistic and Mixed, (including the unintegrated) forms of behavior and types of personality, and each type occurs most often in, respectively, the Ideational, Sensate, Idealistic, or Mixed society'.[25] Since he is only studying key elite persons, mentioned in the ninth edition of the *En-*

cyclopaedia Britannica ('historical persons'),[26] it may seem obvious that they should exhibit the same traits as the cultures they themselves have formed — particularly since later historians (including those writing for *EB*) probably will have a tendency to typify both periods and persons by means of each other — 'he was an exponent of his time'; 'he formed the culture of his period more than anybody else', etc. However, the indicators used in describing the persons are not the same as the indicators used in describing societies, 'according as his Sensate needs were maximal (Sensateness) and his efforts great to satisfy them by the transformation of the external *milieu* (energy), or his needs minimal and his chief energies devoted to non-Sensate and otherworldly values'.[27] Correlations are reported, and Sorokin concludes that he has demonstrated that 'these same principles bring similar order and significance to the welter of fragments and details in the field of human action and reaction, that is, in the field of behavior'.[28] These correlations are, however, of a much lower order than the correlations between different cultural indicators.[29]

At this point, let us summarize some of Sorokin's findings. The point of departure is the definition of the two cultural mentalities — and then he sets off identifying them in terms of cultural and social *realms* (art, epistemology, jurisprudence, social relationships, etc.) and locating them in *time* (the study of fluctuations) and in *space* (he actually concentrates on the 'Graeco-Roman and Western Christian civilization', but gives some illustrations from other civilizations as well). His studies of painting, sculpture and architecture[30] locate an *ideational* period in Greece before the fifth century B.C., followed by an *idealistic* period in the fifth century, then a period of 'visual' (corresponding to sensate) art lasting till the fifth century A.D., then a period from the sixth through the twelfth century dominated completely by *ideational* art. Then came the *idealistic* thirteenth century, and from the fourteenth into our days a new period of *visual* art (with a breakdown in our century, leading to forms that are more mixed than fixed). Music closely parallels this, but here the idealistic period came later and lasted longer[31] — from well before Bach till well after Beethoven. Music is found to be atypical — literature and the numerous divisions of 'systems of truth and knowledge' follow the general pattern[32] (the same applies to the ethico-juridical systems although all with some important exceptions). Of course, to the extent that this is tenable it is important illustration of the general social science claim that societies consist of very interdependent parts and of Sorokin's claim for logico-meaningful integration.

What emerges is a see-saw *rhythm*, ideational-idealistic-sensate, repeated twice during some twenty-five or twenty-six centuries of Graeco-Roman Western history. Although Sorokin is very explicit in stating that 'the sequential order of these alternatives in most cases is probably such as described, but it is not to be assumed that in some cases the sequence cannot be different,'[33] this is nevertheless interesting. His explanation goes along these lines. The extreme mentalities are exaggerations. In the ideational phase there is always this inherent conflict: the value is on the transcendental; nevertheless, life is here and now, in this sensate existence — 'there is a common minimum for all societies, whether Sensate or Ideational.'[34] But in the sensate phase man exploits and changes the external world at the risk of exaggerating; 'man becomes so "wild" that he cannot — and does not want to — "tame himself" and, like a reckless driver, can be brought to his senses only by catastrophic tragedy and punishment, as immanent consequences of his "folly".'[35] Thus, the big turns in history occur when sensate man has driven his existence to such extremes that ideational forms of existence are sought. But the undercurrents of sensate culture will continue and may blend with the ideational in such a perfect combination as to make the idealistic phase — until the sensate forms break fully forth again, untamed by 'the strait-jacket of the Ideational culture'.[36] Whether one agrees or not, this picture of the human drama is fascinating. One should only wish that Sorokin had also discussed the possibility of an integration of his own perspective into either of the cultural mentalities. In other words, is Sorokin's own perspective a meta-perspective, neither ideational, nor sensate, but 'above' either of them; or does it lean more to one side than the other? Is it possible — in the sense of 'logico-meaningful integration' — to be *of* one culture, yet not only understand the other extreme but even appreciate it and hope for their coexistence in both space and time, since they seem to fulfill different human needs?

It is very easy to criticize Sorokin on methodological and other grounds, although there is something commanding in this monumental work that probably has silenced many critics. The work has such grandiose dimensions that criticism of details may seem petty, and not all mosquitoes raise their voices against elephants. Nevertheless, some points that appear to be important in this particular context will be mentioned briefly.[37]

The main criticism would take the form of a suspicion: So many things fit together; could that not be because Sorokin bases his analysis on the work of generations of historians and other scientists who have already typified and purified the periods because of their selective attention, inherited descriptions and interpretations, their traditions concerning articles on *Encyclopaedia Britannica*, etc.? Has there, in the writing of history, been a tradition for or against emphazing the atypical, and what effect has this had? We do not know. Future research may show whether the rewriting of history in each generation leads to more than minor adjustments in Sorokin's data and whether Sorokin has merely contributed to a perpetualization of historical dogma.

Second, although the data are given with pedantic exactness — decimal places, etc. — they are never used in more than an ordinal fashion — and rightly so. This means that his main conclusions are sufficiently unspecific to be invariant under even quite severe modifications of indicators and methods of calculation. And given this 'softness' of the data, the arguments in favor of geometric means[38] are not strong enough to warrant their use instead of the much simpler arithmetic means or the even more appropriate medians. But some sensitivity analyses seem to indicate that his main conclusions stand up well against such modifications, for even if he uses inappropriate parameters his reasoning relapses to the more appropriate, ordinal level.

Third, a well-known difficulty in the problem of seeking for periodicity can be expressed as follows. Imagine that a phenomenon has a period of one hundred years, for instance that it takes place in the last decade of each century. Thus, periodicity would appear if data were given for each decade. But data may be imperfect and the phenomenon neither sufficiently regular nor sufficiently pronounced to be discovered if data were given for each year — and the periodicity would disappear completely if data were given for centuries. Sorokin uses periods of different lengths when data are analyzed, but even more systematic procedures could be desirable, particularly in order to verify or falsify hypotheses of fluctuations that are not periodic in physical time, although perhaps in some kind of 'social time'. The 'periodicity-detectors' employed by Sorokin are too crude; harmonic analysis, for instance, might get more out of his often quite refined data.

Further, one could continue at great length the argument about the selection and use of indicators. More important, however, is another kind of objection. Sorokin has chosen his two polar opposites, and the *social and cultural dynamics* are to a large extent seen as outcomes of struggles and conflicts between forces leading to either extreme. The not-extreme types are often described as inferior; as 'innumerable Tartuffes, so well typified in Molière's comedy; all the hypocrites, the insincere, the dissimulators in speech, writing and action'.[39] Actually, Sorokin's work should stimulate somebody to write a study contrasting *extreme* vs. *in media res* or *mixed* cultures, throwing another perspective on social and cultural dynamics. With these preconceptions it follows as a natural consequence that mixed types are somehow unbalanced, while the pure types are more stable; and this is used as an explanatory principle throughout.

But what if the coordinate system were rotated, using what now appear as mixed types as axes? And finally, what consequences result from Sorokin's using sensate criteria of knowledge, external correspondence criteria rather than internal consistency criteria, to investigate not only sensate, but also ideational forms of cultural existence? What asymmetries arise when one culture is used to describe another? For all his professed disgust for present aspects of sensate culture Sorokin is deeply sensate in his approach. He wants to communicate his findings by making them inter-subjectively communicable and reproducible. But is this instrument more neutral, more unbiased than ideational, non-communicable insights would be?

Against this background, let us now summarize what we consider to be the essential implications of Sorokin's work for any study of the great transition of *our* time.

First of all, a new emphasis is given to the truism that there is nothing unique in this transition, except for us: it takes place in our century. Earlier centuries have witnessed technical, economic, not to mention social and cultural, revolutions and their spread to other civilizations at least as important as the present revolutions, although the scale may be greater today due to the multiplier effects introduced by modern means of transportation and communication.

Second, extreme care should be exercised not to confuse the categories of 'ideational cultures' and 'technically and economically underdeveloped countries'. Greece in the fifth century B.C. would probably have received technical assistance had it been in existence today, yet it was not ideational in its orientation. But relative to its contemporaries Greece would definitely be more among the yielders than among the receivers of that type of 'aid'. In all probability, so-called *technical* assistance will *go from* countries with a longer sensate history to countries that are ideational or recently were predominantly ideational; and in all probability technical assistance will be *received by* people in those countries more sensate in their orientation than the local average. But this will always be a question of degree, of differentials and probabilities, not of either/or. The point — that sensate development will predominantly be the work of sensate man because he wants 'external change, modification of the external milieu, knowledge and control of sensate reality' (Table 1.3.1) — may seem trite, but it has important social consequences to be explored later.

Third, if the great transition of our time to some extent depends on the relative proportion of people with a sensate vs. ideational orientation, then we should have in our possession an important diagnostic and prognostic tool. Not only should a community predominantly sensate in its orientation be more receptive to this kind of social change (that undoubtedly involves control and change of the external world and therefore is a change highly compatible with sensate values) than a predominantly ideational community, but we should also be able to predict where in local society the bridgehead for social change may be, if we know the distribution of ideological orientation, on structural variables. This perspective is largely missing in Sorokin's work: societies are portrayed more often as billiard balls without cracks, as ideational *or* sensate. But in social reality there are always *degrees, dispersions other than zero* and *social distributions* to be explored.

Fourth, Sorokin's perspective gives us no reason to believe in any linear theory to the effect that this great transition is the last transition and that there may not be a reversal in ideological orientation. To what extent such reversals will imply a reduction in the use of all kinds of amenities, conveniences, technical inventions, etc. is not known. But the contemporary transition is one among many, and, more importantly, it will in all probability, like other transitions, exceed some unknown limits through exaggeration and lead to a partial reversal. Thus, one would expect growing ideational segments within the predominantly sensate cultures dominating modern, industrial society. There are signs in this direction, and there are also good reasons to believe that neo-modern, post-industrial society may more easily sustain ideational segments than industrial society could.

Fifth, and this is where a highly practical perspective relating to conflict and peace research in addition to development research enters:

> The periods of transition from the Ideational to the Sensate, or from the Sensate to the Ideational, phase of culture are the periods of notable increase of war activities and war magnitude.[40]

The data given by Sorokin demonstrate this relatively clearly, although there may be several possible alternative explanations. For instance,

43

were the wars due to the transition, or did the wars cause the transition as a reaction against old systems leading to such calamities? Or were they signals of basic incompatibilities within the old systems? However this may be, another significant implication of this principle relating transition to violence is in the field of *inter-group, intra-society* relations, of what Sorokin calls 'internal disturbances':

> Thus we have *three main peaks; in the eighth, in the thirteenth and fourteenth centuries, and in the ninteenth and twentieth.* ... The answer is given by the whole character of this work, namely, all three peak periods are the periods of transition, either in the whole culture of Europe and in its system of social relationships, or in the system of social relationships only.[41]

Of course, no analysis is needed to tell that disturbances are closely linked to transitions — that is a tautology. What is important is that the 'disturbances', external or internal, are linked to transitions of a specific type, from ideational to sensate or vice versa. The practical question is what possibilities there are of reducing these 'disturbances' to a minimum once it is known that they will have a tendency to appear in this context.

To conclude, Sorokin opens great vistas for us, giving an interesting topography to the social landscape in space and time. To him the peaks of high potential energy are ideational, from these peaks the trend is downhill to the sensate forms of existence from which humanity may ultimately (how?) accumulate enough energy to climb or create a new ideational peak.[42] But in these vistas details at the micro-level are easily lost sight of — and one wonders how this functions at a more trivial level of human existence — for instance, a village. More particularly, one wonders what the transition stage looks like, the stage captured by Sorokin's many 'impure' types, but nevertheless somewhat lost in his analysis. In short, the task is to apply Sorokin's basic concepts to the social reality of a more limited social system, avoiding the 'billiard ball' fallacy. An attempt in this direction will be made in Chapter 3.[43]

1.4. *Lerner's theory: the role of psychic mobility*

To move from Sorokin to Lerner is to move from the grand theory of a contemporary classic to modern 'middle range' social science at a high level, and to move from an author unlimited by space and time to an author concerned with the transition of *our* time. The study blends two important traditions of social science exploration: the study of mass media of communication as it was developed by Paul F. Lazarsfeld at the Bureau of Applied Social Research (at Columbia University) and its predecessors, and the particular type of concern with the great transition found at the Center for International Studies at the Massachusetts Institute of Technology. In short, the study gives an approach to the problem of transition or development in terms of the role of mass media of communication, where patterns of media exposure and media response are seen partly as causal agents and partly as effects of change. But even if this were the focus of the research at one of the earlier stages of the project, the scope of the book quickly widens to encompass a much richer set of factors and crystallizes into a highly significant theory.

Some three hundred respondents were interviewed in each of six Middle East countries, Turkey, Lebanon, Jordan, Egypt, Syria and Iran, in 1950–1951 — and in 1953 Daniel Lerner was invited to prepare a book based on the initial analyses. In 1954 he visited the area to get some perspectives on the changes that had taken place in the meantime, and this undoubtedly added much to his insights into the process of transition, in which the book abounds.

The bulk of the book consists of two chapters on Turkey and one on each of the other five countries, with a wealth of information about all of these countries and with intriguing details coming out of the general theoretical framework. However, apart from a charming 'parable' taken from a Turkish village, 'perceived' in 1950, 'revisited' in 1954, it is the rest of the book that contains the general theory on which we shall focus (Chapters Two, Three and Four, and Appendix C).

A particularly impressive aspect of this theory is its ability to operate on two levels, national as well as individual. A set of variables is used as in Table 1.4.1.

Table 1.4.1. *Lerner's variables*

Individual level	National level
Industrial-agricultural	Level of industrialization
Urban-rural	Level of urbanization
Literate-illiterate	Level of literacy
Media participation	Mass media distribution
	daily newspaper circulation
	number of radio receivers
	cinema seating capacity
Electoral participation	Election turnout

Not all of these variables are equally well utilized, however. Thus, the two dichotomies industrial-agricultural and urban-rural have a tendency to be subsumed under each other in Lerner's presentation.[1] Historically, urbanization without industrialization has been rather important, as witnessed by the heavily urbanized countries in Latin America, where the tertiary sector typically has developed more quickly than the secondary sector. As mentioned in 1.2 one may also well imagine industrialization without urbanization, provided problems of transportation of personnel and goods, and problems of control, are effectively solved — there are tendencies in this direction in several countries. However, this is less important: to Lerner *modern* society is an urban, literate, above all participant society — and eventually an industrial society. And *traditional* society is the negation of all this; it is rural, illiterate, non-participant. The latter should be accepted with a certain qualification, however: *traditional* society is typically feudal; it is participant and communicating at the top of society but fragmentalized and non-participant at the bottom, and the 'bottom' comprises the overwhelming majority of the society.[2]

Obviously *transitional* society is located in between the two extremes and is, potentially, of many types. If we subsume industrialization under urbanization we get four indicators from Table 1.4.1 of modernization of the national level, and if we dichotomize them we obtain 16 patterns, out of which one is traditional, 14 are transitional and one is modern. However, at this point Lerner shows that the four indicators are heavily intercorrelated, using UNESCO and UN data. Thus, literacy is shown to have correlations between 0.61 and 0.75 with the three indicators of mass media distribution,[3] and the multiple correlations obtained by correlating urbanization, literacy, media distribution and election turnout (using one of them as a dependent variable and the other three as independent variables) for 54 societies vary between 0.61 and 0.91.[4] Total correlations reported were in the same range.[5] In a sense all this is rather obvious since the variables belong to what most theorists in the field would recognize as the same syndrome of variables — and we do not feel that it adds anything to our knowledge when Lerner states that 'the size of these coefficients demonstrates that the relationship between the four sectors *is* systemic'.[6]

However, what is not trivial is his effort to trace paths of development from traditional to modern, thus reducing the number of transitional patterns. Seventy-three nations were classified according to data on literacy and urbanization, and he found that the nations that were in the 0%–10% range where urbanization was concerned were in the

0%–20% range where literacy was concerned — whereas the urbanization range from 10%–25% was compatible with a literacy range from 20%–100%. Thus, it takes some measure of urbanization to speed up literacy, but once a certain level of urbanization is attained maximum literacy can be obtained. Since this means that 'urbanization high' and 'literacy low' are incompatible — at least in our century and for these 73 nations, Lerner's conclusion is that urbanization comes prior to alphabetization in the process of modernization.[7]

We think this analysis should rather have been performed systematically by testing whether the additive index that can be constructed from the four items can in fact be reduced to a cumulative scale.[8] But according to Lerner's reasoning, urbanization precedes literacy, and since literacy obviously precedes some kinds of mass media participation, one only has to assume that media participation precedes political participation to arrive at Lerner's three developmental phases (Table 1.4.2).

Table 1.4.2. *Lerner's developmental phases*

	Urbanization	Literacy	Media participation	Political participation
Phase 0	low	low	low	low
Phase 1	high	low	low	low
Phase 2	high	high	low	low
Phase 3	high	high	high	low
Phase 4	high	high	high	high

Actually, Lerner only talks about Phases 1–3, and refers to them as the phase of *urbanization*, the phase of *literacy* and the phase of *media participation* respectively.[9] What happens in these phases is relatively obvious from the Table above: 'by drawing people from their rural communities, cities create the demand for impersonal communication by promoting literacy and media; cities supply this demand.[10] One may disagree with Lerner when he says that 'the great symbol of this phase [literacy] is the Sears Roebuck catalogue'. This is perhaps to emphasize unduly the economic consumption aspect of development as against, for instance, political and symbolic participation. But his arguments for media participation are relatively convincing. 'Once people are equipped to handle the new experiences produced by mobility (via their move to the city), and to handle the new experiences conveyed by media (via their literacy), they now seek the satisfactions which integrate these skills.' What is less convincing are his words about the final transition: 'rising media participation tends to raise participation in all sectors of the social system — in the public forum via opinion, in the representative polity via voting'.[11] On the contrary, Phase 3 may probably be a rather stationary point in the development, as in dictatorships protected by a high level of mass economic consumption and strict control of the mass media. Moreover, the model seems to have a built-in North Atlantic assumption of the voter who casts his vote according to stimuli his literacy has enabled him to absorb from the mass media — and to neglect, for instance, direct communication between a charismatic leader and his electorate.

But this diachronic theory is clear and subject to test since it predicts that a synchronic analysis will yield a predominance of the five patterns in Table 1.4.2 and very low frequencies for the remaining eleven patterns. We then proceed to a test of this hypothesis with some of the best data presently available for that purpose, from Yale University's *Political Data Program*. Not that these data are perfect, much better data will probably be available soon or are already available, but it was the best test we could develop for the purpose.[12]

After dichotomizing urbanization, literary, media participation (based on an additive index composed of three standard indicators) and political participation for 104 countries, we got complete data for 82 countries distributed in the following manner (for the remaining 25 countries there were no data available on political participation) (Table 1.4.3).

Of the 82 countries or societies 55 are scaletypes and 27 or 33% are non-scale types, i.e. patterns not predicted by the theory. An ungenerous conclusion would be that this is a refutation of Lerner's hypothesis, a more generous conclusion would mention that most social science predictions are not even two-thirds correct anyhow, so the more cautious conclusion would probably be that the Lerner factor accounts for much, but by no means for everything. The total picture is, as always, 'more complicated than that'.

Some aspects of these complications become more clear if one looks at the frequent deviant patterns, such as numbers 2, 3 and 11. They all have low literacy levels in common but are high on one or two of the other indicators. Without drawing on commonsense knowledge stimulated by the proper names of the particular countries it is rather obvious what kinds of countries they are: number 2 could be a highly traditional country with a charismatic leader commanding a large turnout in even unrigged and relatively pluralistic elections; number 3 could be a country

Table 1.4.3. *A test of Lerner's hypothesis*

Pattern	Phase	Urbanization	Literacy	Media participation	Political participation	N
1	1	low	low	low	low	13
2		low	low	low	high	5
3		low	low	high	low	4
4		low	low	high	high	1
5		low	high	low	low	3
6		low	high	low	high	1
7		low	high	high	low	4
8		low	high	high	high	2
9	2	high	low	low	low	5
10		high	low	low	high	0
11		high	low	high	low	6
12		high	low	high	high	1
13	3	high	high	low	low	0
14		high	high	low	high	0
15	4	high	high	high	low	6
16	5	high	high	high	high	31
					Total	82

with a highly developed (although thinly spread) tertiary sector using the transistor revolution for advertising and other purposes; number 11 would be a more effective (and also more likely) development of number 3, adding urbanization. In short, there are many variations of the theme of development, and Lerner catches only some of them. But it should be mentioned that if political participation is left out, then Lerner's hypothesis predicts correctly 20 of the 23 countries that could not be included in Table 1.4.3, or 80 of the 107 (80%).

However, even if this test (or further data) yielded 90% confirmation instead of 67% or 80%, this synchronic result would by no means imply one specific diachronic trajectory. Non-scale patterns would be unlikely, but regression would not be ruled out by a finding based on synchronic data: a country might develop in jumps, passing the phases in order 0–2–1–4–3 rather than 0–1–2–3–4. This is obvious, but it tends to be forgotten since there is such a scarcity of analyses based on diachronic data.

From this excursion into *national* level analysis let us have a look at Lerner's way of handling his theory at the *individual* level. In principle he could do exactly the same at the national level since the four rates used to describe nations correspond to such social processes as mobility from rural to urban settings of concrete individuals, to alphabetization of these individuals, to their exposure to mass media of communication and their eventual participation in mass consumption and mass politics. However, for some reason that probably has to do with a general methodological predilection for latent structure analysis rather than cumulative scale analysis this is not done. Instead, an analysis of 1.357 of the interviews is carried out with an effort to divide them into two latent classes, class I and class II — the first one 'modern' and the second one 'traditional'.[13]

Recruitment probabilities are calculated for each one of the 32 response patterns and an inspection of these probabilities leads to a relatively clear division of the patterns in 'moderns' where 100% are recruited from class I, 'transitionals' where not more than 90% are recruited from any one class, and 'traditionals' where more than 90% are recruited from class II. It shows up that all moderns are literate and the others are non-literate, and, moreover, that the difference between transitionals and traditionals is that the former have a score of at least three on an additive index based on the five items in Table 1.4.2, whereas the latter have a score of less than three. It would have been interesting to see whether the results obtained by means of latent structure analysis in any sense differ from the categorization one would have obtained by a simple trichotomization of a crude additive index.

In most of the text these three groups are now dissected meticulously and skillfully in all six countries in terms of causes and consequences of their position. However, we are more concerned with the reasoning behind, and the first observation to make is that the categorization for individuals is not based on exactly the individual level variables listed in Table 1.4.1. The first three are there, with media exposure measured on an index from 0–12 depending on the degree of exposure. But then comes SES, socio-economic status, as one more indicator of social position and as the fifth variable the key factor in Lerner's system: the factor of *empathy*. This is defined as 'psychic mobility', as 'the capacity to see oneself in the other fellow's situation' — whether at other places, at other periods in time or in other positions in the society. Let us look more closely at this factor.[14]

Empathy, as developed by Lerner, is a composition of projection and injection — but Lerner leaves aside the psychoanalytic overtones of these concepts in terms of attribution of negative and positive properties. Divested of such evaluative connotations the concept has to do precisely with 'psychic mobility', Lerner's very fortunate term. People are high and low on this capacity as on everything else, and Lerner's thesis is that 'empathy is more functional in Modern than in Traditional society'[15] because 'the higher empathiser tends to become also the cash customer, the radio listener, the voter'.[16] The theory is actually quite simple: in order to take any one of the steps leading from traditional to modern, it is neither a necessary nor a sufficient condition to be able to anticipate, to envision oneself in the goal state be it as urban resident, as literate, as participant — but it surely helps! A minimum of cognition is a condition for positive evaluation, and a minimum of positive evaluation is a condition for taking the step — at least if one keeps in mind that one is talking about high correlations and strong tendencies rather than a deterministic model. For that reason Lerner feels that 'the more empathic respond to the lures'[17] — of cities, of literacy, of participation — so if we only know were the empathic are located and in what quantities then we should also know something about the future of the society.

To measure empathy, a set of nine role-playing questions were used 'that require for responsiveness some capacity to empathize — to imagine what it must be like to be head of government, editor of a newspaper, manager of a radio station or even "people like yourself"'.[18] The measure of empathy consisted of a count of answers different from the 'don't know' varieties. To validate the index, another index of how opinionated a person is was developed, and this index was, of course, highly correlated with urban residence, literacy and participation. And

> ... this left a group which — in terms of literacy, residence, media exposure — should have been homogeneous in the opinion range, but in fact was not. Some of these individuals had significantly more opinions than the others. The only satisfactory way to account for this divergence was by our personality variable — empathy. For what distinguished these illiterate, rural, non-participant individuals from their peers — where opinion-holding is concerned — was a keener interest in impersonal matters, a deeper desire to become participants of the opinion arena.[19]

Thus, Lerner uses empathy as a causal element that may develop even in the most traditional setting and serve as a psychological capacity that stimulates and is stimulated by moves to the city, acquisition of literacy and participation. In other words, it is capital at the intra-personal level that can be converted into modernization. Most theories of development make use of a personality variable at some place in the construction, such as McClelland's n-achievement or the many versions of entrepreneurial capacity, for instance as developed by Schumpeter and Hagen. Some individuals are more responsive to the challenges of modernization; some individuals are more effective as agents of modernization; and there is no doubt that there is a personality residual left when all structural variables are controlled in efforts to account for individual differences. Whether all these theories will converge toward a common basis is difficult to say, but Lerner's contribution is certainly as valuable as any other. There are, however, two comments that can be made, one of a methodological and one of a more theoretical nature.

One reviewer has commented about 'the tautological nature of the argument — concealed in the use of this special term [empathy]'.[20] At the general level where no operations are introduced it does come seriously close to a tautology: actual mobility and capacity of psychic mobility are so close that there is little wonder if the two should be correlated. That there are more car-buyers among car-wanters or even among people who know and dream about cars than among the rest will not startle anybody. But Lerner escapes from this difficulty through his operationalization since the *index* of empathy is based on role-playing items, and it is not trivial that the ability to answer questions like 'Suppose that you were head of the government. What are some of the things you would do?'[21] is related to modernization — both as a cause and as an effect.

But what is gained through operationalization is, in our mind, lost almost completely in the way the five items are combined in the latent structure analysis. The 32 patterns are derived from five dichotomous items, out of which two are clearly structural (urban-rural and SES), two are half-structural, half-personality characteristics (literacy and media exposure) and one, the crucial variable of empathy, is a typical personality variable. Thus, the classification in moderns, three types of transitionals and traditionals is based on a strange mixture of variables which complicates the theory because there is no clear model. We agree with Lerner that there is no need to distribute primacy between 'human nature' and 'social determinism'. But one wonders about the social determinants of empathy, which is lost sight of when empathy is lumped together with four more or less structural variables in even more global categories. Also, it sounds strange and unbelievable that all 'moderns' are literate and vice versa — it is difficult to accept a concept of modernism with so much emphasis on participation that the most tradition-oriented intellectual is classified as modern just because he can read and write.

In other words, it might have been better to leave empathy out of the index of modernism, and define the latter in the term that Lerner

52

actually prefers himself: participation. One aspect of modern society, no doubt, is participation, and at the mass level, mediated through modern mass media, usually based on achieved skill rather than on ascribed status, with a descriptive content in addition to the predominantly prescriptive content found in what Lerner calls 'oral systems'.[22] The difference is not merely in terms of scope — how many are reached — but also in terms of content. Thus, using as a dependent variable a number of indicators of participation in modern society, the role of the urban-rural dichotomy, literacy and SES could have been studied with, possibly, relatively obvious conclusions, and these findings could then have been enriched tremendously by bringing in empathy both as an independent and as a dependent variable, but above all as an intervening variable. The model would be something like that shown in Diagram 1.4.1.

Diagram 1.4.1. *A revision of Lerner's model*

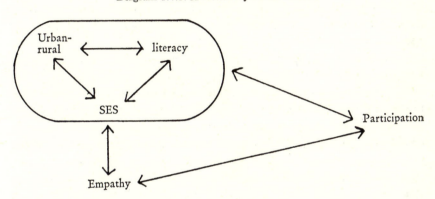

The double arrows stand for causation both ways, with the most structural variables grouped together in one cluster. Unfortunately, detailed analysis of how these variables are interrelated is lost sight of in Lerner's work for the reason mentioned — and the general thesis to be derived is probably that extreme care should be exercised when items are grouped together in an index, lest important propositions get lost because they become tautologies. To say that moderns are more empathic no longer makes sense when empathy already is included in the conceptualization of 'modern'.

Leaving this aside there is another very simple comment which serves as one of the theoretical bases for what we are trying to do in the present work. Lerner is concerned with 'the passing of traditional society' —

we are concerned with a traditional society that shows a remarkable ability to defend itself against change. Lerner looks at his six societies from the vantage point of the developed United States, to our mind too much defining development in terms of the particular trajectory that characterized that nation, immodestly called 'the first new nation' by another theoretician. Lerner sees sectors of modernity expanding and analyzes it in terms of injections or investment of empathy as well as of creation of more empathy. Empathy flows, carried by mobile persons, toward the centers of modernity, the cities, and upward in the social structure, but unlike fuel, the more it is used the more it expands. But implicit in this is the notion that the non-empathic are left behind in their traditional setting and that *the stayers will relate themselves to their traditionalism in a pattern of vicious, circular causation — the antithesis of the pattern of virtuous, circular causation between empathy and modernism presumably found among the leavers.* What is missing in Lerner's general theory is a more symmetrical view of the matter: 'the more empathic respond to the lures', *but they also leave behind the non-emphatic and the empathic that cannot leave for one reason or another.* And how do *they* relate themselves to their local traditional setting, usually at the village level? How do they respond? We know that *the non-empathic not only do not want but also do not know what they do not want.* But what about the people who know that they want modernism but cannot attain it?

To conclude: Lerner presents us with a basic factor: psychic mobility or empathy — empathy with other positions in *space*, in *time* and in the *social structure* — and argues convincingly that this factor plays a significant role in development, although it may be that he stresses empathy as a cause somewhat too much and empathy as an effect somewhat too little. It should be emphasized that to be high in empathy in Lerner's sense is probably a necessary but not a sufficient condition for being a sensate in Sorokin's sense: the empathic may be a dreamer and leave it at that, but the sensate bent on *change* and *control* of the external world must have *some* kind of image as to *where* and *how*. Of course, theoretically his creed may be 'anywhere, only away from here', but in practice some course is chosen, some goal is indicated however vaguely — and that is hardly conceivable without a minimum of ability to project oneself into that goal, even of anticipatory consumption of the goal; and that is already a component in empathy. In short, we would expect the two factors to be related, but in the sense that there is a higher proportion of people high on empathy who are low on sensate ideology than there are people high on sensate ideology who are low on empathy.

Potentially, then, using both factors should give us some additional insight into the dynamism involved.

Unlike Sorokin, Lerner deals with the micro-level, and he tries to locate his hero, the empathic person, in the social structure, but fails to some extent — in our mind — because of some unfortunate tactical decisions in the construction of indices. Strategically, his analysis carries the exploration deeper into the social fabric — but then the problem of asymmetry appears. Lerner focuses on the leavers and neglects those who stay behind, although the idea of *an increasing empathy gap* between the modern and the traditional sectors — more or less the same as the urban vs. the rural sectors — is an obvious implication of his thinking. In short, an important task would be to apply some of Lerner's basic ideas and to try to locate the empathic and the non-empathic, the psychologically more and less mobile, in the social structure — so as to get some basis for speculation about the empathy gap. An attempt in this direction will be made in Chapter Four.[23]

1.5. *Banfield's theory: the role of amoral familism*

To move from Lerner to Banfield[1] is to move considerably closer to the field of the empirical investigation to be presented here. Although Banfield does not deal with data from Sicily he gets the empirical stimulus for his thinking about development almost from the neighbor — at at least in a global perspective. The 'backward society' the book deals with is a village — called Montegrano, located in the province of Potenza in Southern Italy and observed during a stay in 1954–1955. It is on the mainland, but economic conditions are not too different from the Sicilian villages in our study — it is the same arid *Mezzogiorno*. This does not mean that his findings have immediate empirical tenability outside that village itself: if anything should be the moral of his study (and of ours) it is precisely the danger of believing that there is no significant variation between villages even when economic conditions look similar to the outsider, and perhaps also to the insider. As a matter of fact, we are not even very concerned about whether the findings are tenable inside that particular village: it is the basic variable, and its use in developing a theory is our concern.

Banfield is concerned with the same problem as we are: Why this ultra-stability, this tenacious persistence in the pattern of the past — 'past' relative to what the author is used to and that he knows has permeated many other sectors of Italy, to a certain point? He starts by giving a vivid description of Montegrano, based on his field notes and some statistics, and then proceeds by the method of contrast to what he calls 'some usual explanations of the phenomenon'. As the title indicates, these are the explanations with 'a strong appeal to common sense' that he is not going to accept. At the risk of presenting these six alternative hypotheses in an even flatter and more easily rejectable form than Banfield himself does, we shall summarize them as follows:[2] 1) *poverty* is so pervasive that the struggle for existence permits no time for political life in the time budget; 2) *ignorance* is so pervasive that people 'can have no notion of what is possible to accomplish politically'; 3) the *class struggle theory*, that the upper classes exploit and organize to suppress the lower classes; 4) differences in political behavior are due to the circumstances of *land tenure*; 5) the theme of *distrust* is everpresent because of centuries of negative experiences; and 6) *fatalism* as a basic creed and style of life makes it improbable and unnatural for the peasant to expect or hope for much more than he has.[2] Obviously, these theories cannot be used to explain exactly the same things, but they can be used and have been used as levers for analyses. All of them have a certain *prima facie* validity, and it is interesting to see how Banfield proceeds in his efforts to discard them so that his own theory can shine even more brightly when contrasted with all this darkness.

First, he concentrates the problem of stability (in the first page of his book) down into one of explaining why there is almost no concerted action — comparing Montegrano with a small United States town of the same size in Utah. The book is permeated by the idea that *organization at the grass-roots level* is among the most important vehicles of progress. In repudiating these six competing absence-of-collective-action theories, which he feels he must because 'one could not on the basis of any of them ... or all of them together ... predict how the people of Montegrano would behave in a concrete situation'[3], he obviously has to show that even though these theories may explain other elements in backwardness, they do not explain adequately the absence of collective action.

He observes that 'there is hardly a man in Montegrano who could not contribute a third of his time to some community project without a loss of income'[4] and uses this observation to discard the *poverty* hypothesis.[5] Objectively this may be a correct observation, but there is an element of misplaced concreteness about time in it. In a highly organized society it makes sense to divide the day into two parts, work and non-work, and to divide the latter into all kinds of time segments with a certain portion reserved for 'community projects' — improving a road, building a sports field, etc. But in a society of this kind there is never a clear-cut borderline between work and non-work — the peasant cannot afford that. He can perform the well-defined part of his job quickly, in fact he will often have to stretch the job in order to give to his time-budget any kind of work structure. But in his situation the remainder is not leisure, *but non-work that may become work :* it is waiting for something to happen, to turn up. Says a Sicilian peasant,

> Why do I sit here ? Because if I do not sit here you can be sure something turns up, suddenly there is a job to be done, a car breaks down and somebody needs a hand. Last week when I was not here somebody else got the chance. ... [6]

While the problem in organized societies may often be to protect oneself against claims on one's capacity to perform a job, the problem here is to protect oneself both against not being claimed and, particularly, against others being claimed instead of oneself. The villager has to be visible, or at least that is what he believes. Two protective measures in other societies are *competence* and *entitlement :* if these are scarce, visibility is of less avail and waiting less necessary. Where there is a garage and a certified mechanic he will be called upon; where there is a caste system supported by a system of belief in pollution there will be a similar constraint on the relation between jobs and job-seekers — although in the first case the course of the constraint is mainly in the employer, in the second case in the employee. The impoverished *industrioso* in Southern Italy is only partly protected by these mechanisms: there are jobs not everybody would take, partly because they feel others are more able, partly because they do not want to. But there is a vast range of unregulated competitiveness. This does not mean that it may not be more rational to engage in collective action, as Banfield implies; but waiting is neither necessarily irrational, a rationalization of laziness or an expression of *dolce far niente.*

The *ignorance* argument is dispensed with by referring to how much the villagers know about politics, and Banfield found that 'Most of the opinions were reasonable, ... Some were very thoughtful'.[7] It turns out that the two 'opinions' he quotes to illustrate this also illustrate that 'they are not so simple-minded, however, as to suppose that Communist claims can be taken at face value' — so the value bias in Banfield's criterion of 'thoughtfulness' seems clear. This is no essential objection against his argument that formal schooling is neither a necessary nor a sufficient condition for participation on the political opinion market, but it is impossible to dispense that easily with the importance of formal education for active political *participation*. A political leader may draw on the support of uneducated masses if some sociological conditions are fulfilled, but he may not himself easily compete with institutionalized power wielders already on the power market if he cannot legitimize his claim to power by reference to other factors than sheer force and mass size. Nor is Banfield's comparison with St. George in Mormon Utah[8] so convincing: even though 'poverty and ignorance were as great or greater than that of the Montegranesi', the Mormons had the distinct advantage of being given a fresh start. St. George had no prior history when they started; possibilities were unexpored; there would by necessity be new situations to deal with, with no age-old patterns setting precedents for distributions of value, etc., whereas Montegranesi and Silciani can look back at centuries and millennia of consistency, except that the standard of living was higher (but of course also lower) in some parts of Sicily some centuries ago than it is today. Nothing seems to breed stability as much as stability, precisely because it gives a pattern to everything and no necessity for social innovation. Still, if Banfield's Montegranesi, as he has pictured them, migrated *en bloc* to places with unexplored possibilities they would probably to a large extent fall back on the pattern Banfield mentions as his factor. To change their cultural pattern they would probably have to be substantially diluted by others.

Banfield dispenses with the other arguments, much in the same manner without giving them too much of a chance to assert themselves.

For instance, the *class struggle argument* is dealt with rather summarily:

> Like poverty and ignorance, they (class and status relations) are general conditions which, so to speak, form the causal background.[9]

But later on he is more explicit:

> In general the peasant is correct in imputing his motivations to the gentry. But he errs in attributing to them an energy and an ability to act in concert, which they do not possess.[10]

Two such examples of peasant thinking are given; the first was the idea that the upper classes systematically prevented improvement of the schools to keep them illiterate, the second that they had cooperated to prevent circulation of information about emigration. It is quite possible that Banfield is correct when he says that 'if any such circulars existed, the reason they were not distributed was almost certainly ordinary indifference and incompetence'. But a distinction should probably be made between cooperating *for* something to be done and cooperation for something *not* to be done. Given the general reason the upper classes in traditional societies have for resisting almost any change, and given the general asymmetry between preservation and innovation, the upper classes have a tremendous advantage. The innovators can rarely command so high a consensus because innovation implies a choice between alternative *kinds* of innovation, whereas preservation involves only an answer to the much more fundamental question, shall we have any innovations at all? The broad and consensual *no* is at the root of much of the organized activity by the Sicilian mafia, and it would be strange if Montegrano upper classes should not also be favored by this differential in in organizational capacity, dependent on whether it is activity in favor of or against something new.

Banfield discards the theory of *fatalism* in a different way, by pointing out that it does not account for the rationality and perseverance so often exhibited in individual action, upper or lower class; and there is nothing in the fatalism argument *per se* that explains why it should apply to collective action only. Hence, whereas the other factors in Banfield's view explain too little, the difficulty with fatalism is that it explains too much.

At this point Banfield encounters a difficulty: the high Communist vote which certainly would be seen by many as a sign of some capacity for collective action — presumably even in the non-privileged strata of society. For his argument Banfield needs some general refutation of the idea of *structural* causes for the high Communist vote, because he is most interested in the idea that there is a 'tendency of voters to shift erratically between right and left from election to election'.[11] To do this he displays a table which gives percentages of the left-wing vote, illiteracy among men, density of population and proportion of laborers for eleven villages in the Montegrano district. And then he proceeds to some of his frequently encountered reasoning of doubtful validity.

First of all he sets up an hypothesis (which 'is often said')

> ... that the Communist vote is heaviest where the pressure of population on resources is greatest (i.e. where chronic poverty is most severe and widespread), where lack of education — and specifically illiteracy — is greatest, and where the proportion of landless laborers to proprietors is greatest. [12]

It is true that this 'is often said' and for that reason worth testing. But Banfield's way of disproving it is by case inspection of the table:

... these factors do not seem to have any relation to the strength of the Communist vote. As Table 2 shows, illiteracy is highest in the town where the Communist vote was lightest in 1953, population density is not significantly greater where the Communist vote was heavy, and the proportion of laborers is greatest in some of the most conservative towns.[13]

However, if we calculate all possible rank correlations,[14] we get Table 1.5.1.

Table 1.5.1. *Rank correlations between some structural variables (eleven villages in the Montegrano election district, 1953 and 1956).*

	Left-wing vote 1953	Left-wing vote 1956	Illiteracy among men	Density of population	Proportion of laborers
Left-wing vote 1953	1.00	(0.44)	− 0.26	+ 0.57*	+ 0.01
Left-wing vote 1956	—	(1.00)	(− 0.81)*	(+ 0.25)	(− 0.28)
Illiteracy among men	—		1.0	—	+ 0.65*
Density of population	—		—	1.00	+ 0.45
Proportion of laborers	—		—	—	1.00

The Table is actually quite interesting as a basis for speculations that sound much more reasonable in view of other studies of Communist vote: it is precisely the combination of *low* illiteracy with a *high* density of population that may be conducive to left-wing radicalism.[15] A high proportion of laborers might perhaps also be conducive to a radical vote if it were not so highly correlated with illiteracy. Density of population is not correlated with illiteracy and, consequently, may yield a significant correlation with Communist vote (when Banfield says 'population density is not significantly greater where the Communist vote was heavy', this is simply not the case, even if 'significant' is taken in its statistical sense).

But the interesting factor is the negative correlation with illiteracy. Although it is not statistically significant for 1953 the finding calls for a study with similar data for a great many Italian voting districts, which could also include a detailed study of the exceptions to the general trend, the exceptions that have led Banfield astray.[16] For Banfield uses his data to discard the hypothesis that illiteracy is positively linked to Communist voting — a conclusion which Table 1.5.1 would certainly warrant too — but does not explore the much more interesting finding

* Significant at the 0.05 level. This is not really a statistical sample, however, so significance levels do not express much.

that it is negatively related. Again, this seems to be attributable to the value bias mentioned above: if Communism is regarded as a threat or at least as negative it is better to have it as a concomitant of an undesirable condition such as illiteracy than of a desirable one such as education.

However, much more important for our purposes is the logic involved: Banfield seems to feel that a scientific hypothesis can be refuted by the single case method — but every social scientist with some experience with this type of data will safeguard himself by phrasing his pet hypotheses in terms of 'tendencies', 'correlations', etc. As a matter of fact, by Banfield's implicit criterion it would be very easy to refute his entire book — if he had presented data of a kind similar to the data he uses to refute the theories of others. Besides, Banfield would actually need a complete set of zero correlations in Table 1.5.1, because it looks as if he feels a need to discard structural hypotheses in both directions. In short, he fails to satisfy the criteria he uses to judge others.

What we have said so far may be interpreted as rather strong criticism, but we nevertheless agree with Banfield in his conclusion concerning structural explanations:

These theories, it should also be noted, do not explain — and may even be inconsistent with — the tendency of voters to shift erratically between right and left from election to election.[17]

More needs to be explained, but here there are some indications that Banfield may have committed an ecological fallacy: structural analyses of villages never do explain individual votes. What we have shown does not mean that the *people* with high education vote Communist, only that there is something in *villages* with lower illiteracy rates that may foster a higher left-wing vote. Of course, over and above such structural factors *there may be other factors* that account for the 'erratic' variations in space and time, but the structural factors should be known. In short, Banfield should have calculated the rank correlations. But if he had done so he might have rested content with these findings and never developed his own provoking ideas. For Banfield seems to be a victim of the frequently held belief that for his own theory to be valid other theories must be shown to be invalid first — the ideas of coexistence and interaction are rarely found; theories are seen as competitive.

But even though his efforts to refute other theories are unconvincing, Banfield's positive contribution is nonetheless interesting: the Montegranesi act as if they were following the rule: *Maximize the material, short-run advantage of the nuclear family; assume that others will do likewise.*

One whose behavior is consistent with this rule will be called an 'amoral familist'.[18] The rest of Banfield's book is an elaboration of this principle with speculations, mainly based on TAT stories, concerning the genesis and operation of this principle. This, then, is the *moral basis* of the *backward society*, according to Banfield.

But we shall put this hypothesis into a more general perspective, cutting the specific link to the family. Man is equipped with *loyalties* of different strengths that attach him to anything from the smallest micro-unit (a human being) to the largest macro-unit (the world, the human race). In most cases it is reasonable to assume that loyalties are stronger to units of which the individual himself is a number (e.g. to himself, his nuclear family, his extended family, his clan, his village, his class, his region, his nation, his power bloc, etc.). Imagine that the latter is the case; substitute 'power bloc' for 'nuclear family' in the Banfield axiom above, and a rule that can be used to account for much in contemporary international relations, especially when the system is in a polarized phase, will ensue.[19] Correspondingly, substitute 'himself' or 'his class' to get simplified versions of well-known bases for explaining economic and political behavior.

For instance, Banfield's first 'logical implication' of this principle is that 'no one will further the interest of the group or community except as it is to his private advantage to do so'[20] — a relatively trite statement on human motivation — which is sharpened considerably in his thirteenth 'implication':

> In fact, he will vote against measures which will help the community without helping him, because, even though his position is unchanged in absolute terms, he considers himself worse off if his neighbor's position changes for the better.[21]

All this can be taken as interesting propositions about behavior on level n + 1 if loyalties are firmly attached to lower levels — probably especially to the level immediately below since that is usually the strongest competitor as a source of the kind of satisfaction offered at level n + 1. Thus: strong national loyalties will impede international cooperation; strong village loyalties or class loyalties will impede cooperation on the national level; strong family loyalties will be detrimental to collective efforts on the village level. Nationalism, familism, egotism are structurally similar in their consequences, all depending upon the level one has in focus. In general, strong loyalties at level n are highly instrumental for concerted action at that level, detrimental for concerted action at level n + 1 and either or neither for action at lower levels.

We shall not examine in detail the consequences Banfield draws from his principle of 'amoral familism', where the term 'amoral' (though not the same as 'immoral') seems to indicate that Banfield considers the family level of attachment to be short of what is ethically desirable — the village level is 'better'. But from the national point of view the latter might well be called 'amoral village-ism', and the terms 'amoral egotism' and 'amoral nationalism' bring to mind other criteria of moral evaluation. We would actually prefer the neutral term 'familism', although Banfield only wants to point out that they act 'without morality only in relation to persons outside the family'. Banfield analyzes, very ingeniously, how this principle prevents and disturbs collective action, and his analysis is certainly a contribution to the understanding of whimsical political behavior: the interests of one's own family will have priority to the interests of the village, both in terms of salience and importance — hence the villager will vote for the person who can secure his short-run family advantages, not for the person who can give advantages to the village as a whole according to some ideological pattern. To raise the standard in the village, even proportionately to all families involved so that internal rankings remain undisturbed, does not in any real sense help one's own family — what a villager who is an 'amoral familist' really wants is a change in his standing relative to other families. No welfare politician, with no streak of favoritism, can bring this about. Hence, politics becomes highly particularistic and even 'corrupt' — *from the village point of view*. From the familism point of view, politics takes on the most logical form; ballots are used as punishment or reward according to what politicians have done to secure relative advancement of each family, not that of the total collectivity.

Of course, this is schematic and should be seen in our minds only as an erratic 'familistic' component, on top of the structural components alluded to already. Actually, *the essence of the reasoning is that the target of loyalty is maladapted to the level on which new institutions can emerge today*. Banfield seems to think that this is the village level, although there are reasons to believe that even in the *Mezzogiorno* the days of the village as the level of modernized economic activity and basic socio-political change are past, and that some sense of at least regional loyalty is needed to create and maintain patterns of exchange on a level better adjusted to the complexities of the socio-economic realities of modern, not to mention neo-modern society.

So far, so good. It remains only to be seen whether there is any truth to this theory. Banfield makes the theory highly acceptable by means of his many stories and quotes, and he also has some very imaginative and interesting applications of TAT stories and dilemma questions of the 'which is better: 1) he is a miser who works hard, 2) he is generous but a loafer' type.[22] The results all point in the same direction: loyalty to the family, a deep sense of immanent tragedy and catastrophe (especially premature death) and a feeling that the family is the only source of protection. A basic point here is the word 'nuclear' in the basic axiom — the extended family is not seen as sufficiently cohesive to fall back on.[23] Evidence of all this is piled upon evidence, of many different types, none quite satisfactory singly, but quite commanding when combined in Banfield's brilliant manner.

Banfield actually protects himself against efforts to falsify his hypothesis in two ways, of which the first is valid but not satisfactory and the second seems invalid. He says:

> The value of the hypothesis ... does not depend upon the possibility of showing that all, or even any, of the people of Montegrano consciously follow the rule of action set forth here. For the hypothesis to be useful, it need only be shown that they act *as if* they follow the rule.[24]

Nobody would deny the usefulness of the planetary system model of the atoms for, for instance, the chemistry of the first half of this century — regardless of whether there were a more direct sense in which the atoms 'looked' like a planetary system or not. But to *account for* empirical regularities by means of a formula, a principle, is one thing, to *explain* them another. To explain the behavior of the Montegranesi more is needed: one has to develop indicators of familism, demonstrate its presence, show how it works both in theory and with empirical data. It is clear that Banfield also feels this, otherwise he would not have felt the necessity for including all the data, particularly data showing differences among TAT stories told by the Montegranesi, by some Northern Italians from the province of Rovigo and by 'some' (not all) of the rural Kansans to whom the test was administered — the latter 'included here only to provide a contrast which will highlight what is characteristically Italian in the others'.[25]

This last point leads to Banfield's argument about selectivity, sampling and more systematic techniques, about which he is completely frank:

> It was not practical to employ sophisticated sampling techniques. (To have done so would have left no time for interviewing.) Therefore we do not know how

representative our interviews were; our impression is, however, that they were highly representative of that part of the population which lives in the town and reasonably representative of the nearby country dwellers. ... Since our intention is not to 'prove' anything ... we think our data ... are sufficient. There are enough data, at least, to justify systematic inquiry along these lines. Until such inquiry has been made, the argument made here must be regarded as highly tentative.[26]

However, no 'sophisticited sampling techniques' would have been necessary. But the difficulty is not so much with being representative as with applying ideal type reasoning: everything fits too well in the book. Certainly, there must have been nuances and differentials which Banfield does not bring into the limelight: *some* heads of households, for instance, are no doubt *more familistic* than others; and *some* heads of households are no doubt less consistent in their *neglect of collective action* than others. *We would say that Banfield's thesis hinges on the correlation between these two factors, or related factors, on the individual level,* but this is never shown in the book. As the data are presented we have reason to believe that Banfield might have used data about one person to show how familistic he is and about another person to show how he neglects collective action, and then might have done what anthropologists often seem to do: added together some bits of information at the individual level to produce a thesis at the level of collectivity. We shall now look more closely into this.

Imagine that whatever indicators (verbal or non-verbal) we used for 'degree of familistic orientation' and 'readiness for collective action', cross-tabulations showed little or no correlation. If the indicators were chosen to our satisfaction, there would still be the possibility that the 'true' relationship was masked by third factors, singly or combined; but there are good techniques at our disposal for unmasking such relationships, if we have some theoretical insights. But if this does not produce a correlation either, would Banfield's thesis not have been refuted? No, there might still be the possibility that on a regional, national or international scale the average level of familism in Montegrano was already so high, and the average level of collective action so low, that the small differentials present no longer had causal functions — that differences and correlations would only appear if a sample including Montegranesi and some people from towns with a different *ethos* were studied.

To bring some order into this important methodological and substantive problem, consider Diagram 1.5.1.[27]

The Diagram assumes that we have found indicators of both variables

65

Diagram 1.5.1. *The collective and individual levels of analysis,* correlations between familism (F) and lack of collective action (L)*

		Inter-village level	
		Present	Absent
Intra-village, inter-individual level	Present	Case 1 (L, F axes)	Case 2 (L, F axes)
	Absent	Case 3 (L, F axes)	Case 4 (L, F axes)

on both levels. For the village level the percentage that are 'familistic', or some other statistic measuring central tendency of the distribution for the village inhabitants, may do, but *sui generis* characteristics would also be of value. In the Diagram, Cases 1 and 4 are uninteresting. The latter represents no Banfield effect at all, at the individual or village level, and would in our mind constitute a refutation of the hypothesis. Case 1 would constitute a complete verification, at both levels. Cases 2 and 3 are the more interesting ones and can be used to explore the relation between the individual and the collective levels.

In Case 2 the mechanism works at the individual level, so as to produce a correlation, but there is no similar effect ordering the villages on both variables, whereas in Case 3 the total Banfield effect is on the collective level. Banfield reasons as if he were trying to prove Case 3,[28] with Montegrano as the box high up to the right, Rovigo in the middle and rural Kansas, not to mention St. George, Utah, in the lower left corner; but he *proves* neither that Case nor any of the others, since he uses individual level insufficiently to prove a collective level hypothesis. Actually, the ideal type of analysis the social anthropologist is likely to engage in will probably, in most cases, lead to propositions of the type seen in Case 3: explicit or implicit, proved or unproved, valid or invalid. And the type of analysis the survey analyst engages in, with individuals as the only units of analysis, may similarly lead to propositions

* The graphs are for the individuals (dots), but individuals in the same villages have been grouped together (in boxes) to illustrate special cases.

of the type pictured in Case 2. Neither is satisfactory alone, and we turn now to the problem of combining the two levels of analysis.

The most famous case of Case 3 analysis in the sociological literature on 'the great transition' is probably Max Weber's analysis. One quote will do:

> ... the wonderfully purposeful organization and arrangement of this cosmos is, according both to the revelation of the Bible and to natural intuition, evidently designed by God to serve the utility of the human race. This makes labour in the service of impersonal social usefulness appear to promote the glory of God and hence to be willed by him.[29]

This is, perhaps, an apt description of a system of belief, an ethos, charactizering a collectivity which also ranks high on 'entrepreneurship'. But this reasoning applies to a number of other cases as well, as Rostow points out.

> In a world where Samurai, Parsees, Jews, North Italians, Turkish, Russian, and Chinese civil servants (as well as Huguenots, Scotsmen and British north-countrymen) have played the role of a leading elite in economic growth, John Calvin should not be made to bear quite this weight.[30]

And Rostow adds, 'More fundamentally, allusion to a positive scale of religious or other values conducive to profit-maximizing activities is an insufficient sociological basis for this important phenomenon.' He adds two conditions to the 'appropriate value system': 'the new elite must feel itself denied the conventional routes to prestige and power' and 'the traditional society must be sufficiently flexible (or weak) to permit its members to seek material advance (or political power) as a route upwards alternative to conformity'.

The importance of these reflections (to which many more factors might be added) lies in the ideas given for enriching the type of Case 3 analysis given by Weber. In Rostow's model it is not necessary to assume that the entrepreneur *himself* is imbued with the Protestant or Calvinist beliefs — he may actually be even less of a believer than the rest of the community. What matters is that his activities to the believing onlookers may be presented, and indeed experienced, as compatible with a belief system they believe in or want others to believe in (or at least to believe that they believe in). And if it is not only compatible with, but even can be seen to epitomize this belief system, it is even better. The two factors mentioned by Rostow in addition to the value compatibility are societal, not individual, variables — and they may or may not be found within the same belief system. All that is needed is that they are found within the same society and combined by some kind of mechanism so as to facilitate or impede development.

But the difficulty with this collective level type of analysis Weber and Banfield engaged in is that almost anything may be proved that way. A village (or culture) low on Y may be found to be high on X whereas another collectivity may be found to be high on Y and low on X. The imaginative mind is then called upon to find a link between X and Y, and the chances of success are proportionate to the amount of imagination, Of course, if the collective level hypothesis is really tested on more than two villages (often only one village is used!), some constraints are put on the free play of imagination. And if, in addition, relevant data on individuals are not only obtained, but also really cross-tabulated — as neither Weber, nor Banfield actually does — a relationship may be demonstrated, if it is appropriately tested for spuriousness (unless one requires perfect correlation for an hypothesis to be verified — as Banfield does). This not only extends the finding to the individual level and combines Case 3 and Case 2 analysis into Case 1 analysis, but it may in addition be a *test* of explanations offered in collective level analysis. But if this is not done, and only collective level analysis is carried out, there is no way of knowing what mechanisms are really working at the individual level. On the one hand, this makes it too easy to 'explain': a high number of variables of the type Rostow mentions can always be paraded by the experienced analyst. On the other hand it becomes difficult to *really* explain, because collective level analysis is bound to rest on individual level analysis: social scientists explain social action, but not in terms of group actors, only in terms of individual actors. Thus, even though Rostow's entrepreneur does not have to be a Calvinist, it would be good if one could *demonstrate* that he 1) feels mobility opportunities blocked and 2) perceives chances to open new roads — or at least that he 3) is an imitator of others. Another thing is that it may be too much to require that these factors should be present at the conscious level, so it may be difficult to get at this by interview-questionnaire techniques.

The difficulty with Banfield's reasoning consists precisely in this: although it is clear that his theory is based on mechanisms working at the individual, or at most at the family level — with familism constantly interfering with other possible activities — his data are combined at the collective level. He seems to want to prove Case 1, gives up because of 'sampling difficulties', heads for Case 3 instead, but does not quite make it. This is not merely methodological hairsplitting; it does matter both theoretically and practically whether the pattern of familism and lack of collective action presented by social reality come closer to Case 2 or Case 3. In the first case there is a consistent trend *inside the village*, providing all innovators with a nucleus of people low on familism and high on potential for collective action. If these people in addition are not located in too peripheral positions in the society, there may be a possibility for really change-oriented action. In Case 3, however, there is no such consistent tendency on the village level, and hence in all probability less conscious motivation along these lines: there is no polarization on which social action can be built. *On a national or regional level, however*, the village lowest on familism and highest on collective action in Case 3 may take a lead. The decisive pattern, then, is located neither on the village nor on the family level; it is on the level above that Case 3 becomes really meaningful as a potential for change. In an unintegrated, insular economy of the village type we would say that Case 2 represents the optimistic picture in terms of possibilities for change; in a more integrated economy of the regional type we would say that Case 3 gives the brighter perspectives for the future.

Admittedly, this reasoning hinges on the unproved, but plausible hypothesis that there is some relation between correlation and readiness for action, that action is most likely where the combination of important variables is most crystallized (i.e. shows highest intercorrelation). In short, our criticism of Banfield at this point is that he should have given individual level information in cross-tabulated form, since this is such a crucial problem for theoretical and practical reasons. Failing to do this, and/or if he feels that the relation only holds at the collective level, he should have 1) proved that this collective hypothesis is tenable, 2) specified how the collective relation is translated into individual action by indicating mechanisms analogous to Rostow's and 3) demonstrated that they are in fact operative at the individual level. But even with these shortcomings his book still remains a brilliant statement of one of the more provocative and illuminating hypotheses in the field, inspiring other investigators to pursue research along the same lines. More particularly, we would like to see whether familists are, in fact, less development oriented. It seems reasonable to hypothesize that a familistic attitude might, in fact, be embedded in an ideational ideology, but one could also imagine a highly sensate attitude at the family level and a highly empathic capacity on behalf of the family. In other words, familism locates the focus of the loyalty; it does not *a priori* imply anything about change orientation or psychic mobility. But even if this is less fruitful as a line of research, we would like to locate the familists in the social structure in order to be better able to evaluate the effects of their narrow perspective on social affairs. An attempt in this direction will be made in Chapter 5.[31]

1.6. *The plan for the empirical study*

We can now be more explicit as to the plan for the empirical study. On the one hand, we want to be able to classify people on a number of value dimensions, more particularly on:

Cultural mentality, interpreted as *sensates vs. ideationals* (Sorokin)

Psychic mobility, interpreted as (Lerner)
1) empathy in social structure	*social perspective, high vs. low*
2) empathy in space	*space perspective, high vs. low*
3) empathy in time	*time perspective, high vs. low*
4) efforts to move or not	*stayers vs. leavers*

Amoral familism, interpreted as *non-familists vs. familists* (Banfield)

Essentially these are three variables, one based on each author, but psychic mobility has been split into four that to some extent can serve as each others' checks (in addition we shall also make use of two ways of approaching the sensate vs. ideational distinction).

The three, or six, dichotomies given above give the names of *dramatis personae*, where the stage is the village and the drama is 'development'. The hero is called 'modern', the villain is referred to as 'traditional' — but they take on different clothes depending on whether Sorokin's, Lerner's or Banfield's script is used. Together these variables will yield ample opportunity for analysis based on averages and dispersions in value distributions, and even for analysis of the intercorrelation between these attitude orientations. Thus, some images can be obtained of the total value situation of, say, a village. But to gain perspective at the macro-level more than one village should be used, so that some collective level analysis can also be carried out. And to gain in perspective at the micro-level it should not be assumed that the dichotomies above necessarily are real, empirically found persons. They are abstractions that mingle and blend inside living humans; the *dramatis personae* are often *homunculi* rather than humans. Sorokin, Lerner and Banfield have too much of a tendency to reify their heroes and villains and to identify them with persons rather than with propensities and inclinations within persons. But that is legitimate only in consistent and stable cultures and societies, not in transitional societies where most people are, precisely, *members of two worlds*.

On the other hand, the idea announced at the end of 1.2 was to combine personality variables with structural variables, such as age, sex, level of education, economic position, occupational position — the latter both in terms of economic sector and in terms of social rank. The point, made several times in the preceding sections, is that it is insufficient to know *how many* have this or that value orientation, one will also have to know *who* they are. One answer to the question of *who* is to bring in more personality variables, but here the answer will be given in structural terms. *Distribution in the social structure* is the first type of what we have called 'structural analysis'. To illustrate this way of thinking, let us develop an example which will also play some role in the analysis of the empirical data.

For this purpose an image of the social structure of traditional societies is needed, and we shall use the model given in Table 1.2.2, consisting of four combinations: *primary* sector, high and low, and *tertiary* sector, high and low. (A detailed rationale for this analytical scheme will be given in section 3.5.) These are four major structural categories or positions, filled with people who are bearers of more or less internalized, more or less consistent, more or less salient value systems. Imagine that in the total population there is a relatively even split between moderns and traditionals, variously expressed as ideationals or sensates or some other term, but that there is an overrepresentation of moderns, M, in two of the categories and of traditionals, T, in the other two — in fact that the discrepancies are so big that it would matter socially. Since there are four categories altogether we get $\binom{4}{2}$ or 6 possible ways in which this can happen (Diagram 1.6.1).

In the Diagram, types 1 and 2 have been grouped together as *class* models since they presuppose gross differences between classes; types 3 and 4 have been termed *sector* models since they assume differences between sectors; types 5 and 6 have been termed *diagonal* models since like pairs are found on the diagonals. We shall not speculate here on the

Diagram 1.6.1. *Possible value distributions in a traditional society*

	P T	P T	P T	P T	P T	P T
High	M | M	T | T	M | T	T | M	M | T	T | M
Low	T | T	M | M	M | T	T | M	T | M	M | T
	1	2	3	4	5	6
	Class models		*Sector models*		*Diagonal models*	

conditions that might have produced these distributions, but shall look into the *consequences* these six distributions could have for subsequent development.

The first four models have this much in common: the traditional conflicts between classes (high vs. low, haves vs. have-nots) and between sectors (farmers against merchants, countryside against city, etc.) are accentuated by heavy ideological differentials. In other words, the conflicts of interest, latent or manifest, between classes or sectors will structure the conflicts of value over development, and vice versa. This will create conditions for easy mobilization of conflict organizations, for conflict symbolism and conflict terminology, and more so the stronger the correlation. It is, then, to some extent, a question of who are stronger, the moderns or the traditionals. And to this there is no clear and general answer — 'it depends'. However, some theoretical leads can be given.

In the first pattern there is an 'enlightened' upper class with all odds in its favor. It has an image of change, and the power to realize the image — both in terms of efforts to convince the lower class that the changes are in their own interest, to win them over one by one or to coerce them. The only danger for the upper class would be if they went too fast, or their course was too heavily loaded with coercion. They would have in their favor the usual lead the center of society has over the periphery as a pace-setter, as a medium through which new ideas originate or at least pass, to be imitated later on by the periphery, etc. This can be used by the upper classes to make the lower classes equally modern, but it can also be used to turn the techniques of modern society into tools for more refined exploitation of a lagging lower class.

In the second pattern all this is reversed. The upper class no longer fulfills its role as a provider of guidance but sticks to the status quo, for instance on the basis of, and to preserve its vested interests. The roles are reversed, with the lower class as the center from which new ideas originate, an incongruous combination pregnant with conflict potential and easily absorbed in general class conflict. The result may be an accumulation of frustration with subsequent aggression at the bottom of the society with individual or collective outlets, the first in the form of migration, criminality and mobility, the second in the form of mass apathy or revolution, with subsequent victory or corruption of the modern ideas.

The third pattern is similar to the second if we assume that the tertiary sector, generally speaking, has a more central position in society than the primary sector does. It usually possesses more power in the sense of being better organized, having more financial power and more information and more access to means of communication at its disposal. Again, the results may be as indicated above: an accumulation of frustrated hopes, due to the resistance from the tertiary sector, that turn into withdrawal or aggression at the individual or collective level.

Correspondingly, the fourth pattern is similar to the first. The ideas and techniques that can modernize the primary sector may emanate from the city or tertiary sector in general (for instance via agricultural colleges), but so may techniques that can be used to expand the tertiary and secondary sectors precisely by keeping the primary sector traditional (for instance by means of the famous Latin American pattern of 'colonizacion interna', whereby blue-collar or white-collar workers in the cities can be paid low wages because all the products from the primary sector are cheap and because the peasants are paid badly — thereby liberating profits made in the secondary or tertiary sectors for consumption or investment).

The last two models differ from the first four because the conflict between moderns and traditionals crisscross both with the class and with the sector distinctions. There can be no clear way of mobilizing a class or a sector in an evolutionary struggle either in favor of modernism or in favor of the status quo. On the one hand, this creates a more complicated situation with less structural basis for revolution or status quo, and, on the other hand, there seems to be the kind of basis where many things can happen, none of them very dramatic. All that can be said with certainty is that what happens will depend considerably on who can cooperate better, the two modern cells or the two traditional cells. This, actually, also applies to the other four models: we have tacitly presupposed that people in the same class can cooperate across sector borders and that people in the same sector can cooperate across class borders — but this may not at all be the case. All we can say is that it seems reasonable to postulate a potential for such cooperation, not that it actually will take place even if they recognize their ideological similarities.

And this brings us to the second type of what we have called 'structural analysis'. In the first type *actors* were distributed; in the second type the focus is on *the pattern of interaction*. A society can only function when there is some kind of interaction connecting all structural positions so that no position is completely isolated, but we cannot assume that direct interaction is equally strong for all pairs of positions or even that there is direct interaction for all pairs. Since there are four positions in our model of traditional society, the maximum number of interaction links is six (strongly connected structure), and the minimum number is three (weakly connected structure).

Let us imagine that there are four, so that two are either missing or so weak that they do not count. In other words, in the day-to-day interaction in the village there is a low or zero level of institutionalized interaction in two of them. Of course, nobody would deny that new lines of interaction can be opened in emergencies or in special situations, that old lines may die out because they are no longer functional or that informal relations such as friendship or kinship patterns may superimpose themselves upon the pattern found in the economic and/or formal interaction pattern. But already existing and institutionalized interaction is a basis for concerted action if a conflict defines conflict groupings — such lines of interaction can serve as nuclei for conflict organizations to crystallize around.

Of course, in addition to these organizational potentials *between* positions there are also all the possibilities for concerted action *within* positions, with actors sharing the same position. But then it should be remembered that sharing a status does not necessarily imply interaction. There may be little or no training in interaction at all, or even a neccesity to open completely new channels even within the same position. Trade unions are the obvious examples of this.

The total number of possible between position interaction structures would be $\binom{6}{2}$ or 15, whereas there would be six possibilities if there were only one weak link and 20 if there were three weak links (the maximum possible). We shall not spell out all these possibilities, only mention that we get 90 different models if we combine the six distribution patterns in Diagram 1.6.1 with the 15 possibilities with two interaction links missing. To illustrate, let us just look at four of them in Diagram 1.6.2. The four examples come out quite differently in terms of potential for development, even two and two when read horizontally or vertically. Thus,

74

Diagram 1.6.2. *Four combinations of value distributions and interaction patterns*

Interaction patterns   *Value distributions*

T	T
M	M

No. 2

M	T
T	M

No. 5

Traditionals can cooperate, primary low have crucial position in influencing upper class

Traditionals can cooperate, moderns mutually isolated

Traditionals can cooperate, tertiary low have crucial position in influencing upper class

Moderns can cooperative, traditionals mutually isolated

there is every reason to take into account both of these structural factors since the same quantity of moderns may lead to completely different consequences depending on distribution and interaction patterns.

And the number of possibilities even in this simple system is quite high, not only 90 but $[\binom{4}{1} + \binom{4}{2} + \binom{4}{3}]\ [\binom{6}{1} + \binom{6}{2} + \binom{6}{3}] = 574$. It would be foolhardy to trace the theoretical consequences of all of them *a priori*, for the good thing about empirical social science is the existence of methods for picking *one* of them on an empirical basis, or perhaps rather a class of them, since the empirical basis can usually be disputed. All we can say is that it would be quite hard to arrive at a good guess as to which one on the basis of intuition and participation in the community alone. Social science research is needed.

We have given this example only to indicate one type of analysis that should be done. Others could equally well be mentioned, for there are so many other ways in which the 'structure' of a society can be presented, for the location of *actors* or for the location of patterns of *interaction*. Then, one does not necessarily have to use the same model for these two types of structural analysis, although it is helpful. And we are interested in not only one but six value dimensions. All of these value dimensions will probably shed some light on the societies studied, and this light will be more lively, giving more realism and more details the more it is combined with structural analysis. But this cannot be done as here on a purely taxonomic basis, in the air so to to speak, if for no other reason than because the number of categories becomes too high. We need data to focus our reasoning on the empirical case at hand and to be stimulated by the richness of social reality. So we now turn to the data, to how they were obtained and to how they can be used.[1]

2. Data background and data collection

2.1. *Three villages in Western Sicily*

For the purpose of this study, three villages were selected in Western Sicily, in the region where Danilo Dolci and his collaborators have worked since 1952. Actually, we originally wanted five villages, but this turned out to be impossible for various reasons, partly of a practical nature, partly because of skillfully organized resistance against the project in one particularly mafia-ridden village. The reason why we wanted five or four villages, rather than three, was to facilitate collective level analysis, using the villages as units of analysis — but much can still be done with as few as three villages.

We shall certainly not claim too much in terms of a theoretical foundation for picking these particular three villages among the many possibilities. There is nothing remarkable about them in the context of Western Sicily except in the sense that everything human can always be individualized and will always defy some generalizations thrust upon it. The three villages are all located in the poor zones of Western Sicily — in the mountains, in the hill district closer to the coast and at the coast itself, respectively. We shall call them by names reflecting their ecological basis: 'Montagna', 'Collina' and 'Marina'. Needless to say, one will search in vain on the map for these names. The purpose of this anonymity is actually not to conceal anything. The analysis is couched in such general terms that it could hardly be offensive to anybody, unless they should believe that these three particular villages are the real object of the study. They were chosen not to represent three types of villages or anything similar, but in order to be *different* enough to provide us with levers for speculation. It should not be inferred that Montagna is the prototype of the mountain village, Collina of the hill village or Marina of the fishing village — these were just three villages chosen from several hundred possible ones to give data to the study.

Essentially, they had this much in common: an almost incredible degree of impermeability to change — technically, culturally, socially — with poverty bordering on misery and an air of almost bottomless sadness. Collina had extremely poor districts as did Marina — some of the fishermen live or lived until recently under conditions that must be among the poorest in Europe — whereas Montagna had a more evenly distributed poverty, with about one half of the population in the *elenchi dei poveri* — registered as 'poor'. In Lampedusa's town, Palma di Montechiaro, this applied to more than 70% of the population.

This does not prevent *Montagna*, for instance, from being extremely attractive at first glance. It is located near the top of a mountain, the houses highest up looking over the peak and down at the town below with its houses nestling in and clinging to each other and to the mountain's slope. The view is as from an airplane: the landscape takes on an unreal, distant quality, much like a sea seen from above — but this time not the sea with 'waves into frenzy' that Lampedusa speaks of, but rather a wrinkled carpet with nuances of color indicating degrees of dryness. From the village the fields can be seen; the work place is always there; but the patches of the individual farmer are scattered kilometers and hours apart (making underempoyment functional in view of the necessary walking time). And the sky is almost always blue, blue with no promise of rain.

Collina is not only less picturesque, it has an ugliness and poverty which not even the most superficial tourist would fail to see. It has a noticeable class difference in its ecology, with an old palace in its midst — one of these Sicilian 'palaces' that looks just like the rest of the village to the uninitiated until one discerns the lines and carvings that speak of richer periods and ambitions. But in the steeper streets of Collina are sights that are only sad — children slightly deformed by malnutriton, young mothers who look like grandmothers, grandparents who look already dead. Montagna has almost no roads; the town is too steep — not even bicycles belong — but it has stairs, some of them very beautifully fitted into the conglomeration of houses, leading at steep angles from the lower to the upper storeys of the town. But in Collina even the stairs are falling apart; this and Montagna's steepness make both villages difficult to cross, even for the villagers themselves. And in the offside stair roads of both villages rubbish, filth, flies, dogs and children accumulate and spell misery.

77

Collina is in the hills, not above them like Montagna, with its solace of the bird's perspective. It is closer to earth, to barren earth that is, and the smell of decay is much more easily discernible. Yet, it is not atypical. It provides the setting for that unholy alliance between the top of society and the bottom, called the mafia, which gives traditionalism and transition in Sicily a special quality not found in other parts of the Mediterranean world. Collina is ugly, but certainly not the ugliest example of how poverty can be linked to an extremely efficient resistance to all change.

Marina is, relatively speaking, better off. It is small, yet has parts that are almost elegant. Its waterfront, not what it could be, has the natural blessing of a lovely beach. But it too fits into the recurring pattern that potentials, mercilessly exploited in other parts of the world, are here still waiting for their redeemer and profit-maker.

All three villages are served by good, all-year, surfaced roads, but it should be mentioned that the road to Montagna is long, steep and curved and passes through very deserted places. There is bus service in Montagna, and Marina even has a railway station (and Collina has the beginnings of a railway that never was completed). Big cities like Agrigento, not to mention the region's capital, Palermo, are only a couple of hours away, so the villages are closer to regularly served airfields than many other parts of Europe. In short, these are not villages that are isolated for lack of adequate communication; they are not isolated by earthquakes, avalanches or inundations (except very rarely); mountains are neither high nor impenetrable; and the Mediterranean is certainly not known for its resistance to efforts at efficient communication. We mention these geographic factors only to point out that these villages are not physically isolated — if they are outside the mainstream of twentieth-century life, it is for other reasons.

So then, why did we select these three villages? Partly because of their similarities, partly because of their dissimilarities. On the one hand we wanted them to reflect conditions in Western Sicily. If we could have found *the typical Western Sicilian village* then we might have concentrated the study on that village. But we know of no way to find *le cas pur* among Sicilian villages. Hence, one has to work with a sample, and this sample could have been drawn at random. However, a better strategy was to work with a purposive rather than a probabilistic sample, with the villages chosen in such a way as to reflect the three major ecologies in the region: one village in the mountains, one in the hill district between the mountains and the sea and one coastal village, engaged among other activities, in fishing. There are two advantages to this sampling method.

First of all, heterogeneity among the villages is guaranteed — with a random procedure the probability of ending up with three villages with the same ecological basis is far from negligible. And this built-in heterogeneity can then be put to important work by *using the villages as each others' replications*. A finding based on one village alone may be interesting, yet reflect only idiosyncratic aspects of that particular village. If this finding is later replicated in two other villages with the same ecological basis, then it has been generalized, but only to that set of mutually homogeneous villages. However, if it has been generalized to a set of mutually heterogeneous villages, *more or less spanning the spectrum of ecological diversity in the region*, then we might venture to say that we know something about the region as such — not only about one village or about one milieu. In other words, *similarities* in findings become much more meaningful when they are based on dissimilar villages; if replication is to increase the degree of confirmation, it will have to be based on units that come from the same universe (villages in Western Sicily), yet sufficiently diverse not to make the replication trivial.

Secondly, if the villages are heterogeneous, then some of the findings will generally also turn out to be *dissimilar*. And these dissimilarities can now be put to use in contextual analysis, *using the villages as units of collective level analysis*. If they were too homogeneous, then the data might not offer sufficient dispersion to warrant an analysis of this type.

However, a note about the *number* of villages. We have argued that they should span the spectrum of villages in the region relatively well. Imagine this 'spectrum' described by means of one dimension only. In collective level analysis this dimension could then be used an independent variable and be related to any dependent variable — global, analytical or synthetic, to use those terms. To test hypotheses on few units, the information has to be utilized fully, which means that both independent and dependent variables must be used to rank all villages. If the hypothesis is that the order should be the same (or the opposite), then this predicts the rank odrer on one of the variables, which means that with n villages one of the n! possible rank orders is hypothesized. But if they are equally probable *a priori*, then the *a priori* probability of falsifying an hypothesis of this kind is n!-1/n! which is equal to 50% for n = 2, 83% for n = 3, 96% for n = 4 and less than 1% for n = 5. Hence, one should ideally have four or five villages in a study of this kind to arrive at a sufficiently high level of falsifiability, but three villages are not too few either — better at least than two, not to mention one. However, a low number of villages can also to some extent be compensated for by using more than one indicator.

But, given these methodological principles, the villages were picked for reasons of convenience rather than for any additional methodological reason. We now have to look more closely at them.[1]

2.2. *Some statistical information about the villages*

As a point of departure, let us see how much information can be gained by letting the census data speak. One census was taken on November 4, 1951, and another one on October 15, 1961, and data have been obtained for both censuses and all three villages from the *Istituto Centrale di Statistica* (ISTAT) in Rome about a number of important demographic characteristics. Thus, we are in the fortunate position of having census data before and after the study was carried out so that the types of social change that are reflected in demographic data can be taken into consideration. Montagna and Collina did not constitute any problem here, since they appear in the data as separate *comuni*, but Marina was not a *comune* in 1951. Hence, we had to make estimates for Marina by assuming exact proportionality for all categories, multiplying the data for the total *comune* with the fraction the population of Marina makes of the total. Unfortunately, we have no way of controlling how appropriate these estimates are, but have no reason to believe that they should be substantially in error.[1]

As of 1959 the population in Montagna was approximately 9,000, in Collina close to 6,500 and in Marina slightly more than 3,000; in 1961 it was about 500 less in all three. In other words, they are very different as to size, yet in the same size category: beyond the small site or congregation of houses where everybody knows everybody else and there is a low degree of institutional self-sufficiency, and below what can with good reason be called a town. We are confronted with three villages, although a closer investigation with the village as a unit certainly would make distinctions between these size categories.

Let us first look at age and sex for the three villages (see Table 2.2.1). There is nothing particularly remarkable in the Table. Relative to Norway, to compare with a 'rich' country, the population is young (with about 30% in the lowest age bracket, as against about 25% for Norway) — relative to the population in a poor Indian village it is old (in the Indo-

Table 2.2.1. *Age and sex composition, three villages, percentage*

	Census 1951								
	MONTAGNA			*COLLINA*			*MARINA*		
Age	Men	Women	Total	Men	Women	Total	Men	Women	Total
0–14	29	28	29	30	29	29	31	31	31
14–25	23	22	22	22	20	21	20	19	20
25–55	34	34	34	36	37	37	36	35	36
55 and older	14	16	15	12	14	13	13	15	14
Total	100	100	100	100	100	100	100	100	100

	Census 1961								
	MONTAGNA			*COLLINA*			*MARINA*		
Age	Men	Women	Total	Men	Women	Total	Men	Women	Total
0–14	29	29	29	29	29	29	27	28	28
14–25	18	18	18	18	16	17	19	21	20
25–55	36	36	36	38	38	38	40	35	37
55 and older	17	17	17	15	17	16	14	16	15
Total	100	100	100	100	100	100	100	100	100

Sex ratio, men per 100 women									
1951		103			100			96	
1961		102			100			95	

Norwegian project àrea near Quilon, Kerala, there would be more than 45% of the population in that youngest age-group). There are no differences to speak of within the villages or between the villages; except, perhaps in the sex ratio. This may be indicative of higher migration rates for men only from the coastal village. But the differences in sex ratio are not sufficient in our judgment to be of real consequence for social relations in the villages.

But the comparison between the data from 1951 and from 1961 reveals the impact of out migration: the age-group 14–25 is most vulnerable, in the order Montagna — Collina — Marina, with percentage differences of 5%, 4% and 1% respectively for the males. The obvious consequence, that the population staying behind becomes less productive both in terms of work and in terms of procreation, will be considered in more detail in Chapter 4. We shall estimate the magnitude of the migratory

Table 2.2.2. *Crude birth rates and death rates, three villages 1955 and 1959, percentage*

	MONTAGNA	COLLINA	MARINA	Norway 1946–1950
1955				
Birth rate	26	21	20	21
Death rate	7	8	6	9
B–D:	19	13	14	12
1955				Norway 1951–1955
Birth rate	25	25	23	19
Death rate	7	9	5	9
B–D:	18	16	18	10

movements, beginning with a consideration of birth and death rates (Table 2.2.2).

We have given some figures for Norway to show the consistent similarity. Although the differences between the villages are small, they may be meaningful and lead to two ways of ordering the villages:

In terms of *rate of increase:* Montagna — Marina — Collina
In terms of *living standard:* Marina — Montagna — Collina

We have used the crude death rates as an indicator of living standards, although it is certainly not the only possible indicator. It is only meaningful if the relatively high death rate in Collina cannot be ascribed to a higher proportion of people in the oldest category. But Table 2.2.1 gives evidence that the contrary is true: Collina had the highest death rate in spite of having the lowest proportion in the highest age category in 1951. The conclusion must be that relatively few people become old precisely because of the conditions leading to the high death rate. This serves as a prelude to a theme which was mentioned in the introduction and will recur quite often: the relative misery of Collina.

This does not mean that Montagna is well off. In 1960, for instance, we were informed by the *municipio* that about 4,500 were registered as 'poor',[2] i.e. that around 50% of the total population were in principle eligible for relief. Nor does it imply that Marina was a place of abundance. The quarters for the fishermen were among the poorest districts of the three villages combined — but there was nevertheless an easier atmosphere in Marina. The total impression, however, is the obvious presence of a strong pressure to leave the place, and this must have had some effects on the variation in the populations (Table 2.2.3).

Table 2.2.3. *Variation in populations, three villages, 1959 = 100**

Year	MONTAGNA	COLLINA	MARINA
1861	54	50	—
1901	72	88	—
1951	99	105	75
1954	101	101	91
1956	102	101	94
1957	101	101	97
1958	100	100	99
1959	100	100	100

The stability during recent years, except for Marina, is remarkable. Since we know the rate of increase the villages would have had if they had existed in a vacuum, completely isolated, with no other changes than those due to births and deaths alone, we can calculate what the population changes might have been.[3] We shall use only the period from 1955 to 1959, and the average rates of increase for that period we can get from Table 2.2.2.

Table 2.2.4. *Variations in populations under the assumption of complete isolation, 1955 = 100*

	MONTAGNA	COLLINA	MARINA
Population end of 1954	100	100	100
Average percentage rate of increase, B–D	1.85	1.45	1.6
Population end of 1959, complete isolation	110	107	108
Population end of 1959, real situation	99	99	110
Difference due to migration	+ 11	+ 8	− 2

As we see, the differences are quite conspicuous, except for Marina, and lead to the same ordering that emerged from Table 2.2.1:

In terms of *net migration :* Montagna — Collina — Marina.

This can only lead to the rejection of the hypothesis of 'splendid isolation': there is no doubt that these villages lose population in ways other than through deaths alone. We do not know the migration into the two villages, but can safely conclude that there is a heavy emigration still taking place, keeping the population at an almost constant level. This, of course, is confirmed by all kinds of verbal evidence.[4]

* Information is lacking for 1861 and 1901 for Marina.

We notice that the three variables of Tables 2.2.2 and 2.2.4 order the villages differently, but that the only village not touched by the net migration out of the villages is the village that is, relatively speaking, better off by the criterion of death rate. This, however, is hardly sufficient as an explanation. Let us look at these vital statistics in a world perspective. Dennis Wrong, the demographer, says:

> Crude rates of 6–9 per 1000 are found only in exceptionally youthful populations and it is exceedingly doubtful that death rates can be reduced any further below this level. Indeed, they are likely to rise in the next few decades as populations grow older.[5]

If we can trust these statistics at all, they seem to indicate that these villages are in the phase which Wrong and others call 'transitional growth', 'those in which a rapidly falling death rate is diverging from a high and relatively stable birth rate to create large surpluses of births over deaths'.[6] It remains to be shown that the birth rates are 'high'. In Wrong's terms,

> ... today a crude birth rate of over 30 can be considered very high, one of 20 to 30 moderately high, and one of less than 20 suggests a recent history of fertility decline.[7]

The three villages are in the middle group: it is a very well-known phenomenon that death rates decrease as soon as infant mortality is conquered and antibiotics are used and as long as the population has not yet been aging long enough to die from what we prefer to call 'natural' illnesses. As indicated in Table 2.2.2 the death rate in Norway is even higher than for the villages, but then the Norwegian population is older, with 10% 65 years or older (as against 7%, 6% and 7% for the three villages). The higher birth rates make for a younger population in these villages.

With regard to age composition, birth rates and death rates, these villages are similar to such countries as Argentina, Spain and the whole of Italy, for that matter.[8] They are not even comparable with the most underdeveloped parts of the world if we look at statistics for such countries as Egypt and India.[9] Thus, the first step in the demographic transition has already been taken, and there is no doubt that the villages are even entering the third phase (Wrong's 'incipient decline'), where both rates are low: the birth rates will decline even further, and the death rates will remain constant for a while due to the balancing effects of somewhat better conditions and an aging population until the latter factor will be more important and the death rates will increase again. Then, some decades ahead, the villages may well experience even the phenomenon of voluntarily increased birth rates, although this is not likely in the near future.

We are actually driving at two conclusions. First of all, the excess of births over deaths does create a pressure on the villages, but is not by itself a sufficient reason for the misery or the great outflux from Montagna and Collina. The population pressure, measured as rate of increase, is 1.9% in Montagna and 1.3% in Collina, but on a world scale[10] this is low compared to Mexico's 2.9% and Egypt's 2.2%. On the other hand it is higher than Italy's 1.0% and Spain's 0.9%, and if a situation is bad there is little comfort in knowing that others are even worse off. But the really crucial argument is Collina: it is low in population pressure, still high in net migration. Hence, the relationship is not linear for our villages; other explanations of the outflux are needed.

The second conclusion is based on the same kind of reasoning. If the misery leading to escape through death[11] should also lead to escape through migration, then Collina should be higher than Montagna in net migration. But either the differences are too small to override, for instance the differences in population pressure, or death rates are poor indicators of the kind of misery that is important here — or (less likely!) misery is not important. At any rate, our three villages indicate that net migration seems to be related both to death rates and population pressure but that these are not the only factors at work. With a large sample of villages we might have estimated the relative effects and interaction between these two factors in predicting, and to some extent also explaining, migration. But that is not our purpose; we want this information only as a background in order to investigate how these factors operate on the individual level.

In conclusion, one might be tempted to say something like this: the death rates are actually very low, since the most immediate factors of a hygienic nature seem to have been eliminated. The population pressure is present but is not excessive, and it will probably decrease. This means that the flexibility permitted by the demographic variables has, at least partly, been exploited — although there is still quite a distance to go from Montagna to the Italian average. This, in turn, seems to indicate that when the net migration over five years is of the order of 10% it must be because other factors *that perhaps are even less flexible than the demographic ones* create a tremendous pressure. In other words, what may look like a factor of relief, the demographic transition, may turn

Table 2.2.5. *Occupational structure in the three villages, percentage*

Census 1951

Occupation	MONTAGNA			COLLINA			MARINA		
	Men	Women	Total	Men	Women	Total	Men	Women	Total
Agriculture	80	11	77	76	32	73	74	42	72
Industry	5	6	5	6	8	6	8	0	8
Construction work	9	0	8	9	0	9	7	0	7
Transport	1	2	1	2	1	2	3	2	3
Trade	2	45	4	4	44	6	5	31	6
Public administration	3	36	5	3	15	4	3	13	4
Total working population	100	100	100	100	100	100	100	100	100
Working population, percentage of total	65	3	34	61	5	33	64	2	33

Census 1961

Occupation	MONTAGNA			COLLINA			MARINA		
	Men	Women	Total	Men	Women	Total	Men	Women	Total
Agriculture	72	44	69	64	62	63	76	16	74
Industry	19	13	18	24	13	23	15	39	15
Other occupations*	9	43	13	12	25	14	9	45	11
Total working population	100	100	100	100	100	100	100	100	100
Working population, percentage of total	62	5	34	55	10	32	64	3	33

* Unfortunately, detailed breakdowns were unavailable for 1961.

out to be a factor of despair because economic takeoff is less easily implemented, *ceteris paribus*, than the administration of elementary hygiene and some measure of contraception.

After this examination of population pyramids and the movement of the population, let us turn to the occupational structure (Table 2.2.5).

Two facts of importance stand out from this Table: the villages are remarkably similar in occupational structure, and they are highly agricultural villages. There is the difference that a sizable proportion of the people listed as working in agriculture in Marina are also engaged in fishing, but with the dismal state of Mediterranean fisheries very few people would have fishing as their full-time occupation. The small differences we find rarely exceed a couple of percentage points, except for the women who are gainfully employed; they are working in shops in Montagna and Collina and in agriculture in Marina.

With more than 70% of the working male population engaged in primary occupations it is certainly correct to classify these communities as non-industrial. Moreover, the category 'industry' in the census is very generous indeed, including, for instance, construction and transport. From our point of view the villages are well chosen insofar as they represent about the same degrees of non-industrialization; we do not have to take a differential in the occupational structure into consideration to explain findings. But there is a difference in the number of men gainfully employed, which again singles out Collina as the place of heaviest misery.

A comparison between the census data for 1951 and 1961 shows changes in the occupational structure, although we hesitate to attribute too much meaning to the figures since they look somewhat erratic (as evidenced by the figures for the female working population). Montagna

Table 2.2.6. *Changes in occupational structure, Italy 1954–60, percentage*

		Agriculture	Industry	Other occupations	Total
1954	Nord	32.7	38.1	29.2	100.0
1954	Mezzogiorno	49.3	26.0	24.7	100.0
1956	Nord	28.3	40.1	31.6	100.0
1956	Mezzogiorno	46.3	27.2	26.5	100.0
1958	Nord	26.6	41.2	32.2	100.0
1958	Mezzogiorno	40.9	29.4	29.7	100.0
1960	Nord	24.4	43.5	32.1	100.0
1960	Mezzogiorno	31.9	30.9	37.2	100.0

and Collina show the usual trend from primary to secondary industries. The figures shown in Table 2.2.6 are compatible with the general figures for Italy for this period.[12]

This being the general (and extremely fast) trend, one would certainly expect pronounced tendencies in this direction even in the interior of Western Sicily during the 1950's. But we would have to invoke very *ad hoc* explanations to account for the failure of Marina to exhibit the same tendency.

Let us then turn to the scholastic situation, perhaps the most fundamental variable in the development of a society (Table 2.2.7).

Four facts of importance stand out from this Table. First of all: the overall level of instruction is low, with less than 5 % in all villages having more than the five years of elementary schooling. The elementary school certificate does not imply, however, as the census data may lead one to believe, that the person is literate: on the contrary, what is quickly learned may be quickly forgotten when there are few stimuli to counteract that process.

Secondly, there is a significant difference between the sexes. *More men than women are illiterates*, in all three villages. The differences are small, but meaningful, and probably contribute to a definition of literacy as somehow 'feminine'. It may be a differential of importance for female emancipation, but as there are few things to read anyhow, it probably does not matter much. Causally, what it means is probably that the boys have been taken out of the schools and put to some or any kind of work very early, whereas the girls have been left in peace. This is a pattern found quite frequently in underdeveloped countries, and may be worth studying if a rapid change suddenly takes place. For instance, to what extent is this factor responsible for the relative speed with which emancipation takes place in countries like Mexico, Cuba and India?

Thirdly, the villages are different, with Marina being much better off educationally. The low number of illiterates there is probably attributable to the relatively high number of classrooms and teachers. This fits in well with what we already have found about Marina's relatively low death rate and absence of pressure to migrate. On the other end of the scale, however, we do not find the miserable place called Collina, but Montagna, where almost half of the men are illiterates. This is probably due to the degree of isolation of the place: it is a mountain village with little communication with the outside world — even though communication is physically possible.

Fourthly, even though the data from the 1951 and the 1961 censuses

Table 2.2.7. *Scholastic situation in the three villages, percentage*

Census 1951

	MONTAGNA			COLLINA			MARINA		
	Men	Women	Total	Men	Women	Total	Men	Women	Total
Illiterates	49	45	47	30	28	29	26	23	25
No school certificate, but literate	7	9	8	7	4	5	14	8	11
Elementary school	39	43	41	59	66	63	56	66	61
'Junior high school'	3	1	2	2	1	1	3	2	2
'Senior high school'	2	2	2	2	1	2	1	1	1
University	(0.7)	(0.1)	(0.5)	(0.3)	(0.2)	(0.3)	(0.7)	(0.1)	(0.4)
Total, population 14 years and older	100	100	100	100	100	100	100	100	100
Percentage of pupils of population from 6–14 years		64			69			65	
Number of pupils per classroom		63			51			29	
Number of pupils per teacher		28			26			29	

Census 1961

	MONTAGNA			COLLINA			MARINA		
	Men	Women	Total	Men	Women	Total	Men	Women	Total
Illiterates	37	36	37	26	20	23	30	13	16
Elementary school	57	59	58	69	75	72	75	85	81
'Junior high school'	3	3	2	3	3	3	3	1	2
University	3	2	3	2	2	2	2	1	1
Total	100	100	100	100	100	100	100	100	100

are not completely comparable there seems to be little doubt that illiteracy was substantially reduced during that decade. This is even more apparent if the percentages for 1961 are calculated relative to the total population 14 years or older, and not only relative to the number of people for whom information is available (we presume). The percentages of illiterates in the male population 14 years or older are: Montagna 33% (16% down from 49%); Collina 24% (6% down from 30%) and Marina 16% (10% down from 26%) — so the change seems to be considerable. In a sense this is the once again theme we developed in connection with health; although nobody would overestimate the quality of this educational development, there is nevertheless some development; and this creates an imbalance relative to the economic stagnation. On the other hand, positive imbalances in favor of health and education may be converted into economic growth by obvious mechanisms, so it would be rash to conclude that this imbalance is necessarily unfavorable — just as rash as it would be to conclude that it necessarily leads to growth.

Finally, let us look at another indicator of standard of living, housing conditions (Table 2.2.8).

Table 2.2.8. *Housing conditions in the three villages. Census 1951, figures for 1961 in parentheses*

	MONTAGNA	COLLINA	MARINA
Number of rooms per house	2.3 (2.4)	2.2 (2.1)	2.3 (2.3)
Number of residents per room	2.0 (1.6)	2.3 (1.8)	2.2 (1.7)
Houses with drinking water	30%	38%	22%
Houses with well water	7%	2%	4%
Houses with toilets	62%	89%	94%
Houses with electricity	50%	82%	90%
Houses with bathtubs	2%	1%	1%

There are few with more than two rooms in any of the villages, and this remained constant during the decade — since most houses were very old. This is the typical pattern: small one- or two-storey houses with two or three rooms. The villages are similar in this regard, and one major implication is the overwhelming preponderance of one-family houses. 'Family', on the other hand, may mean anything from an incomplete nuclear family to different kinds of extended families (stem families as well as 'joint' families). If there is any tendency at all in the Table, it is to show that rooms are slightly more crowded in Collina than in the other two;

90

but the differences are certainly minute. Moreover, as a consequence of the migratory movements, the number of residents per room is decreasing.

When it comes to modern conveniences like toilets and electricity there is a clear pattern, however: the more isolated the villages the more remote they are from the centers of production and modern life in general — the lower is the percentage of people having these conveniences. Bathtubs are in another category; they are evidently defined as luxuries by almost everybody and far beyond what can be expected. The data for water, on the other hand, probably tell more about natural conditions in the neighborhood than about economic conditions in general.[13]

2.3. *The collection of data*

The problems we have set for ourselves at the ends of 1.2, 1.3, 1.4, 1.5 and 1.6 are obviously of a kind that can never be answered by means of even the best political, economic or demographic data alone. More information is necessary, even relatively detailed information about *individuals*, about their social setting, about their attitudes and opinions, however ephemeral. And even the best observational data will not do here. Ideological orientations, desires and wants are not easily revealed by observing behavior alone — verbal data are indispensable. There are two ways of eliciting verbal data, but in communities with the percentages of illiteracy revealed by the census data presented in the preceding section, where they are certainly not exaggerated, questionnaires would be ridiculous. Hence, interviewing became a major tool of investigation.

Since interviewing consists in bringing together a sample of *respondents* and a sample of *stimuli*, by means of a sample of *interviewers*, the question is: How adequate were these obtained samples? And how adequately were they brought together? We shall discuss these questions in this section.

1. *The respondents.* Our sample consists of 408 respondents. It is a two-stage sample, with individuals chosen at random from a purposive sample of three villages. The first stage of the sampling, that of the villages, has been described in 2.1, so we turn here to the sampling of the respondents.

The respondents were obtained in the following way. We obtained, from the provincial administrations, maps of the villages; the houses were numbered; samples were drawn randomly. The prospective objects for interview were then plotted on the maps; the villages were divided into suitable ecological units. and the units distributed randomly among the interviewers, so as to reduce bias resulting from unfortunate matching of interviewers with respondents, while at the same time attempting to minimize walking distance and to maximize aquaintance with particular districts. The maps were not quite up to date, but sufficiently accurate for our purpose, and the overwhelming proportion of the families lived in housing units drawn as single houses on the maps. The *capofamiglia,* the head of the household, was then interviewed, which means that the sample consists mostly of males (88%). If there were more than one consanguinal family in the house, only one of them was interviewed; but the underrepresentation this leads to of families sharing houses is of no numerical importance. Hence, in this study *the family is the sampling unit, represented by its head of household.* And the reason for this is the general difficulty, in traditional societies, of obtaining interviews with anybody else without causing intolerable suspicion and anxiety.[1] The results are summarized in Table 2.3.1.

Table 2.3.1 *The size of the samples and the results of the interviewing*

	MONTAGNA	COLLINA	MARINA	Total
Total number of houses selected at random	207	231	175	613
Houses with residents permanently absent	17	24	25	66
Houses with residents temporarily absent	28	26	29	83
Refusals	10	30	16	56
Interviews obtained	152	151	105	408
Total	207	231	175	613
Percentage of refusals (based on people actually contacted)	6	17	13	12

All houses drawn at random were visited, but a number of them (14%) were uninhabited. These houses are to a considerable degree the tomb-stones of migration (but kept for a possible return and as a symbolic presence), whereas the houses with owners temporarily absent are mainly the signs of work activity, for instance in distant fields.

The refusal rate is high in Collina[2] which, as has been mentioned,

92

is the village among the three where the mafia had the best control. We do not imply that the mafia actually issued directives to the effect that interviews should not be granted, rather, that a high level of mafia control is caused by or causes a general atmosphere of suspicion and anxiety. Since the order of mafia control as estimated by people acquainted with the region is Collina — Marina — Montagna, this is well corroborated in the ordering of the refusal rates.[3]

We plotted the refusals on the maps, since geographic location was the only factor known about them, to check for geographic clustering. For Montagna and Collina nothing at all was found: the refusals were completely scattered around the village. This indicates three things: 1) that there is no 'neighbor effect' in the sense that a neighborhood may decide against participating, 2) that refusals cannot have a strong correlation with socio-economic factors, since these factors are known to correlate relatively highly with geographical location (there are poor districts and well-to-do districts) and 3) that refusals were not related to the interviewer, which was also proved directly. For Marina we actually found almost the same scattering, but of the sixteen refusals, six were three pairs of neighboring houses. This is more than we would have expected by chance[4] and could probably have been overcome if the neighboring houses in the sample had been approached simultaneously, so that one of them could not build up resistance in the other.

By and large we are well satisfied, however, and plotting of the interviews obtained yields a very good scatter of the respondents. We shall return to an evaluation of the data at the end of this section.

2. *The questions.* It is safe to say that social science interviewing was a new experience for most of the respondents — and also for the interviewers. This is both an advantage and a disadvantage. On the one hand, the respondents were curious and many of them expressed their desire to continue talking for an extended period after the interview was finished. Lack of experiments with social science interviewing might have led to refusal for some, and to over-acceptance for others — but in any case we had to take their relative naiveté into account by constructing a *simple* schedule. Moreover, it would have to be *short* in order not to be too nauseating for untrained interviewers and respondents, yet include the variable we needed. After many versions had been discussed and a pre-test had been carried out in Partinico, the author, the local advisors and the team of interviewers finally agreed on a questionnaire the content of which is shown in Table 2.3.2. (For the whole question-

Table 2.3.2. *The content of the questionnaire*

	Number of questions
1. *Value-orientations*	
Cultural mentality (Sorokin, Banfield)	12
Psychic mobility (Lerner)	
social perspective	1
space perspective	12
time perspective	9
efforts to move	2
Miscellaneous attitudinal questions	8
2. *Structural variables*	
Background variables	17
Participation variables	8
3. *Evaluation of interview*	1
Total	70

naire see Appendix 1.) The questionnaire has a very simple structure, designed to test exactly the hypotheses we were interested in, although it is insufficient where precise interaction questions are concerned. Much work was spent on making the questions as simple as possible, and it may well be that we have actually exaggerated the need for simplicity. On the other hand, we know that this schedule worked; we do not know what might have happened with other schedules.

3. *The interviewing.* The interviewers had all been selected by the the *Centro studi e iniziative per la piena occupazione* at Partinico. The author directed the interviewing in Montagna and took care to supervise the training of the interviewers beforehand, particularly of the three interviewers that would also take part in the interviewing in the other villages.[5] Some of the interviews in Montagna were also carried out by the author. On the average, the interviews lasted slightly more than half an hour.

For many reasons (economic, 'interview-strategic', etc.) it was decided to use the method of the 'short, sharp shock' in concentrating the interviews on as few days as possible in each place.[6] Usually, it is advisable to include a Sunday in a field expedition of that kind in order to cover different phases of the weekly routine, thus minimizing the number of refusals and absences. On a Sunday people unobtainable during the week because of heavy work schedules might be interviewed, so to know who these 'hard to reach' people are, the Sunday should be at the end of the field expedition.[7] The field work was done as indicated in Table 2.3.3.

Table 2.3.3. *Character of the field expedition*

	MONTAGNA	COLLINA	MARINA
Number of interviewers	7	7	7
Number of days	4	3	4
Period	Late August 1960	Late September 1960	Early October 1960
Number of interviews	152	151	105
Number of interviews per interviewer	21.6	21.7	21

The similarity in the average number of interviews per interviewer is indicative of the similarity in the way in which the field work was organized.

Of the interviewers, the three who constituted a permanent nucleus did altogether 209 or 51% of the interviews. Thus, we consider the interviewing to have been under control during the entire period, since the teams worked in very close cooperation and with frequent discussions. For the interviewers this was reported to be an experience of considerable value, yielding an insight into Sicilian life which is unobtainable by other means, even (or precisely) for Sicilians.

We shall now turn to two problems of considerable importance in the evaluation of the data: *sampling bias* and *interviewing bias*. Both are important sources of error that should lead to a general distrust of the data and our findings — if they are prevalent. A sampling bias may lead to distorted estimates for the total population, and an interviewing bias may lead to severe changes in the internal structure of the response patterns.

4. *The sampling bias.* The best way of controlling *sampling bias* lies in a careful reexamination of the sampling (which usually leads nowhere because one does not know how systematically refusals and absences are scattered in the population) and to a comparison of the sample with population data where they exist. We know the sampling was as good as we could obtain; houses were revisited many times if interviews were not acquired at once. Hence we turn now to a comparison with census data. We shall use the columns for the *men* in section 2.2, for these compariaons, since the respondents in most cases are male *capifamiglia*.[8] And we shall use the census data for 1961, since they come closest to the data collection.

To start with the simplest, age, comparisons are of little value since

95

Table 2.3.4. *Age composition for the three villages, sample, percentage*

Age	MONTAGNA	COLLINA	MARINA
less than 20	1	0	0
20–39	30	29	29
40–59	43	52	48
60–69	15	7	15
70 and older	11	11	8
NA	—	1	—
Total	100	100	100
(N)	(152)	(151)	(105)

we do not have census age distributions for *capifamiglia*. What we can do, however, is to look at the sample distributions and compare them to check for possible biases (Table 2.3.4).

As we see, the three are remarkably similar, as reflected in the median ages of 49, 48 and 51 years respectively. The Table squares well with Table 2.2.1 if we interpolate and delete the lowest age category that cannot possibly recruit heads of households. In other words: 1) the sampling seems to represent the universe well where age is concerned, and 2) the sampling seems to be uniform for the three villages at least in this case where there also is a high degree of universe uniformity. So far, the sample has stood the test.

Let us then turn to occupational categories; they usually bring more difficulties.

Table 2.3.5. *Occupational composition in the hreet villages, sample and census compared*

	MONTAGNA			COLLINA			MARINA		
	Census 1961	Sample 1960	Differ- ence	Census 1961	Sample 1960	Differ- ence	Census 1961	Sample 1960	Differ- ence
Agriculture*	72	49	+ 23	64	74	− 10	76	80	− 4
Industry**	19	14	+ 5	24	7	+ 17	15	8	+ 7
Other occupations	9	37	− 28	12	19	− 7	9	12	− 3
Total	100	100	0	100	100	0	100	100	0
Average percentage difference			19			11			5

* This includes fishermen for Marina.
** This includes construction and transport.

At first glance it looks as if there are great discrepancies, especially for Montagna, but it turns out that most of the differences stem from difference in terminology and from the category 'other occupations', which in the sample includes people who have retired. If they are distributed according to their past profession a more congruent picture develops. Further, the category of 'craftsmen, artisans' is not included in the census classifications, and they had to be distributed between agriculture and industry. It is almost meaningless to assign only *one* source of income to the villagers; as it is said about the inhabitants of Roccamena:

> Che si siano ottenute 106 fonti de sussistenza per 70 famiglie si spiega facilmente: la maggior parte sono constretti, per vivere, ad 'industriarsi', *a fare un po' di tutto.*[9]

They feel they have to know something about everything within the lower occupational range in the villages, to be able to get some return from any possibility that might open up. The consequence is versatility bought at the expense of skill — a problem they then will have to cope with as in-migrants in Milano or immigrants in France, Switzerland, Belgium and Germany; Australia, Canada and the United States. The level of education is shown in Table 2.3.6.

Table 2.3.6. *Scholastic situation in the three villages, sample and census compared*

	MONTAGNA			COLLINA			MARINA		
	Census 1961	Sample 1960	Differ- ence	Census 1961	Sample 1960	Differ- ence	Census 1961	Sample 1960	Differ- ence
No school certificate	37	56	− 19	26	77	− 51	20	82	− 62
Elementary school	57	28	+ 29	69	19	+ 50	75	14	+ 61
Secondary school and above	6	16	− 10	5	4	+ 1	5	4	+ 1
Total	100	100	0	100	100	0	100	100	0
Average percentage difference		19			34				41

Here the differences are very wide and an explanation must be found. The common feature from all three villages is the much lower percentage in the sample of people with the elementary school certificate. This does not mean that those without are illiterate, or at least not complete illiterates, but it does mean that the sample gives a less flattering image of the scholastic levels. If the sample is correct, then the census is biased so as to present a more favorable picture than is warranted of social reality. If the census is right, then the sample shows an overrepresentation of the uneducated which is tantamount to the underrepresentation of the upper classes hypothesized above. One reason why one might feel that the sample is to blame is that the major difficulties are in the two villages with the highest refusal rates; on the other hand, the refusal rates are not sufficient to explain the discrepancies. The *direction* is compatible with the reasons already advanced for lower refusal rates in the lower classes, but the magnitude is too great to be explained fully in these terms.

But the census percentages are based on population 14 years old and the sample on a much older population of heads of household. This certainly contributes to an understanding of the differences, because the older the population, the less schooling do they have for the simple reason that schooling on a mass scale is a relatively novel phenomenon. This is not sufficient to explain the very big discrepancies, however. And since we know of no conscious or unconscious source of bias that could have been responsible for such gross discrepancies we are forced to conclude that even though the sample data may under-report scholastic achievement somewhat, it looks almost certain that the census data overestimate the level of education considerably. But this argument would be more convincing if we could also show that census data and our own data coincide better on some other point where there is less leeway because of different interpretations of categories, and perhaps also less desire to exaggerate the level of achievement. And we have such data, relating to the housing situation, where the highly visible and consensual variables show a higher level of agreement between census and sample (Table 2.3.7).

Table 2.3.7. *Housing conditions in the three villages, census and sample compared*

	MONTAGNA			COLLINA			MARINA		
	Census 1961	Sample 1960	Difference	Census 1961	Sample 1960	Difference	Census 1961	Sample 1960	Difference
Rooms per house	2.4	2.4	0.0	2.1	2.0	+ 0.1	2.3	2.1	− 0.2
Residents per room	1.6	2.1	− 0.5	1.8	2.7	− 0.9	1.7	2.7	− 1.0

We now feel entitled to draw three conclusions, since these data are comparable (the building style did not change noticeably during this period; besides, little building was needed with the exodus taking place). First, the discrepancies are very small as long as the houses alone are involved; they become higher when residents are included (second line). Secondly, this time the differences are small enough to be relatively explainable on the basis of the refusal rates reported — setting Collina and Marina apart from Montagna. Thirdly, the discrepancies go in the direction of an overrepresentation of houses with many residents per house and per room — in short an overrepresentation of lower classes. Since this is compatible with the reasons advanced for the refusals in Collina and Marina, it looks as if *we have to admit a certain underrepresentation (but of a relatively modest magnitude) where the relatively well-to-do are concerned.* At the same time we get one new demonstration of the good quality of the Montagna sample. Further, the similarity of the samples where age is concerned serves to support the contention that the bias is confined to the class dimension.

But the consequences of this bias are not serious for the type of analysis we want to carry out. Almost all of our analysis is concerned with *inter-individual* comparisons, and we have no reason to assume that the overrepresentation of 'lower' classes will affect appreciably the *correlations* between variables at the individual level. But they do affect the rates, so it is clear that we have to be careful in connection with *inter-village* comparisons, not so much because of the underrepresentation as because of the differences in underrepresentation, and because we do not know whether class has a different impact on other variables in the different villages. On the other hand, since we have no reason to assume that the bias has affected correlations, correlations can still be compared across villages; and the whole replication strategy indicated in 2.1 above is essentially based on this assumption.

5. *The interviewing bias.* Let us then turn to the question of the *interviewing bias.* Essentially, the interview is biased if the characteristics of the interviewer are not spuriously correlated with the responses recorded from the respondent. Hence, if there is interviewing bias, it should show up as predictable differences between interviewers who are different, in a relevant way, when they interview similar respondents. If there is no such difference, it may be due to absence of interviewing bias; but it may be due to lack of comparability of respondents (the idea being that both respondents and interviewers are different, but in such a way that the

differences cancel out) or to lack of relevant differences between the interviewers.

We want to examine the most difficult case we can imagine from this particular collection of data, the case of asking questions about religious attitudes. It is evident that how one asks a question like 'Who ought to have more to say about things in general in a village, a priest or an engineer?' or 'What is better in your opinion, to participate in religious activities or to improve the living conditions of the village?' may depend on one's own answer to these questions. This is true everywhere and true *a fortiori* for such ideologically central questions as these. It so happened that during the interviewing in Montagna two very devout Catholics participated, and they reported difficulties with these questions, both their own difficulties and difficulties attributed to their respondents. Let us see what differences there are in the end results (Table 2.3.8).[10]

Table 2.3.8. *A comparison of devout Catholic interviewers with the others (data from Montagna, indices of ideological orientation), percentage*

	Occupation items		Allegiance items	
	Devout Catholics	*Other interviewers*	*Devout Catholics*	*Other interviewers*
Ideationals	24	34	37	39
Medium	52	30	43	27
Sensates	24	36	20	34
Total	100	100	100	100
(N)	(46)	(106)	(46)	(106)

We have used both indices of ideological orientation, and together they seem to tell this story: there is not so much of a tendency for the two 'devout Catholics' to over-report responses that 'favor' their own, possibly less sensate orientation, but there is a definite tendency for them to under-report answers in the middle, DK's, etc. But this may have been exactly their way of solving the dilemma: they may have been 'members of both worlds' in the sense that they felt the answer to the choice between religious activities and improvement of village conditions is *both*, that both are good and that one is conducive to the other. Very conscientious as they were, they would hardly have biased the recorded responses systematically in an ideational direction. This is nevertheless a case of interviewing bias, although of a relatively mild kind.

But there are also two other possible explanations: that these two interviewers have a *general* tendency to report or extract middle answers, regardless of the nature of the question, and that they have happened to be also allocated to a sample where there is a propensity to such answers. Let us see what results they got on the second principal value-orientation variable, and on two other questions picked at random (Table 2.3.9).

Table 2.3.9. *A comparison of devout Catholic interviewers and the others (data from Montagna, three variables), percentage*

Ever tried to move?			Who has the power here?			Where have you learned most?		
	Devout Catholics	*Other interviewers*		*Devout Catholics*	*Other interviewers*		*Devout Catholics*	*Other interviewres*
Stayers	26	39	Clear answers 'all of them'	67	69	Clear answers 'equally much'	91	91
In betweens	39	29						
Movers	35	32		33	31		9	9
Total	100	100	Total	100	100	Total	100	100
(N)	(46)	(106)	(N)	(46)	(106)	(N)	(46)	(106)

As can be seen from the left hand side of the Table, there is also here a certain tendency to get 'middle answers'. However, this tendency does not generalize to all kinds of 'dustbin' answers, as can be seen from the two other sub-tables in the Table.

As long as their bias is in the direction of middle answers, it may be argued that the danger is not great. But there is also a tendency, as can be seen from Table 2.3.8, to report fewer sensates relative to the other interviewers. Based on our knowledge of the interviewers, however, we are inclined to believe that this is because they simply met fewer sensates than the others, but it is difficult to prove this. The standard techniques call for the introduction of variables correlated with ideology, to see whether the two devout Catholics happened to have in their sample people who, on the basis of the general findings, would be suspected to be more on the ideational side regardless of what interviewers

Table 2.3.10. *The composition of the sub-samples for the two categories of interviewers (data from Montagna, occupational groups,) percentage*

	Primary high	Tertiary high	Primary low	Tertiary low	Total (N)
Devout Catholics	24	39	26	11	100 (46)
Other interviewers	14	38	25	23	100 (106)
Difference	+ 10	+ 1	+ 1	− 12	0

they happened to meet. In Table 2.3.10, an inspection of the data reveals the following composition of the samples interviewed by the two groups.

One category is overrepresented and another underrepresented, but they are *both* predominantly 'ideational' or 'not sensate' according to Table 3.5.4. Hence, what is lost in one should be gained in the other, so we cannot explain the bias on this basis (as a matter of fact, we would even have predicted a slight increase in the number of sensates for the devout Catholics). A closer inspection of the data shows that the devout Catholics have the same rank order of ideationals vs. sensates for the four occupational categories on both indices as the other interviewers except in two cases — and these cases are different for the two indices. Hence, the chances for significant distortions are small but will have to be kept in mind in the analysis.

We also asked the interviewers to give their own evaluation of the contact obtained during the interview. It is difficult to arrive at inter-subjective criteria for such evaluations, and this is reflected in a very high percentage of the interviews (26%) that was not evaluated. We give the information for what it is worth (Table 2.3.11).

Table 2.3.11. *Evaluation of the contact obtained during the interview, percentage*

	Insufficient	Medium	Good	Total	(N)
MONTAGNA	5	19	76	100	(128)
COLLINA	13	36	51	100	(120)
MARINA	8	17	75	100	(52)
Devout Catholics	5	23	72	100	(43)
Other interviewers	5	16	79	100	(85)

The picture that emerges is the same as the one we already obtained from Table 2.3.1, where the relative difficulty encountered in the three villages is concerned. The devout Catholics have had more difficulties than the rest, but not many — but this may again be an expression of their predilection for the middle category. Had they really encountered major obstacles, however, then we would have expected this to show up in 2.3.11.

Moreover, why should devout Catholics necessarily be considered to be more problematic than devout socialists or devout communists that also were represented on the staff of interviewers? There is no particular reason for preferring one or the other. Rather, it seems that we were fortunate to have a certain mixture of ideological orientations present on the interviewer staff, that the interviewers encountered respondents that were well scattered in the social structure (Table 2.3.10) and that by and large we have reasons to assume that the biases that might have been introduced have been relatively randomly distributed and to some extent cancelled each other.

6. *'Don't know'* and *'no answer'*. We checked the data for the number of 'don't know' and 'no answer' responses (there were actually so few of the latter that they were included in the former). The distribution shows that the number was high; with a median number of 9 'don't know' responses and 67% of the distribution located between 6 and 13 'don't knows'. But this is not interpreted as a sign of bad interviewer contact. Rather, 'don't know' is seen as an answer which is particularly meaningful in a setting with a high level of cultural ambivalence, where one part of the culture, of the village, even of the person himself, asks questions the other part does not know the answer to or does not even understand. For this reason the 'don't know' answer will be used systematically and analytically particularly in connection with time and space perspective.[11]

3. The sensates and the ideationals

3.1. *Two measures of cultural mentality*

We shall now take the first steps on a long and cumbersome road, where the aim is to arrive at a judgment concerning where in the social structure of these villages the 'spirit of modernization' is located. The difficulty is that there are so many concepts and ideas concerning modernization that we have to make a choice, and, as already mentioned in section 1.3, we shall make use of Sorokin's ideational-sensate dimension as a point of departure. In other words, we shall try do three things. First of all, an effort will be made to locate our respondents on this dimension operationally and to see what other characteristics people we shall call 'ideational' and 'sensate' have, to test the validity and fruitfulness of the dimension. Secondly, if the typology turns out to be useful and valid, efforts will be made to bring it to bear on a number of the ideas already put forward in the first chapter concerning the relationship between this dimension and various other attitudes and structural characteristics of individuals in transitional societies. Finally, when this is done, an effort will be made to assess the consequences of our findings for a theory of social change in the communities in this region, and more generally for socio-economic development anywhere.

Everything now hinges on a measure of ideological orientation, and the basic question is: How does one go about measuring where a person belongs on a scale from the extreme ideational to the extreme sensate? One of the difficulties lies in the fact that these concepts are defined in terms of philosophical concepts beyond what can be reached in a traditional survey interview. To get some insight into what a respondent considers to be the nature of 'ultimate reality', what he sees as 'primary' in his existence, what he sees as 'intrinsic change' or 'extrinsic change' is not impossible — but it is impossible if a randomly selected sample from a semi-literate population is approached by survey methods and direct questions are asked. These philosophically phrased concepts do not belong to the sphere of everyday activities and thoughts that a simple questionnaire should be geared to. But as this attitudinal variable is central to our investigation, some kind of indicator *must* be found — otherwise we shall have to content ourselves with the usual idle speculations encountered only too frequently.

Ideological orientations are value orientations, and as indicators of values only other values can serve. Hence, some value-loaded manifestations of the more latent concepts of ideational and sensate in the day-to-day routine of a village must be made use of. We have chosen two approaches to the problem, and selected the manifestations in the *field of occupations* and the *field of general spheres of value orientation*. To evaluate occupations is tantamount to suggesting a rank order among them, and to evaluate 'spheres of orientation' is tantamount to suggesting a rank order of spheres of allegiance. The question is only which ones to pick, and how to arrange them intuitively on a scale ranging from ideational to sensate.

Four occupations held by us to be representative of different parts of the ideational-sensate continuum were picked,[1] *viz.*, *priest*, *lawyer*, *physician* and *engineer* — and four spheres of allegiance were picked, *viz.* the spheres of *religious activities*, *family life*, *oneself* and *conditions in the village*.

We wanted the *occupations* ranked in terms of *legitimate authority* attributed to them by the respondent, and to elicit this we asked: 'In your opinion, who ought to have more to say about things in general in a village, a priest or a lawyer?' Partly to get more detailed information, and partly to avoid the difficulties arising from the fact that not everybody is able to rank simultaneously as many as four items, we used the method of *paired comparisons*. Out of four items $\binom{4}{2} = 6$ pairs can be formed, these pairs were then randomized as to order (and as to order of elements within the pairs) and presented to the respondents. Ideally, there were two possible answers — for instance *either* priest *or* lawyer, but in interview practice possibilities like 'equally important' and 'I just do not know' always appear. All these 'middle answers' were grouped together in a third, middle category.

We wanted the *spheres of allegiance* ranked according to subjective *importance*, and simply asked: 'What is better in your opinion, for instance, to look out for oneself or to improve the life of one's family?'

Methodologically, we proceeded in exactly the same way with these items; they were combined into six pairs, randomized and presented to the respondents.

On the ideational-sensate continuum the items were placed by us as shown in Table 3.1.1.

Table 3.1.1. *The items in the indices of ideational-sensate orientation*

	Ideational		Sensate	
	Very typical	*Less typical*	*Less typical*	*Very typical*
Occupational items	priest	lawyer	physician	engineer
Allegiance items	religious activities	family life	oneself	improve village conditions

To justify this way of looking at the items it should first of all be noticed that this must be decided on the basis of analysis of the content of the items, not on how the sample reacted to the paired comparisons. If we had been able to get at a person's orientation in its purest form, we might certainly have used statistical techniques to arrive at a decision as to how these items rate on an ideational-sensate scale. But no such external criterion exists, so we have to rely on our own judgment as to where the items belong. And had the 'external criterion' existed, then we would of course rather have used it than the items above.

There can be little doubt about the items termed by us as 'very typical' in Table 3.1.1. The 'priest' is concerned with *intrinsic* change; his entire profession is an institutionalization of the overriding importance of the transcendental existence; his status is geared toward the soul. In practice he may do many other things, but this is his *raison d'être*. Similarly, the 'engineer' is concerned with *external* change of this mundane existence; his task is to change nature, not man. Correspondingly, 'religious activities' have as their extreme counterparts efforts to 'improve the living conditions of the village'. They are comparable insofar as they are activities, and opposite in so far as they can be seen as heaven directed and world directed respectively.

The 'less typical' items may look more problematic. The 'lawyer' is seen as a person who is concerned above all with the normatively given, and with the preservation of stability, with the control of deviations from the normatively given — whereas the 'physician' is seen as a person engaged in extrinsic changes; his activities are *body* directed, not *soul* directed.[2] This does not mean that there is no physician, the *medico*, in the traditional society with its overriding ideational orientation — nor that he is not seen as an important man — only that insofar as his *medical* activities in our sense are concerned, he is not given that much authority. But he can derive considerable authority as a medical man if his activities are not defined as purely a-religious. Since he is in control of matters of life and death, an admixture of ideational elements very easily takes place. We feel, however, that the *medico* in present day Sicily is perceived in more 'modern' terms — as an academic man, a professional who may or may not be religious as a person, but not as a status. For this reason, he is put on the sensate end of the scale, but obviously not as far out as 'engineer'.[3]

The relative position of 'family' and 'oneself' does not follow from the more philosophical connotations given to the ideational-sensate dichotomy. It is rather a social correlate of it, and as an empirical correlate not logically necassary. What we feel is that the idea of 'looking out for oneself' is more indicative of a sensate orientation, because it implies a change of external conditions for the benefit of oneself. Of course, one might argue that a person may be 'looking out for himself' in his striving for religious salvation, but this is hardly the interpretation in the cultural setting in which this study was carried out. 'To look out for oneself' has a connotation of the sensate, not of the ideational — but not so much so as the 'improvement of village conditions'.

In short, we feel that the positions of the extreme items in Table 3.1.1, and also the positions of these items relative to the other items, are well justified. There can be some doubt, however, in connection with the relative position of the two middle items. This means that out of the six pairs of each kind the meaning of the choice is clear for five of them — and we feel we have the right to establish the meaning of a choice for the sixth pair by convention. Thus, if in a pair the respondent chooses the item to the *right* in Table 3.1.1, this is taken as an indication of a *sensate* orientation; if he chooses the item to the *left*, this is taken as indicative of an *ideational* orientation. On this basis two indices were constructed (by giving a '0' to an ideational choice, a '1' to a choice in the middle and a '2' to a sensate choice), one index based on the occupational items, the other index based on the allegiance items.

One major difficulty with this method is that we do not and cannot ask directly we want to know; we cannot apply Sorokin's definitions directly but have to rely on indicators related to an unknown manner to the latent dimension. Thus, when a person feels that a physician should have more of a say than a priest, this may be an expression of a general feeling of reverence for the high status of the physician, and not so much an expression of a sensate orientation. For this reason the occupations selected for comparisons had to be within the same social stratum. In practice this is impossible in a status-conscious community like a village with relatively few statuses — but these four academic professions are at least not too far apart in rank distance. And economic sector is also kept constant: they are all tertiary professions.

Similarly, there may be many reasons for a choice of a sphere of allegiance other than the more abstract kind of orientation in terms of 'sensate' and 'ideational'. Thus, a person may have an inclination in the direction of changing village life, but the idea that it *can* be done may be so farfetched that he does not pick the item when he has the chance. Nevertheless, these value orientations seem to be closer to the latent dimension than the occupational items, where the differences in rank may interfere. For that reason we shall have to give some justifications for our assertion that the four occupations selected are relatively similar in rank, so that ranking in terms of preferred power distribution can be seen at least in great part as due to ideological convictions. Among the innumerable studies of social stratification we have selected some for reference. Unfortunately, we know of no relevant study from the area, so we had to make use of the principle according to which 'what is similar in many parts of the world is probably similar here too'.

Svalastoga[4] gives a ranking of 75 occupations with our four occupations located as physician (number 11), attorney (number 16), engineer (number 17) and minister (number 24). Thus, they occupy a span of about one-sixth of the order scale, but only one-tenth of the total rating range available: from 2.00 to 2.51 — with all prestige ratings ranging from 1.00 to 5.00 theoretically, from 1.20 to 4.79 empirically. This is actually quite narrow. Moreover, there are one sensate and one ideational both among the two highest and among the two lowest of the four occupations, so there is no systematic value bias. However, it may be objected that Denmark, although not highly industrialized, is nevertheless a modern country, so data from a more traditional society had to be located.

Tiryakian[5] presents such data. He makes the respondents rank 30 occupations and gets our four occupations located as physician (number 1), lawyer (number 3), engineer (number 4) and priest (number 6); in other words, exactly the same ranking as Svalastoga found in Denmark. The span is one-fifth of the total, and we still have the ideational and sensate occupations well interspersed. Tiryakian also has a number of references to studies from Great Britain, New Zealand, Australia and Japan showing similar similarities.

But the main summary of such studies is given by *Inkeles and Rossi.*[6] The comparison is between U.S.A., Germany, Great Britain, New Zealand, Japan and U.S.S.R. For U.S.A. the four occupations are ranged physician (score 93), minister (87), lawyer (86) and civil engineer (84) — with the total range being 93 to 33. This differs from the rankings above, but we still have the ideational and the sensate well mixed. For the other countries we do not find all four, but those we find cover ranges from one-quarter of the total (for Germany) to much less for the other countries. In all six countries the physicians are either on the top or very close to it. Thus, the cross-national consensus is most impressive, and there seems to be little reason to believe that Sicily should constitute an exception.

On the other hand, instead of asking *why* this or that horn of the dilemma is chosen, we may ask instead what the *consequence* is of answering as the respondents do. If we look at Table 3.1.1 again, and try to grasp the meaning of the four items listed under *ideational*, as opposed to the meaning given by the four items listed under *sensate*, the idea is typically that of a very ideational vs. sensate orientation in the sense outlined in the first chapter. *A person who makes choices that place him on the ideational end of the scale will, if these choices are acted out or repeated verbally in his social life, contribute to the creation and maintenance of an ideational atmosphere* — even though his reasons for making these choices may be quite different. Socially, he *is* ideational, although psychologically he *may* feel different and, correspondingly, if he consistently makes sensate choices. Thus, the *face validity* of the dimensions seems to be high.

As the indices were constructed (each with six items that could take on the values 0, 1 and 2), they ranged from 0 to 12 — but adjacent categories were collapsed symmetrically so as to get seven categories. The extreme categories obtain if and only of the respondents make a completely pure choice — completely ideational, or completely sensate. But very few made such choices.

Let us compare the three villages in terms of these distributions (Table 3.1.2). We were particularly anxious when we first arrived at this Table, since we could not possibly know in advance (although we had done some pre-testing) whether our items could really discriminate well. In other words, we wanted *symmetric distributions*, and this is more or less what we got. Conceivably, the items might have been so extreme relative to the local philosophies that practically all respondents appeared

Table 3.1.2. *The distributions of the ideological orientations (original form, percentage)*

Index	Occupation items							Allegiance items							Total	N
	Idea-tional						Sen-sate	Idea-tional						Sen-sate		
Value	0	1–2	3–4	5–7	8–9	10–11	12	0	1–2	3–4	5–7	8–9	10–11	12	Total	N
MONTAGNA	0	11	20	37	17	12	3	3	5	18	54	14	6	0	100	(152)
COLLINA	1	5	18	34	28	12	2	0	3	17	52	27	1	0	100	(151)
MARINA	0	5	12	47	20	13	3	0	3	14	41	35	7	0	100	(105)
Average	0	7	17	39	22	12	3	1	4	17	50	24	4	0	100	(408)

either as 'ideationals' or as 'sensates'; but for all six distributions the modus is in the middle of the total range.

On the other hand, we would of course have preferred the additive indices to yield *U-shaped distributions* rather than the peaked, A-shaped distributions we have for all villages and both indices. The distributions we got are due to two factors. First of all, the correlations between the items are relatively low, which was to be expected since they do not correspond directly to concrete issues with accompanying polarization in the villages. And secondly, the 'both important' and 'don't know' answers contribute heavily to this concentration in the middle. But much more important than these methodological considerations is a substantive comment: the A-shaped distributions indicate that *there is a low degree of crystallization of attitudes*, that most people have inconsistent, confused patterns of thinking. In other words, as mentioned in 1.6, the majority are people in transition; they are *members of two worlds*.

Although the distributions are symmetric in the sense that the modi are always in the middle category, they are not completely symmetric in the sense that there is no skewness. Actually, the two distributions for Montagna are tilted to the ideational side, and the four distributions for Collina and Marina to the sensate side, which indicates an important difference between the villages to which we shall have occasion to return later. But by and large we have been fortunate as the indices divide the samples in three relatively meaningful parts, and, *grosso modo*, in the same way.

We shall not use the index in the form it is given in Table 3.1.2, however; it is much too refined and the extreme frequencies are too small. With samples of our size, three-point indices are generally preferable, and we want to be guided by these rules of thumb in choosing our cutting points:

1) The cutting points should be symmetric around the middle so that the semantic meanings of the terms 'ideational' and 'sensate' are symmetric.
2) The cutting points should be the same for all three villages so that the results are directly comparable.
3) The cutting points should make the categories as equal as possible in terms of frequency of respondents.

We may call these the *semantic* rule, the *comparability* rule and the *statistical* rule, respectively. Clearly, they do not yield the same results and may, hence, lead to conflicts and a need for rules of priority. We shall make use of the ordering of the criteria above as a priority order. The semantic rule seems to us so important to retain the degree of symmetry we have obtained, that we have put it first. For instance, for the index based on the occupation items all we have to do is to retain the middle category (5–7) and collapse the categories on either side, calling them 'ideational', 'medium' and 'sensate', respectively. 'Ideational', then, means a preponderance of ideational choices, but with the differences we have between the villages this division will also lead to a low number of respondents in the category of ideationals for the least ideational village, i.e. Marina. Nevertheless, this seems to be the best choice.

For the second index, based on the allegiance items, we run into the difficulty that 50% of the sample is in the middle category. Hence, we make use of the original variable from 0 to 12 and concentrate on index value 6 alone, in line with the semantic rule above (a combination of 6 and 7 would have yielded a better statistical distribution, because of the general tilting to the sensate side — but the semantic meaning of the categories would no longer have been symmetric) (Table 3.1.3).

Table 3.1.3. *The distributions of the ideological orientations (collapsed form, percentage)*

Index	Occupation items			Allegiance items			Total	(N)
	Ideational (0–4)	Medium (5–7)	Sensate (8–12)	Ideational (0–5)	Medium (6)	Sensate (7–12)		
MONTAGNA	31	37	32	38	32	30	100	(152)
COLLINA	24	34	42	31	25	44	100	(151)
MARINA	17	47	46	26	20	54	100	(105)
Average	24	39	37	32	27	41	100	(408)

From this Table the ranking of the three villages in terms of being ideational (Montagna — Collina — Marina) is both consistent and clear, and is, in fact, invariant of changes in reasonable cutting points for both indices. Hence, it was not strange that the distribution for Montagna was leaning to the ideational side.

In everything that follows, the cutting points introduced in Table 3.1.3 will be retained, unless otherwise indicated. The first thing to look for is the *interrelation* between these two indices designed to measure orientation along the ideational-sensate continuum (Table 3.1.4).

Table 3.1.4. *The relation between the two indices of ideological orientation (for the three villages, percentage)*

	MONTAGNA				COLLINA				MARINA				
	Ideational	Medium	Sensate	(N)	Ideational	Medium	Sensate	(N)	Ideational	Medium	Sensate	(N)	Total
Ideational	50	26	24	(46)	44	28	28	(36)	44	29	17	(18)	100
Medium	41	32	27	(56)	33	23	44	(52)	33	20	47	(49)	100
Sensate	24	38	38	(50)	22	25	53	(63)	8	10	81	(38)	100

The trends are very consistent and the correlations are, especially for Marina (gamma = 0.62), high enough to warrant the assumption of interchangeability of the indices for some analytical purposes. But at the same time it is clear that the two indices do not measure exactly the same things. This puts us in the same situation as for the sampling of the villages discussed in 2.1: the indices are similar enough to warrant their use as each other's replication, yet dissimilar enough to make the replication non-trivial.

Our instrument is now presented, and in conclusion let us mention five problems of a general methodological nature and of considerable importance in connection with this entire chapter.

1. *The problem of validity.* But — is this *really* what Sorokin means when he writes about 'ideational' and 'sensate'? Evidently it is not; the extreme richness inherent in Sorokin's concepts can never be caught completely by means of some indices based on survey items. At best, indices can catch a fragment of the ideas and translate them into meaningful questions and answers.

We have three lines of defense, however.

First of all, the indices are based on value choices which we feel are meaningfully related to the overriding value dimension of ideational vs. sensate, and our reasoning in this connection has already been presented in this section. Secondly, we have constructed two different indices, not only one, thus catching at least more of the ideas than with one index alone; and we shall make use of both as each other's control. Finally, although we have no external criterion that corresponds exactly to what Sorokin has intended, there are some variables we can use for validation purposes. For instance, whenever it comes to questions concerning changes in what nature gives, we would not only expect but actually *require* that our sensates have a more active and accepting attitude, and the ideationals a correspondingly passive and even rejecting attitude. Thus, we would expect the sensate to suggest industrialization and to be in favor of birth control, the ideationals to be against both. This will be discussed in section 3.2.

2. *The problem of reliability*. As demonstrated in Table 3.1.4, the two indices are correlated, but not very strongly. Hence, we cannot pick one of them and discard the other with the justification that 'they measure the same'. Besides, we have no *a priori* reason for preferring one to the other. For this reason and for the reason mentioned above, *we shall use both indices singly, not combined*. Thus we shall not accept correlations as 'findings' unless they hold for both indices.

3. *The problem of speech reactions vs. non-verbal behavior*. This is an old methodological problem of considerable generality: in real life, the *speech reactions* we can register are of little consequence, what matters is how the respondents act out their cultural inclinations in their *behavior*. We shall not attempt to discuss this fully here, only indicate some arguments for the validity of a 'both/and' position. To act out a sensate orientation in a village where the *ethos* is predominantly ideational and the material conditions are very traditional is difficult if not completely impossible; so it is quite likely that we would not even discover the would-be sensates by purely observational means. Conversely, an ideational orientation may not necessarily express itself in terms of, for instance, church attendance — all 1001 external conditions may interfere and make overt behavior less of a true indicator of attitudinal belongingness than the kind of answers we can elicit. This is not to deny that observations of behavior would be extremely valuable, and we

wish we had such data in addition to what we have — but this study is predominantly a study of values and attitudes and perceptions, and we feel that these can best be obtained by means of a survey. However, we shall return to an aspect of this problem in section 3.3.

4. *The problem of classification.* Our cutting points have been chosen in accordance with three principles, but they are nevertheless arbitrary because our items are to some extent arbitrary. Further, even though we have six items in each index, this does not mean that a respondent is given a complete chance to indicate the different shades of his own philosophy. But — and this is the main point — the classification of the respondents may be faulty because the respondent answers as he does for *other* reasons than his latent inclinations in terms of ideational vs. sensate. We have already mentioned this point, and our principal answer lies in the *switch from causal to functional reasoning :* if he answers as he does, he is by definition what we call him — and let us then see what consequences follow from the relations between these answers and his other answers. For even if the cutting points are arbitrary they have to be placed somewhere, even if it does violence to some individuals. How fruitful it is, is another question.

5. *The problem of fruitfulness.* If one accepts the comments given to the four problems above, one may still ask: But is this of any real value ? Concepts and typologies abound, but they are only useful if they are fruitful in the usual sense that respondents belonging to the same group have other interesting characteristics in common. And is this the case here ? This, of course, is the major problem of our empirical research and will be answered in two steps in the usual manner recommended[7] for new indices:

a) *by rediscovering what is already known,* i.e. by testing some obvious hypotheses relating ideational-sensate to some other attitudes and some structural variables, partly to validate the instrument, partly to know its properties better. This will be done in sections 3.2, 3.3 and 3.4.

b) *by exploring what is not known,* i.e. by exploring new relations between ideational-sensate and other attitudes, not to mention with other structural variables benefiting from the experience already gained in the use of the instrument. This will be done in sections 3.5, 3.6, 3.7, 3.8 and 3.9.

At the end of the chapter, in section 3.10, an effort will be made to summarize and evaluate the meaning of the findings for general development theory.[8]

114

3.2. *Who the sensates are : traditionalists or innovators*

The task confronting us in this section is a double one. First of all, we want to find out whether our indices show what we know they must show if they are to be of any use at all. And secondly, we want to get some additional insights over and above the trivial 'He who is more influenced by modern values is also likely to accept and want industrialization', etc.

For this purpose the ideal would be to place the respondent in his local situation and ask him questions that address themselves to problems of everyday concern, and to problems of relevance to everybody: *the local village situation.* Thus, we asked simple, open-ended questions concerning the diagnosis and the cure for the difficulties in the villages: 'What is the main problem?' and 'How can conditions be improved?' The answers were ordered according to how much activity and innovation they expressed, starting with 'don't know' as the most apathetic one and ending with 'to get industry'. An obvious request to our indices would now be that the sensates should be clearly overrepresented among those who have an active attitude and see both diagnosis and cure in terms of *change.* Thus the suggestion that the cure should consist of 'improving what exists' should be overrepresented among the ideationals, for the simple reason that this implies a basic conception of stability — amelioration, but not innovation. The results, starting with the occupation index, are shown in Table 3.2.1.

Table 3.2.1. *Ideological orientation and diagnosis and cure for the villages (occupation items, total sample, percentage*)*

	What is the main problem?			Can conditions be improved?				
	Don't know	To get work	To get industry	Don't know	Improve what is	To get work	To get industry	Total sample
Ideationals	45	22	16	43	33	24	15	25
Medium	42	34	37	39	41	41	38	38
Sensates	13	44	47	18	26	35	47	37
Total	100	100	100	100	100	100	100	100
(N)	(31)	(168)	(49)	(28)	(55)	(90)	(93)	(408)

* Other answers were also given, but the frequencies are too small to warrant comparisons.

The Table should be read horizontally, and the first and third rows give uniformly the same impressions: *the more active and innovative the answer, the fewer ideationals and the more sensates.* This holds uniformly for both parts of the Table, and the percentage differences between the two most extreme and most clear answers, don't know' and 'to get industry', are about the same. Moreover, if we compare the eight corner percentages in the two parts of the Table with the corresponding percentages for the total sample, we see that the hypotheses about over- and underrepresentation have been well confirmed. In short, we feel relatively confident, although the differences probably would have been higher if we had an even more valid instrument — but this is the best one we have.[1]

At this point one should pause for a moment and ask whether this is trivial or not. Of course, it may be said to be trivial that he who places the engineer higher than the priest also is industry-oriented — but this is only one of the six items in the index. The index as a whole relates to the relative ranking of four academic professions, derived from a theory concerned with a basic orientation to society and culture, and it turns out that this orientation is quite strongly related to one's basic orientation in everyday village affairs. We assume that the answers recorded in Table 3.2.1 would also be the ones that will color the respondent's *piazza* conversation — and the Table suggests not only two distinct camps and schools of thought in the villages, but also a vast middle category of people with one foot in either camp. Thus, the villages as a whole and a substantial portion of the villagers seem to be members of both worlds.

Let us then see what happens to the other index. In a sense we should expect even more correlation because it refers so directly to values. On the other hand it has a more abstract content and is less related to the immediate problems of village life (Table 3.2.2). Again, we find exactly the same tendencies and differences but less pronounced. Why less pronounced? Probably for the reason indicated: the abstract values are less directly related to the content matter of these questions. But the reason may also be that there is something wrong with this index, some basic inconsistency that decreases correlations. So far, our conclusion must be that both indices yield correlations in the direction we want, but whereas the percentage differences are around thirty points for the occupation index, it is only about half of this for the allegiance index. Thus, if we should use only one of them, we would certainly use the best one, the occupation index; but we should also require that

Table 3.2.2. *Ideological orientation and diagnosis and cure for the villages (allegiance items, total sample, percentage)*

	What is the main problem?			Can conditions be improved?				
	Don't know	To get work	To get industry	Don't know	Improve what is	To get work	To get industry	Total sample
Ideationals	39	36	24	32	40	32	26	32
Medium	35	27	27	32	24	26	27	27
Sensates	26	37	49	36	36	42	47	41
Total	100	100	100	100	100	100	100	100
(N)	(31)	(168)	(49)	(28)	(55)	(90)	(93)	(408)

the second index show some correlation. This will be our general policy in what follows, but the complete data will not always be given for reasons of space.

Let us then turn to another highly important question of everyday concern — the *number of children* — both the number they have and the number they think is appropriate for a family (Diagram 3.2.1).[2]

The figures are clear enough: whereas the mode for the number of children they *have* is three, there is a certain consensus around the figure

Diagram 3.2.1. *Real and ideal number of children per family*

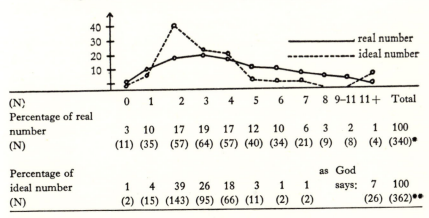

(N)	0	1	2	3	4	5	6	7	8	9–11	11+	Total
Percentage of real number	3	10	17	19	17	12	10	6	3	2	1	100
(N)	(11)	(35)	(57)	(64)	(57)	(40)	(34)	(21)	(9)	(8)	(4)	(340)*
Percentage of ideal number	1	4	39	26	18	3	1	1	as God says:		7	100
(N)	(2)	(15)	(143)	(95)	(66)	(11)	(2)	(2)			(26)	(362)**

* The question did not apply to 68 respondents (17% of the total sample).

** Forty-six respondents have been omitted, 34 because the question was not asked or answered (it was an embarrassing question to many), 12 because they 'did not know'.

two as the *ideal* number of children (the medians are also very close to these figures). The arithmetic means show the differences even more clearly. The number of families with a high number of children contributes to a mean of 3.9, against a mean of 2.8 for the ideal number.[3] *Evidently, nature's average is too high, but not overwhelmingly so.* Further, there is much more consensus about what is ideal than there is similarity in actual practice. Evidently, there must be a number of people who have more children than they think is suitable for a family. But there are also some people who want more — they are mostly young and still in the process of building up a family, however.

How great is the discontent? To see the relation the two variables have to each other, Table 3.2.3 can be used.

Table 3.2.3. *Ideal number of children as a function of the real number of children, percentage*

		Ideal number				
		0–2	3+	as God says	Total	(N)
	0–3	54	46	0	100	(152)
Real number	4 +	36	52	12	100	(157)
	Average	45	49	6	100	(309)

Within an ethical system where the production of children is legitimate but the destruction of children strongly proscribed, there is only one cell in the Table that can be said to represent a situation of conflict. Thirty-six per cent of the people with 'many' children want less, even much less. As the minimum discrepancy in this Table is from four children down to two, we can be confident that this is a sincere desire — it is not just a question of having one child less. The discontent in the other corner is more easily dissolved, provided the couple are not too old.

Keeping the number of children they have constant, how does the ideal number of children depend on ideological attitude? We would expect the attitude to play some role, although other factors (e.g. socio-economic standing) may also be of importance.

Table 3.2.4. *Ideological orientation and the desire to have only 0–2 children (based on people who have four or more children), percentage*

Index	Ideational	Medium	Sensate	Total sample
Occupation items	23	34	47	36
Allegiance items	33	37	38	36

118

The correlation is substantial and in the expected direction for the first index, but insignificant (although the direction is correct) for the second index. Again, we find the same: the occupational index gives a better indication of the relationship. The index based on the allegiance items supports the finding but more like a voltmeter calibrated for very high tension only, whereas the index based on occupation items is calibrated for more refined measurement.

Let us see in Table 3.2.5 whether this also holds regardless of the real number of children, and whether it holds for each single village.

Table 3.2.5. *Ideological orientation and ideal number of children*[*]

	MONTAGNA				COLLINA				MARINA			
	1,2	3–7	Total	N	1,2	3–7	Total	N	1,2	3–7	Total	N
Ideationals	42	58	100	(36)	48	52	100	(27)	6	94	100	(15)
Medium	49	51	100	(41)	52	48	100	(42)	35	65	100	(45)
Sensates	68	32	100	(41)	54	46	100	(50)	41	59	100	(37)

The Table gives a clear confirmation, although the correlation is very weak for Collina (percentage difference of six). Evidently, the attitude expressed in the index affects many spheres of the ideology, the family as well as the social order. On the other hand, the correlations are not perfect and indicate resistance in the sensate camp as well as acceptance in the ideational camp. That is, the Table indicates attitudes toward the idea of having few children, fewer than nature's average in these villages, but it should be noticed that the idea that one or two children are 'best' is not the same as accepting the idea of contraception, and far from trying to acquire and use contraceptives. The important facts for us, however, are 1) that the idea of few children is widespread, and 2) that the idea is to some extent accounted for by general ideological orientation and has a much stronger foothold in the sensate camp.

It would be strange if age did not play a role, however, and since it is up to the younger generation to decide on the shape of the future population pyramid, their attitudes are particularly important. We get the distribution shown in Table 3.2.6. The general tendency is clear as seen from the Table for the total sample, and the role of age is conspicuous. Curiously enough, the oldest generation seems to be more positive to the idea of a limited number of children than the middle generation. This is probably a result of their life experiences. But the

[*] We have only made use of clear answers to the question.

	Born							
	1871–1900		1901–1920		1921–1940		Total sample	
Number of children wanted	1,2	3–7	1,2	3–7	1,2	3–7	1,2	3–7
Ideationals	35	65	19	81	74	26	36	64
Sensates	58	42	47	53	65	35	55	45
Difference	—23	+23	—28	+28	+ 9	— 9	—19	+19

youngest generation are far above the other categories when it comes to favoring a low number of children.

More interesting, however, is the difference between the sensates and the ideationals. In the youngest age category the ideationals have not only an equally 'positive' attitude to few children, but actually surpass the sensates, although the difference is not statistically significant with the low number of respondents. What is certain is the sharp reduction in the difference with decreasing age. *One interpretation of this is that the whole problem of family planning is gradually being taken out of its religious-ideological context and has become a question of a new generation's way of viewing these matters.* For proponents of family planning this is a highly optimistic finding, for it implies a sharp reduction in the ideological polarization in this field — if not at the level of public debate, at least in the more private sphere where these things are decided anyhow.

There is another aspect of family life prior to begetting children, also subject to choice and possible influence from ideologies: *the age of the spouse.* Four variables come into play here: at what age the respondents married, how old the spouse was, when the respondent feels a man should marry and when he feels a woman should marry. Let us first look at the distributions of these variables in Table 3.2.7.

The important differences in this Table are across sex lines, not between the real and the ideal. Although the proverbial saying in the region 'uomo ventinove, donna dicianove' exaggerates both the real and the ideal age difference between the spouses, it is approximated in reality as well as in ideology. The many functions of this pattern — e.g. postponement of sexual gratification for the man, premarital chastity preserved for the woman but not for the man, sexual maladjustment because the woman enters her optimum age a decade after the marriage (perhaps fifteen years after the husband passes his); high numbers of

---

* We have only made use of clear answers to the question and have excluded the middle ideological category since it adds nothing to the understanding.

Table 3.2.7. *Real and ideal age at marriage, both sexes (total sample, percentage)*[*]

Age	16–17	18–19	20–21	22–24	25–27	28–30	31–35	36 +	Median	Total	(N)
Real age, respondent	1	3	8	21	30	18	11	8	26.7	100	(356)
Real age, spouse	13	20	20	26	12	6	2	1	21.7	100	(356)
Ideal age, man	1	1	6	11	54	24	2	1	26.7	100	(378)
Ideal age, woman	7	38	38	10	6	1	—	—	20.3	100	(378)

widows surviving their husbands, many children with old fathers, the perpetuation of the authority of the man because it is also built into the age differential, practically no opportunity for the woman to seek higher education, strengthening of 'the male society' because of the prevalence of young adult males with no immediate family attachment, etc. — are too well known to warrant any comment here. It should only be noticed that this pattern is a part of traditionalist society of extreme importance. It should be said, however, that it is also a pattern that permits the man a certain choice, not only of women before he marries, but also of traveling, seeking experiences of all kinds, before he settles down to family life. Hence, if reduction of discrepancy in marital age is reduced by lowering the age at which the man enters marriage, this may well lead to a reduction in the value flow in the local society. In more sensate societies, such as Norway, this factor is counteracted by the relative ease with which social and geographical mobility of the whole family and particularly of the newly wed couple takes place. The other way of reducing the discrepancy is by higher marriage age for the woman, to permit her education and other emancipatory necessities and to reduce the power differential in the family. But this does not seem to be in accordance with local, male ideology: whereas the median marriage age for the women is 21.7 years, the median ideal age for women is about one and a half years lower, 20.3 years. This is even more interesting because there is no difference in the medians for the ideal and real marriage ages for the men. Evidently, quite a few males want the women to be even younger — and the interesting question is: Does ideology in our sense play a role here?

There is little reason why it should. One might guess that sensate males are exposed to cross-pressures: on the one hand the ideal male

* Unmarried people and DK's and NA's have been omitted.

superiority, on the other hand a vague idea that social change can make use of the emancipation of women, which again may have something to do with a higher marriage age for girls. But this latter part is uncertain and has hardly penetrated into the villages of Western Sicily yet, whereas the first part touches on very basic values. And since the latter part is the only part which should be ideologically relevant, we would expect little or no correlation. To test this, we looked at three relations shown in Table 3.2.9. The correlations obtained are about the same and very slight, but in the opposite direction of what one might have expected. An *ad hoc* explanation is needed, and the only one we can think of is that 'waiting' for marriage to take place is somehow not considered 'modern'. Whatever factor may be at work here, however, its effect is a minor one, and this is further substantiated by the data in Table 3.2.9.

Table 3.2.8. *Ideological orientation and ideal marriage age for women (total sample, percentage)*

	Occupation index					Allegiance index				
	16–19	20–21	22+	Total	(N)	16–19	20–21	22+	Total	(N)
Ideational	44	32	24	100	(93)	37	43	20	100	(125)
Medium	44	41	15	100	(144)	49	33	18	100	(92)
Sensate	45	39	16	100	(140)	48	36	16	100	(160)

Table 3.2.9. *Ideological orientation and relative ideal marriage age for women (total sample, percentage)*

	Relative to real marriage age for the woman				Relative to ideal marriage age for the man			
	Occupation index				Occupation index three +		Value index three +	
	Prefer younger	Prefer the same	Prefer older	SUM	Groups younger	Same	Groups younger	Same
Ideationals	50	31	19	100	31	(2)	34	(4)
Medium	45	29	26	100	32	(5)	30	(4)
Sensates	50	28	22	100	33	(5)	33	(4)

The Table reveals no differences at all: when seen relative to the real marriage age for the wife, or the ideal marriage age for a man in our sense, ideology plays no role at all in determining attitudes in this field.

The issue has not yet crystallized and been absorbed into this ideological cluster. Thus, it is worth noting how extremely small the number of people who want the spouses to be in the same age bracket is.

In conclusion let us summarize our impressions from these first experiments with the indices, in the following points:

1) Where correlations were expected, correlations were found and in the expected direction. In other words, we rediscovered what we already knew.

2) Although this holds for both indices, the occupation index has so far yielded more clear results than the other index. They have never yielded results that contradict each other, but since the occupation index gives higher correlations, it seems probable that we shall discover relationships more easily by means of that index than with the other. Hence, if only one index is used, it will be the index based on occupation items.

3) The best procedure seems to be to use the occupation index with the allegiance index as a control. If the latter gives a correlation in the opposite direction, findings should be disregarded or explained; if the latter gives no correlation at all, findings must be evaluated very carefully.

4) Of the values examined in this section it is clear that values relating to the economic sphere of life correlate best with the ideology expressed by the indices. When it comes to the institution of family, indications are that 'family planning' has gained a bridgehead in the sensate camp, whereas changes in absolute or relative age at marriage have not yet been included in this ideological cluster.[4]

3.3. *Who the sensates are: social participation*

We have studied some ideological concomitants of these orientations and turn next to some behavioral variables. In our data there is information for each respondent about how often he reads a newspaper, reads a weekly, listens to the radio, watches TV, goes to a movie and was in church last week. This gives us an opportunity to study in some detail both the quantitative and qualitative aspects of participation: how much do they participate, and where? We had actually no precise ideas as to what to expect — except some vague notion that the ideationals probably would go more to church and less to the movies — because this was what one would expect extrapolating from superficial ideas about how 'religious' people behave. From the same notions, we

Table 3.3.1. *Ideological orientation and amount of participation, percentage*

	Occupation index Participation			Allegiance index Participation		
	Low	Medium	High	Low	Medium	High
Ideationals	23	27	22	29	38	34
Medium	43	28	44	26	26	28
Sensates	34	45	34	45	36	38
Total	100	100	100	100	100	100
(N)	(210)	(124)	(74)	(210)	(124)	(74)

would also have expected that the ideationals would be overrepresented among people with a generally low degree of social participation. This, however, did not turn out to be true (Table 3.3.1).

With one index showing no and the other low correlation it seems relatively safe to say that ideological orientation is neither directly and strongly caused nor does it express itself in differential total participation rates. To the extent that there is a correlation, however, it is indeed worth noting that it is in the opposite direction from what we expected, with the sensates participating *less*. We shall pursue this when we look at the different items — for it seems intuitively obvious that this similarity must mask differences when it comes to *kind* more than *amount* of participation.

Let us start out with the more critical institution in this connection, what one might expect to be the bulwark of ideational orientation: the *church*. The logical question to ask is this: If a person gives away ideational 'speech-reactions', should we not expect him to implement this some way or another, for instance by going to church (Table 3.3.2)?

Table 3.3.2. *Ideological orientation and reported church attendance 'last week', percentage*

	Occupation index			Allegiance index		
	MONT-AGNA	COLL-INA	MAR-INA	MONT-AGNA	COLL-INA	MAR-INA
Ideationals	76	53	28	83	62	26
Medium	82	67	39	69	55	43
Sensates	58	52	40	62	60	40
Average	72	58	37	72	58	37
Ideationals attending church	31	24	17	38	31	26
Sensates attending church	32	42	46	30	44	54

124

This Table, where both indices as usual show the same thing, gives a much deeper insight into these villages. First of all, it should be noticed that the differences in church attendance are substantial: from close to three-fourths in Montagna, to one-half in Collina and down to little more than one-third in the more cosmopolitan Marina. This must mean that the church does not have a uniform power of attraction but a very differential influence in the three villages — which it is necessary to take into account as a warning against stereotyped talking about the influence of a social institution. For instance, if our sample had been drawn from Montagna only, generalizations about the heavy church attendance in Western Sicily might easily have been concluded from the data; had the sample come from Marina alone similar generalizations about how the church 'loses its hold' on people might have emerged.

We shall encounter the ordering Montagna — Collina — Marina a number of times. It is the same as the order of the villages in terms of proportions of ideationals (see 3.2), proportions of 'locals' (see 3.8), proportions having no relatives abroad, etc. In a sense, all these single items are compatible, and a systematic comparison of all findings when the villages are compared will be carried out later. But the finding in Table 3.3.2 is more interesting: it is *not* true that ideationals generally go more to church than sensates. With heavy church attendance in the predominantly ideational Montagna, there are more of the ideationals than of the sensates present, with medium church attendance in the mixed Collina, they are about equally well represented, and with low church attendance in the predominantly sensate Marina, the sensates are better represented than the ideationals! How can this be explained? Let us try some speculations based on these three villages.

First, look at these relations from Tables 3.3.1 and 3.3.2 graphically.

We shall certainly not claim too much on the basis of three villages, but it looks as if the claim for an increasing or monotone relationship with increasing proportion of ideationals in the village but with decreasing returns in general church attendance and ideational attendance, is warranted. The curves based on the two indices are also remarkably parallel. Of course, we would expect a heavier general church attendance in cities with a more ideational climate, and we would also expect this climate to cause and to be caused by a heavy attendance among the ideationals. The church is theirs, not only by ideological compatibility, but also by majority possession. It is easy to understand that the sensates stay away more than one should expect by chance: the church is certainly not theirs, nor is the village theirs.

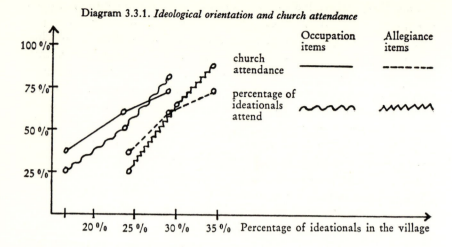

Diagram 3.3.1. *Ideological orientation and church attendance*

	Occupation items	Allegiance items
church attendance	——————	— — — —
percentage of ideationals attend	∿∿∿∿∿	∧∧∧∧∧

Percentage of ideationals in the village

But when the village becomes predominantly sensate, as is the case for Marina (Table 3.1.3), does it really also follow that the *church* becomes predominantly sensate in its attendance? After all, is the church an ideational institution? Since church attendance drops in general with increasing sensateness in the population, we do not get a rise in the proportion of sensates present in church, but the proportion of church-going sensates drops much more slowly, so that the proportion of the sensate church-goers actually becomes higher than the proportion of ideational church-goers. If we omit all mediums, we can calculate the ratio between ideationals and sensates in town and church (Table 3.3.3).

Table 3.3.3. *Ratios ideationals/sensates, in the villages and in the churches (occupation index only)*

	MONTAGNA	COLLINA	MARINA
Church attendance	72%	58%	37%
Ratio I/S, town	0.97	0.57	0.37
Ratio I/S, churches	1.27	0.58	0.26

Evidently, the model of the church as an institution designed to meet the needs of ideationals only or mostly, and perceived as such, is not tenable. This will not be news to people knowing the region, but to outsiders it constitutes an interesting bit of evidence bearing on the role of the church. We have two explanations to offer.

126

The first explanation sees the church not so much as an ideational or even Christian institution, but above all as *a social institution, dominated by the majority*. It is 'catholic' in the sense that it belongs to all, gives to all and receives from all, but like all other social institutions there are people who are inside and people who are outside. This may be defined in terms of ideology, in terms of whether they are 'true' Catholics or not — but it may also be defined in more structural terms: in terms of whether they really belong to the typical in the village or not. If they belong to the dominant orientation, one might expect them to be over-represented and the deviants to be underrepresented. In fact, one might expect the deviants, which in Marina means the ideationals, to be increasingly skeptical of church attendance and stay away even more, leaving the ground for the sensates. The more the ideationals withdraw, the weaker becomes their position unless they do as very ideational people in Protestant countries when 'secular' powers take over the sacred institutions: they form a sect. But there seems to be no organizational basis for sect formation in these villages (except some Protestants in Collina).

The second explanation is not incompatible with the first, but rather a second version of it. It presupposes the idea of a priest who does not satisfy the ideational needs of that segment of the population so that they withdraw and leave the ground for the sensates. We inquired in Marina and got hearsay evidence that seems to confirm this idea. But what the primary factor is here, the priest, the image of the priest or the ratio of ideationals to sensates, we do not know.

Thus, the church is a general social institution more than an ideational institution. Had it been a purely ideational institution attracting ideationals only, all ratios in the third line in Table 3.3.3 would have had to be higher and even much higher than the corresponding ratios in the second line and would also have to decrease less than them: we might have expected an ideational minority to be even more devout relative to the sensates than an ideational majority. Of course, there is also the possibility that the indices do not measure what we believe they measure, but the uniformity of the results makes us believe that the findings are quite valid.[1]

Let us then turn to the range of participation shown in Table 3.3.4. This Table tells us a lot about social life in these villages.

First of all: for all villages there are more people attending church than any other activity or exposure to mass media. The church outdoes newspapers, weeklies, radio, TV and movies — which says something

Table 3.3.4. *Social participation in the three villages 'last week', percentage*

	Read a newspaper	Read a weekly	Listened to the radio	Watched TV	Been to movies	Been to church
MONTAGNA	24	19	46	34	15	72
COLLINA	19	11	35	29	17	58
MARINA	18	2	47	25	30	37

about its power relative to those other sources of influence. There is only one exception to this: more people listen to the radio than go to church in Marina. The radio is actually the only serious competitor in the other two villages, too.

Secondly, the rates of attendance seem generally to be in this order: Montagna — Collina — Marina. This is also the order of degree of isolation, and a reasonable explanation seems to be compensation: people in Marina have somewhat higher chances of having their needs satisfied by *other* means than local institutions of mass media. They may go to Palermo or some other medium-sized town in the neighborhood — and, in particular, they may more easily go to the movies, which is the only consistent exception to the rule above (there is also the more idiosyncratic exception of radio listening in Marina).

But how is this related to the ideological variable? The answer is: there is absolutely no consistent trend at all, consistent in the sense of holding for both indices and all villages. Again, this does not mean that no such relationship exists, only that it may be masked by some other variable. Before we proceed along that direction, however, it should be noticed that the consequence of this almost complete lack of correlation is quite important: *neither camp is at any advantage here; they cannot claim legitimacy based on superior knowledge, insight, level of information, etc.* And this makes insight into how the value orientations are distributed in the formal categories defining social structure — age, education occupation, etc. — even more significant.

3.4. *Who the sensates are: age and education*

We shall now approach the problem of exploring how the ideological categories are located in the social structure, with particular focus on the sensates. This will be done with a double purpose in mind: to consider both the *causal* and the *functional* aspects in order to get insights into *why* people have the ideological inclinations they have, and the *consequences* that derive from it. If we find a preponderance of, say, sensates in one specific structural category, such as the well educated or the poor or the old, the task would be to look for the factors that may have contributed to that distribution and for the consequences the distribution may have. With this in mind four structural categories will be used: age, education, social position and economic position.

Let us start out directly with *age* and give the results for all three villages since it is such an important variable and since the hypothesis is so obvious. We would not be willing to use a measure of modernism that did not show consistent increase with decreasing age (Table 3.4.1).

Table 3.4.1. *Ideological orientation and age, percentage*

	MONTAGNA			*COLLINA*			*MARINA*		
	1871–1900	1901–1920	1921–1950	1871–1900	1901–1920	1921–1950	1871–1900	1901–1920	1921–1950
Ideational	36	32	23	22	27	20	21	16	13
In betweens	36	39	36	52	27	36	46	50	43
Sensate	28	29	41	26	46	44	33	34	44
Total	100	100	100	100	100	100	100	100	100
(N)	(39)	(65)	(47)	(27)	(79)	(44)	(24)	(50)	(30)

The correlations are low, but consistently in the expected direction with the old being ideational and the young being sensate, so the correlation between age and this special kind of ideological orientation constitutes one further item in our list of validations of the index. In short, and exaggerated: the young people prefer a sensate and reject an ideational orientation. This entire perspective has entered these Sicilian villages at the bottom of the population pyramid, and undoubtedly above all on the masculine side, although we do not have data to substantiate that. This, in our mind, has two consequences and raises an important problem with theoretical and practical ramifications: *What will happen to these young people when they become older?*

If they stick to their beliefs, it will sooner or later have social consequences one way or the other, for with increasing age they will get an increasing share in the total power of the community. But there are at least three important reasons why we believe they may change orientation as they grow older. First of all, increasing age means a certain

129

decrease in life chances. The future, where oneself is concerned, is less uncertain; the number of possibilities will have decreased. This means less concern with change, more with routine; less with innovation, more with maintenance. A sensate ideology may become more of a burden than an asset for people who grow up to take positions in a predominantly ideational society. And secondly, as one grows older, one's set of acquaintances will also be older. If this were restricted to the people with whom one has been young together, in other words one's own age-group, the simple fact of growing older would be of no significance. But chances are that the forty-five-year-old can stretch his acquaintances into the power wielders even if they are ten to fifteen years older than him; he will have more access to people older than himself than the thirty-five-year-old. And finally, these sensate ideas are not that new. Since there is some correlation with age, chances are that this correlation also existed one generation ago, and chances are that many people now old *have* already changed their minds. In other words: chances are that much of the younger people's sensate orientation is structural, an expression of generational conflict, and due to disappear when the person crosses the generational watershed.

Essentially, Table 3.4.1 inspires a certain distrust of the established ethos among the young, which is certainly not exceptional as a finding. What is interesting are the possible consequences of this distribution. For instance, does it mean that young people will be in opposition politically? Does it mean that they will form an organization to further their views? The latter is highly unlikely, since it is not obvious that they have other interests in common than this elusive ideological orientation, which they may not even be aware of themselves. But could it be that this correlation between age and ideology is particularly pronounced for certain occupational categories (Table 3.4.2)?

The tendency of a more sensate orientation among the young is present in all groups, but particularly pronounced in the lowest occupational group. For the group of *braccianti* taken alone, 29% of the old as against 50% of the young have a sensate orientation. This is a highly important specification. An important bridgehead of the sensate orientation among impoverished *braccianti* is precisely where it has the least immediate effect — except, of course, as a voting potential for left-wing parties. Since this group is found in all villages, we also get correlation in all three — whereas the other occupational groups show little or no age differential.

What is there about the group of *braccianti* that makes age an important

Table 3.4.2. *Ideological orientation and age, for occupational groups (percentage, total sample)**

	Topdogs (tertiary high)			Farmers (primary high)			Farm-hands, laborers, etc.		
	1871–1900	1901–1920	1921–1950	1871–1900	1901–1920	1921–1950	1871–1900	1901–1920	1921–1950
Ideational	19	24	20	33	30	31	29	24	16
Medium	38	31	30	42	42	38	47	38	43
Sensate	43	45	50	25	28	31	24	38	41
Total	100	100	100	100	100	100	100	100	100
(N)	(21)	(49)	(30)	(24)	(33)	(16)	(45)	(112)	(74)

variable where ideology is concerned? Objectively, it is the group that has the least reason to be satisfied — not necessarily in the sense that they want to move, but in the sense that they do not want things to remain the way they are. Since it is generally axiomatic that new ideas catch on easier among the young (but not among the quite young), Table 3.4.2. actually amounts to showing one thing: that there is more unrest among the *braccianti* and the *industriosi* — but that this unrest is either of relatively recent date or may lose its hold on people in these categories when they grow older. The latter seems to us to be a more reasonable interpretation of the age differential, since this group will have difficulties in anchoring an emerging ideology in any kind of organization, both in their own minds and in the social system. The whole system is systematically biased against them, as we shall later have ample occasion to see.

Let us then turn to *education*. We would certainly not have been surprised if the ideological orientation had been substantially correlated with education: presumably, higher education may predispose for more 'modern views'. On the other hand, having an idea about what education is like in Sicily, we were not surprised at this almost complete lack of correlation either (Table 3.4.3.)

This does not mean that education plays no role, but rather that whatever role it plays is efficiently counteracted by some other social factor. If there is a tendency at all, it is in the direction that education predisposes for a more *ideational* orientation. Or, let us put it this way: the school teaches the *ethos* of the society, which is ideational. In a sense

* For definitions of occupational categories, see 3.5. For four respondents, information about age was missing.

Table 3.4.3. *Ideological orientation and education (total sample, percentage)*

	Formal training			Vocational training	
	0 years	*1–4 years*	*5 years and over*	*yes*	*no*
Ideationals	28	20	30	28	23
Medium	35	41	36	31	42
Sensates	37	39	34	41	35
Total	100	100	100	100	100
(N)	(96)	(192)	(118)	(119)	(289)

this is obvious: *it is not education as such, but what is taught that counts.* At the same time, however, any schooling may also widen general outlooks and perspectives and provide instruments for independent pursuit of knowledge, so these two forces may well almost cancel each other out so as to yield a net balance of zero.

We would not expect this to be the case with regard to the respondents' educational philosophy, however, if by 'educational philosophy' we mean the answer to the very important question: 'Where have you learnted the most? At school, in the family, at work, in military service, or by yourself?' (Table 3.4.4). The tendency is quite clear: the school educates its own children; its true adherents are also the people who adhere to the official ethos of the villages. The sensates are people who seek their own ways — which is logical. Where else should they turn to pick up the fragments of a sensate orientation? The Table is quite consistent, insofar as the maximum percentage for the sensates (characteristically enough for 'by myself') is at the same place as the minimum percentage for the ideationals, and vice versa. So we repeat the conclusion here: *the school above all trains ideationals; the sensates have to seek their training by themselves.* (This finding holds, as usual, for all three villages, both indices.)

Evidently, what is lost when the church becomes a general social institution instead of a meeting place for ideationals (section 3.3) is gained by invading the educational establishment and making it a breeding ground for ideationals (the present section). Strategically, from the point of view of the church, this may be a good allocation of scarce manpower resources. But the situation is hardly stable with growing secularization. And it should also be added that the totals (bottom row) reveal a general devaluation of the school: local opinion does not attribute much positive importance to it. This is, of course, related to the low level of schooling.

Table 3.4.4. *Ideological orientation and educational philosophy (allegiance items, total sample percentage)**

			I have learned the most			
	At school	*In the family*	*At work*	*In military service*	*By myself*	*All of them*
Ideationals	60	30	34	29	25	39
Medium	17	33	27	32	27	22
Sensates	23	37	39	39	48	39
Total						
	100	100	100	100	100	100
(N)	(35)	(67)	(92)	(38)	(98)	(31)

Finally, let us look at the influence age has on this general relationship or lack of relationship between ideological orientation and education. In other words, let us look at age and education combined. The important features are quite clear, judging from Table 3.4.5. First of all, education is improving here as almost everywhere else in this century: the percentage having had no schooling drops from 38% to 24% to 13% with decreasing age. Secondly, the effect of schooling on ideology seems to depend on age in an interesting way. The younger people are the more sensate they are, as we already know; but this tendency is four times as pronounced if they have *no* schooling. The interpretation of this depends

Table 3.4.5. *Ideological orientation as a function of age and education, percentage*

			Born			
	1871–1900		1901–1920		1921–1940	
Schooling	*0 years*	*1 or more*	*0 years*	*1 or more*	*0 years*	*1 or more*
Ideationals	29	27	33	23	13	20
Medium	47	41	28	40	31	40
Sensates	24	32	39	37	56	40
Total	100	100	100	100	100	100
(N)	(34)	(56)	(46)	(148)	(16)	(105)
Percentage of total	38	62	24	76	13	87
Percentage difference, ideationals	− 2		− 10		+ 7	
Percentage difference, senates	+ 8		− 2		−16	

* The other index yields exactly the same result, but not quite as pronounced, an exception to the general finding that the occupation index yields the most clearcut results.

133

on whether one assumes the content of the formal education to have been relatively constant or not. If we assume it to be constant, it looks as if it takes time for a Sicilian to overcome the ideational training he has been given at school and to develop a sensate perspective. The older he is, the higher is the excess of sensates in spite of schooling, from -16% to -2% to $+8\%$, whereas the ideational gain tapers off. According to the Table it looks as if it takes time before the effect of the schooling tapers off, probably because it will be one of the main concerns of the church to keep alive the ideational spirit imbued in the pupils. However, we cannot disregarded the possibility that the schools have changed during the age span of our respondents — although it seems unlikely that they have changed as much in an ideational direction as the data would require. Hence, barring the effect of a fourth variable (the finding holds when one controls for social position), we are left with the interpretation that *the school loses its ideational grip as time since leaving school passes.*[1]

3.5. *Who the sensates are: social position*

With our instruments, imperfect as they may be yet apparently able to reveal hidden factors in the social order, we shall now turn to the most important background variable, directly related to economic and political structure: the *social position* as expressed by the *occupational status*. Even though the status sets of these Sicilian villagers are poor, they are not that poor; and even though age, sex and kinship may be given more importance than in most parts of Europe north of Southern Italy, occupation seems nevertheless to be the pivot or dominant status. Since social change will have to imply a change in occupational structure according to most views presently held concerning the conditions for development, it is crucial to know where in the social fabric the ideological categories are overrepresented.

As a point of departure let us express occupational status in terms of *social rank* and use a simple dichotomous vertical dimension: the 'topdogs' and the 'underdogs', or *high* vs. *low*. Let us further assume that there will be a clear trend in the sense that the sensates and the ideationals will be distributed in a complementary way: where one is 'high', the other will be 'low', etc. In the line with the generally inductive strategy employed in this work, we feel we have little reason to offer more than these two simple theories concerning the distribution of ideology:

1) *The sensate ideology will be overrepresented at the top* because of the compatibility between the easier access to new ideas found in the upper layers and the (presumed) recency of sensate orientations in this part of the world.
2) *The ideational ideology will be overrepresented at the top* because of compatibility between the vested interests of the upper layers and the utilization of the ideational ideology as a justification of the desire for stability.

Unfortunately, both hypotheses seem perfectly convincing. The upper layers have readier access to new ideas by virtue of their positions and may also have more of a potential for risk taking; on the other hand, they are the only ones who may have anything to lose, *relatively speaking*, by a change. Thus, *causal* reasoning seems to favor the first hypothesis and *functional* reasoning to favor the second. Since the hypotheses are mutually incompatible, and we have no *a priori* basis for assuming that one of the factors is stronger than the other, we may expect to find positive, zero or negative correlation. In short, we have no basis for prediction; anything can happen. In a case like this it is useful to look at the data shown in Table 3.5.1.

Table 3.5.1. *Ideological orientation and social rank, percentage*

	MONTAGNA		COLLINA		MARINA		Total sample		
	Top-dog	Under-dog	Top-dog	Under-dog	Top-dog	Under-dog	Top-dog	Under-dog	Differ-ence
Ideationals	32	28	27	22	14	19	26	23	3
Medium	32	43	33	35	43	49	36	41	— 5
Sensates	36	29	40	43	43	32	38	36	2
Total	100	100	100	100	100	100	100	100	0
(N)	(84)	(68)	(48)	(103)	(42)	(63)	(174)	(234)	(408)

The dividing line between topdog and underdog here is *ad hoc*, and most of what is classified as 'topdog' would certainly not pass as such in more developed societies. We have classified as *underdogs* farmhands (141), day laborers (19), people on relief or retired (6), housemaids, servants, waiters etc. (55) and people 'who do a little bit of everything' (13). That leaves for *topdogs* the professionals (9), the tradesmen (9), the white-collar workers (13), the artisans (43), the skilled workers (26) and the farmers (74). Our main doubt in this classification has to do with the skilled workers working in small enterprises, but the permanence of their jobs as well as their slightly higher level of education[1] makes it difficult to classify them with the unskilled workers: the *industriosi*, the *braccianti* and the *casalinghe*. However, even if we move them to the underdogs the conclusions of this section do not change.

Table 3.5.1 is quite clear insofar as it says the following: *there is no correlation at all*, either for the total sample or for the villages (except a tendency for Marina).[2] The first, very tentative explanation in line with the very rudimentary theory above would be that the lack of correlation is the net outcome of two processes in different directions, for instance the two factors mentioned. We shall look into this later, but shall first concentrate on a second type of explanation: that the unidimensional type of stratification used in Table 3.5.1 defies Sicilian reality, or the reality of any other society for that matter.

Thus, although there are good *a priori* reasons to believe that some topdogs will have easy access to new values and that some topdogs will have vested interests, these are not necessarily the same topdogs. Correspondingly: some underdogs may be sensate because of rebellion against ideational topdogs; others may be ideational for lack of access to any new values and because they are symbiotically tied to ideational topdogs — and these are not necessarily the same underdogs. The question is whether we can derive a horizontal division of these societies that splits them so that the different kinds of topdogs and underdogs are kept apart. In methodological terms the problem is to find a socially relevant third variable that can be used to divide the societies into sectors so that the zero correlation of Table 3.5.1 is split into one negative and one positive correlation.

Whereas the vertical ordering of statuses in terms of rank has always been a primary concern of sociological analysis, their horizontal ordering has received relatively scant attention.[3] In analyses of simple social systems this is perhaps inconsequential since there will probably be fewer horizontal groupings of interest. But in the analyses of complex systems, not to mention societies, a theory for the division of the society into sectors is crucial, and *institutional analysis* is one traditional answer. However, it does not answer the problem of dividing individuals, only statuses. Thus, each *villagero* participates in such institutions as economy, polity and religion — for instance with the status set (farmhand, voter, church abstainer). The traditional community analyses would have these and other institutional realms as their chapter headings and would probably fragmentalize the individual without putting his status set together again. But we are interested in even less, in the status the individual has in the economy institution alone and in a division of these statuses into sectors that can be classified as 'traditional' and 'modern' (at least relatively speaking).

Since the occupational structure is in the cross section of the professional interests of economists and sociologists it seems natural to look across the fence and explore the classical division economists have been using for more than a generation now, into the 'primary', 'secondary' and 'tertiary' sectors of the economy. We shall show that this division fits our theoretical needs in more than one sense, and shall thus be able to link our empirical analysis to the general view on (horizontal) development presented in 1.2.

This classification goes back to Sir William Petty, who noticed in 1691 that 'there is much more to be gained by *Manufacture* than by *Husbandry*; and by *Merchandise* than by *Manufacture*'.[4] This statement contains the two elements in the theory: the conceptualization and the proposition. As to the conceptualization, these terms and definitions may be compared in Table 3.5.2.

Table 3.5.2. *Dividing the economy institution of a society*

	Primary sector or industry	*Secondary* sector or industry	*Tertiary* sector or industry
Current terms	extraction	processing	services
Petty's terms	'husbandry'	'manufacture'	'merchandise'
Clark's definitions[5]	agriculture, livestock farming, hunting, trapping, fisheries, forestry	manufacturing, production, public works, mining, electric power	commerce, trade distribution, transport, public administration, artisanry, domestic service, professionals, building, construction
Leibenstein's definitions[6]	considerable utilization of natural forces, such as those provided by land and sea	manipulating materials or non-human factors, without substantial aid of the forces provided by nature	selling services, something with no physical material elements in it

Many more lists could be given. Clark's relatively extensional definition should be contrasted with Leibenstein's effort to give an intensional definition in terms of energy and type of commodity provided by the productive unit. Both authors agree that 'it is the activity of the *production unit* rather than the activity of the individual which counts'.[7]

We shall not concern ourselves with the many difficult borderline cases (e.g. mining). Some of them are solved by the distinction between 'occupation' and 'production unit' or 'organization'. Obviously, the tertiary sector has a tendency to become a rather heterogeneous residual category, and it has been suggested to split it up and introduce a fourth and a fifth sector. However, with the definition given by Leibenstein and similar efforts to attach some precise meaning to the three categories, they nevertheless constitute an important tool in the analysis of economic and social change, as we have already tried to demonstrate in 1.2.

According to Fisher,[8] the three sectors not only form a classificatory scheme, useful in making inventories of the economy of a country, but also represent a development sequence. As mentioned in 1.2, a country or region would start with the overwhelming majority of the population in the primary sector, which is primary in two senses: first by being close to what is given by nature — hence involving little technical sophistication — and second, in the sense of satisfying primary needs like hunger and thirst. Then comes manufacturing, which brings in its wake satisfaction of less elementary needs, but at the expense of increased technical sophistication — and finally comes the tertiary sector. Or at least that was the model in the modern, Western world. In ancient and medieval history and in the non-Western world the tertiary sector expands first.

According to Leibenstein, this development takes place because of increasing specialization and increasing *per capita* income, which gives a neat theoretical basis for explaining the regularity. Since the proportion of income used to cover industries is subject to diminishing returns whereas secondary and tertiary industries are subject to increasing or at least constant returns, a transfer of manpower from the former to the latter should follow. But in addition to this comes the specialization argument: 'increased income implies an increased division of labor, which, in turn, implies a decrease in the variety of activities performed by the individuals in the community',[9] and,

We note that there is no shift from manufacturing to primary industries since, to begin with, primary activities are not performed to any extent by secondary industry. Tertiary industry cannot lose to other classifications because of further specializations but only as a consequence of a greater integration of activities.[10]

In short, Leibenstein's thinking is based on increasing division of labor, where the primary sector 'loses' to the secondary and tertiary sectors, and the secondary sector to the tertiary. This is well documented historically, as a general trend, but is perhaps somewhat limited to our own period. It is certainly not inconceivable that at some time in history the inter-sector losses due to specialization may be in the other direction — but that need not concern us here either.

If we accept this thinking, the classification gives us not only a useful descriptive tool, but also a rough indication of *where* on the curve of socio-economic development a country is located. Francisco Sánchez López,[11] among many, has an interesting application of this idea where he distinguishes between 'chronological time', the ordinary time scale and 'social time' (a better term might be 'socio-economic time'), which measures how far the country has come on the road from a predominantly primary to a predominantly tertiary economic structure. Comparing data, he makes statements of this kind:

... España se encuentra, desde este punto de vista, en un período de tiempo social aproximado al que se encontraba Estados Unidos a fin del siglo XIX, mientras que Méjico se encontraría en un período semejante a los años veinte de España.[12]

For our purposes the important thing is the 'social time' of the three villages. According to Table 2.2.5, the agricultural proportion is around 75%, which Clark thinks is a maximum,[13] and there is no secondary sector. In these terms the villages are located at time Zero, but that misses the pre-traditional stages. The question is what this means translated to ideology.

From the propositions that the classification in primary, secondary and tertiary sectors is fruitful and that economic growth implies and is implied by a reproportioning of the population *from* the primary and *toward* the secondary and/or tertiary sectors, it does not follow that there is a correlation between sector belongingness and ideology in general. A sector may be structurally modern, yet be populated by completely ideational men and women. Structurally speaking, the primary sector is the traditional one, and the tertiary sector, not to mention the absent secondary sectors (absent from these villages by Clark's as well as by Leibenstein's definitions), is the less traditional

139

one, the foreboding of times to come. But, as is rather obvious, there are many ways of doing agriculture or commerce, and they can all be ordered along an axis of degree of modernism. What today is known as industrial farming or industrial fishing may be difficult to classify as belonging to either the primary *or* the secondary sector; they may even have admixtures of distributive, tertiary activitie built into them that make them small-scale models of the entire economy. But the important factor is that there is room for initiative in both sectors. The sensate ideology of external change and control *can* be implemented in both sectors; it is not ruled out by theoretical thinking based on the definitions.

Thus, just as for the vertical dimension of society, we have little basis for offering more than these two simple theories for the distribution of ideology on the horizontal dimension we now have introduced:

1) *The sensate ideology will be overrepresented in the tertiary sector* because of the easier access to new ideas in the tertiary sector, since their service activities bring them into contact with more people, and other positions.

2) *The ideational ideology will be overrepresented in the tertiary sector* since they are, relatively speaking, at the top of the local society and will feel that they may have most to lose from a change.

Again, the reasoning is based on the two pillars of 'differential access' to new values and the 'vested interests' argument. We have not tried to base anything on a presumed inherent compatibility between ideational ideology and primary activities, for the simple reason that there is no reason to believe that there should be more 'change or control of external circumstances' in tertiary activities of the classical kind one finds in these villages than in primary activities. As mentioned, activities in either sector can be carried out in traditional and in modern ways.

But the argument about 'differential access' to new values seems to be valid. Often this is the argument used to contrast the urban and rural environments, and this is proper *since the tertiary sector is the projection of the city on countryside* and the sector with most contact with the cities in general. As will be argued later, the flow of value is more rapid in this sector, and at least some of it should, theoretically, rub off.

The argument about 'vested interests' is weaker and less clear. In the two sections to follow we shall show how the tertiary sector is seen as the more prestigious sector, probably precisely because it represents modern life. But from this it does not follow with any necessity that they will be more set on preserving the existent structure and in general adopt a more conservative ideology. They may want more, for themselves or for the village, as may the upper classes, to switch argumentation for a moment from the horizontal to the vertical division. Besides, even if the primary sector wanted more change for themselves, this desire may not translate itself into a sensate ideology, but rather take the form of wanting to exploit fully, for themselves, the possibilities offered by the existing structure.

However this may be, we feel we can go no further with idle speculations but must to look at the data again. According to the hypotheses anything can happen, but what actually happens is just as in Table 3.5.1 — *nothing*.

Table 3.5.3. *Ideological orientation and economic sector, percentage*

	MONTAGNA		COLLINA		MARINA		Total sample		
	Pri-mary	Ter-tiary	Pri-mary	Ter-tiary	Pri-mary	Ter-tiary	Pri-mary	Ter-tiary	Differ-ence
Ideationals	25	34	24	23	13	21	22	27	— 5
Medium	44	32	32	39	50	44	40	37	3
Sensates	31	34	44	38	37	35	38	36	2
Total	100	100	100	100	100	100	100	100	0
(N)	(64)	(88)	(103)	(48)	(48)	(57)	(215)	(193)	(408)

The dividing line between the primary and tertiary sectors is, as far as possible, drawn according to the Clark-Leibenstein criteria. In the primary sector there are only two occupational categories, the farmers and the farm-hands (corresponding to the poverty of division of labor in this sector), and the rest are all classified as tertiary occupations.

The only difficult categories are the 'skilled workers' and the 'artisans'. The question is whether or not they should be combined into a special secondary sector, but we have decided against it. Two quotes from Clark about these two special occupations seem to be not only economically but also sociologically meaningful, and to justify our decision:

... (the secondary sector) has been defined as a process, not using the resources of nature directly, producing, on a large scale and by a continuous process, transportable goods. This definition excludes the production of untransportable goods (buildings and public works), and small-scale and discontinuous processes such as the hand tailoring of clothes, or shoe repairing.[14]

A man's 'occupation' is the nature of the work he actually does; his 'industry' is defined by who he does it for ... our first object must be to examine industrial rather than occupational distribution.[15]

The best argument for placing the artisans in the tertiary sector is the highly commercial nature of this small-scale village artisanry — they are engaged in mending and changing much more than processing, and certainly rarely on anything that can be called a large scale. And the 'skilled workers' are engaged in such public utilities as waterworks and electricity, which are clearly tertiary *industries* even though their occupations may look more secondary. Their 'industry' is their social context, and this, more than exactly what they do within that organization, defines them socially.

The lack of any consistent correlation in Table 3.5.2 is interesting. Again, the reason may be that the two factors of differential access and vested interests draw in different directions and cancel each other. And we now face exactly the same problem as in connection with the vertical dimension. Some people in the tertiary sector may be sensate because of easy access to new values, and some may be ideational because of vested interests — and these people are not the same people. Also, some people in the primary sector may be ideational because of their location in a self-sufficient, autonomous sector of the economy, whereas others may be sensate because of their desire for changes in the power distribution. Parenthetically, it should be noticed that the main instrument, the ordered pairs of occupations, should give answers independent of where the respondent is located, since all four occupations are professions, classified as 'tertiary, high'.

Time has now obviously come to combine the vertical and horizontal ways of thinking about these social structures.[16] What should one expect from a combined classification? Take the primary sector where high and low are both outside the mainstream of modern life but where 'high' has something to lose whereas 'low' has nothing. Thus we would expect the primary topdog to be ideational because he is *both* isolated *and* motivated against change, whereas the primary underdog is isolated *but* possibly with a strong class motivation for change. We would expect him to be sensate, but of a variety that is less motivated by access to ideology and new values than by dialectical reaction against the topdog for whom he works and the social order he represents.

142

As to the tertiary sector we would predict the opposite pattern for the following reasons. There is more access to modern life, but only of the higher levels. And these levels have their chances of further expansion tied to modern values, whereas the lower, unskilled levels have their meagre outcomes linked to the existing society, which treats them better than it treats the *braccianti* and also provides them with less clear and definite focuses as class enemies. As will be shown in 3.7, this group has a possibility of mobility that is denied the *braccianti*, and consequently has more unused possibilities inside the existing structure. Thus, both for lack of access to sources of influence and because of vested interests we would expect them to be ideationals, and the tertiary topdogs to be sensates. The scheme of hypotheses is shown in Table 3.5.4.

Table 3.5.4. *Ideological orientation and social position: hypotheses*

		Horizontal dimension	
		Primary, 'traditional' sector	Tertiary, 'modern' sector
Vertical dimension	High, topdog	Predominantly *ideational*, vested interests	Predominantly *sensate*, easy access
	Low, underdog	Predominantly *sensate*, reaction	Predominantly *ideational*, vested interests

The two ideational combinations are relatively isolated, and both have their vested interests in *stability*, in the existing structure. The two sensate combinations have their interests in *change*, but they differ in being extremes as to access to the outside world. Thus, the scheme predicts something more than the distribution of value orientations; *it also predicts more ideological similarity between the primary high and the tertiary low than between the primary low and tertiary high.* The data is shown in Table 3.5.5.

This time we are richly rewarded, through the simple device of multivariate analysis of type 3.2 (three variables, keeping two variables constant). If the percentage differences in this Table are compared with the percentage differences in Table 3.5.1, we see an increase for the ideationals from $+3\%$ to $+14\%$ and -10%, and for the sensates from $+2\%$ to -16% and $+23\%$ — all in the predicted direction. Similarly, if we

143

Table 3.5.5. *Ideological orientation and social position (total sample, percentage)*

	Social position					
	Primary high	*Primary low*	*Differ-ence*	*Tertiary high*	*Tertiary low*	*Differ-ence*
Ideationals	31	17	+14	23	33	—10
Medium	41	39	+ 2	31	44	—13
Sensates	28	44	—16	46	23	+23
Total	100	100	0	100	100	0
(N)	(74)	(141)	(215)	(100)	(93)	(193)

compute the differences between sectors within strata and compare with the differences in Table 3.5.3, we get an increase for the ideationals from –5% to +6% and –16%, and for the sensates from +2% to –18% and +21%. The ratios between the old percentage differences and the new are higher than 3% (and as high as 11%) in seven out of eight cases, so we regard the hypothesis as confirmed (which does not mean that we have to accept the theory). This finding is so important that we also give the data for the villages separately, in concentrated form in Table 3.5.6.

Table 3.5.6. *Ideological orientation and social position in the villages (percentage differences)*

	Primary high — primary low			Tertiary high — tertiary low		
	MONT-AGNA	*COLL-INA*	*MAR-INA*	*MONT-AGNA*	*COLL-INA*	*MAR-INA*
Ideationals	+22	+14	+10	—14	— 9	—17
Medium	+ 4	— 2	— 9	—17	— 6	— 6
Sensates	—26	—12	— 1	+31	+15	+23
Total	0	0	0	0	0	0
(N)	(64)	(103)	(48)	(88)	(48)	(57)

If we as usual disregard the middle category, we see that *all twelve differences are in the predicted direction* (and only one of them is not statistically significant). Almost all of this also holds for the other index, so the pattern is very clear and the differences are probably on the conservative side because of the rather blunt instrument we have applied.

Thus, we have dissolved two surprising zero correlations into two very meaningful correlations, one positive and one negative. We have indicated *one* possible causal explanation, to which we shall return, and we also have important data for a functional analysis. Above all, the problem of distribution in the social structure has been solved: the answer comes closest to type 6 in Diagram 1.6.1, one of the two 'diagonal' types.[17]

3.6. *Who the sensates are : economic position*

We shall now attack the same problem of how ideology is distributed in the social structure from a different angle: *economic position*, as expressed by the *living standard*. Although economic position no doubt is correlated with social position, and in these villages quite strongly, it is not the same. There will always be economic variation within the same social category. Social position is what you *are*, economic position what you *have*. Both can be potential as well as actual. But economic position has one important property social position does not have: it is divisible. A person can throw away one-fifth of his economic position but his social position is much more of an all-or-none affair: either he is or he is not. The problem now is what relation this has to his ideology.

Our principal difficulty in this connection consisted in finding a measure of economic position. 'Income' is not very meaningful in communities where barter economies still prevail in many spheres of economic life, nor did we want to bother the respondents with questions of this kind or to destroy the study with questions that were reminiscent of the tax collector. This also applied to 'fortune': after some considerations we gave it up. The answers would probably be extremely unreliable, or even if they were not, there would be no way of excluding the possibility that they were. Above all, they would be so multi-dimensional, involving dimensions with such complicated relations to each other, that this would be a subject of an economic treatise in its own right. Hence, we chose an easier and perhaps even a more relevant way out.

Whether economic status is due to one's own efforts or is inherited, it is bound to manifest itself in different indicators of standard of living, unless it is all spent in immediate consumption of non-durable goods. But what is standard of living? We have given it a relatively narrow interpretation, based on the word *living* : it is defined here as the standard of the dwelling. Thus, we have used the simple index shown in Table 3.6.1.

The index runs from 0 to 6, and we have designated as 'low' 0 to 3, as 'medium' 4 and as 'high' 5 to 6, so as to produce as equal classes as

Table 3.6.1. *Standard of living: the composition of the index*

	Low (0)	Medium (1)	High (2)
Number of residents per room	3 or more	2–2.9	less than 2
Running water	no		yes
Animals in the house	yes		no

possible. Obviously, the index classifies as 'medium' or 'low' the wealthy spendthrift who believes more in the pleasures derived from immediate consumption than from the investments in durable consumer goods needed to get the animals out and the running water in. Correspondingly, he who has nothing but a good house is classified as 'high'. But we feel that even this can be justified. These villages are clusters of family houses; the family is present in the village by way of their house, in a w.y that is not similar to the Northern European apartment dweller. The family not only live in it, *they are the house and the house is them* in the small village characterized by its high visibility. Even the most superficial tourist cannot fail to see the enormous difference between 'all those picturesque houses', and these differences are to some extent captured in the index.

However, we would never have used the index if it did not correlate as it should with two good criteria. First of all, it should correlate with the villages, where we would predict the same rank order in terms of standard of living as we derived from the death rates in 2.2: highest Marina, then Montagna and then Collina. This is indeed the case (Table 3.6.2).

The differences are quite pronounced and also give a good illustration of the mafia theory that sees the mafia (Collina) as an expression of low standard of living in general. At the same time, although the relative

Table 3.6.2. *The villages and standard of living, percentage*

Standard of living	MONTAGNA	COLLINA	MARINA	Maximum difference
High	28	18	36	18
Medium	21	21	34	13
Low	51	61	30	−31
Total	100	100	100	0
(N)	(152)	(151)	(105)	(408)

146

difference is important, it still does not go sufficiently below subsistence level to cause gross differences in the mortality rates. For this kind of analysis, however, a higher number than three villages would be necessary, but the Table nevertheless constitutes a validation. As mentioned in 2.2, this is also the rank order based on more intuitive impressions.

The second criterion would be by means of social position. We would expect heavy correlation, and heavy correlation we get. However, since it may rightly be objected that the inclusion of animals as a criterion is mostly relevant for the primary sector of the villagers, we have to correct for sector (Table 3.6.3).

Table 3.6.3. *Standard of living and social position, percentage*

| Standard of living | Social position | | | | | |
	Primary high	Primary low	Differ- ence	Tertiary high	Tertiary low	Differ- ence
High	26	9	+17	50	28	+22
Medium	28	18	+10	24	31	− 7
Low	46	73	−27	26	41	−15
Total	100	100	0	100	100	0
(N)	(74)	(141)	(215)	(100)	(93)	(193)

The differences are already considerable, and higher differences can easily be found by dividing the tertiary topdogs a little. Thus, the clearest expression of how tightly social and economic positions are tied together can be found by comparing the profile for the *braccianti* with the profile for the professionals, tradesmen and clerical workers: we get (9%, 18%, 73%) against (74%, 13%, 13%) and percentage differences higher than 60% between the high-ups and the low-downs. The wretched condition of the farm-hands is very conspicuous. But it should again be remembered that one item in the index is the presence of animals in the house, and this *may* be said to be a part of their occupational equipment — like books for the professional. On the other hand, it may also be argued that precisely this apologetic thinking is wrong: the presence of domestic animals in the family's living room is a health risk and an indicator of low standard, regardless of how necessary the animals are for the daily work.

If we now take the index at its face value and apply the intuitive knowledge we have of these villages, relatively typical as they are of

Western Sicily, the Table gives a dramatic picture of how much social position means in Sicilian village life. The highest and lowest among the occupational classes are almost perfectly polar in terms of standard of living; there is not much overlap — yet they live geographically very close. Visibility is high and may lead to envy, hatred, contempt and fear, or to emulation, respect, protection or paternalism, as the case may be. The basic drama in human existence, due to differential distribution of scarce goods, can be acted out on the stages provided by these villages any day, any year. The characters are readily identifiable by virtue of these massive correlations: it is more like a Hindu caste system than the inhabitants of, for instance, a small Norwegian town where there is a certain similarity in standard of living. On the other hand, indicators and cutting points can be devised for such a town, too, and can be used to demonstrate high correlations, though we doubt it would be easy to find high correlations with such simple and important indicators.

But what does this mean, for instance, in terms of social participation? It means surprisingly little, according to the data. Of course, we always get the difference in social participation (newspapers, weeklies, radio, TV, movies, church) between the social strata. Here the differences lie typically between the tertiary high on the one hand and all the others on the other hand — in full agreement with the theoretical basis for our hypothesis about distribution of ideological orientation in 3.5. But living standard does not add or subtract much from this. Thus, whereas 48% in the tertiary high with high living standard did *not* read a newspaper 'last week', the number was 85% for the *braccianti* in the same category, 84% for the *braccianti* with a medium living standard and 87% for the *braccianti* with a low standard. In other words, they are excluded from certain kinds of social participation by their social position, by what they are — not by what they have. The same applies to the tertiary low, whereas the upper strata, especially in the tertiary sector, are more influenced in their social participation by their living standard. *Economic position plays a role at the top — not at the bottom — of the society.* Thus, the percentage of farmers listening to the radio decreases rapidly with decreasing standard of living, but the percentage of farm hands listening is unaffected — it is always low.

There are two interesting exceptions to this, though, and quite revealing in one sense. With decreasing standard of living, both upper and lower classes increase one kind of participation: *the upper classes go to the movies* (36%–42%–50% for the tertiary high) and *the lower classes go to church* (31%–48%–56% for the primary low). For the lower classes

Table 3.6.4. *Ideological orientation and standard of living, percentage*

Standard of living	MONTAGNA			COLLINA			MARINA			Total sample		
	High	Med-ium	Low	High	Med-ium	Low	High	Med-ium	Low	High	Med-ium	Low
Ideationals	40	29	26	18	28	22	26	14	10	30	23	21
Medium	35	26	42	41	31	36	37	50	55	37	36	41
Sensates	25	45	32	41	41	42	37	36	35	33	41	38
Total	100	100	100	100	100	100	100	100	100	100	100	100
(N)	(43)	(31)	(78)	(27)	(32)	(92)	(38)	(36)	(31)	(108)	(99)	(201)

the church is about the only tie they have to organized society — and with increasing standards they seem to sever even that tie without getting new ones, because of the extremely low level of organizational activity in the villages. The upper classes have so many other things that they can better take the blow of a lower standard of living; the lower classes have almost nothing to lose — and hence very little to gain with increasing standard.

Let us then return to our major theme and present the data for the relation between ideology and standard of living (Table 3.6.4).

The Table is remarkably similar to Table 3.5.1. For the total sample there is some, but not much, correlation — only percentage differences of 9% and ÷ 5% — indicating that the sensates are found among the poor people and the ideationals among the better off. But if we look at the data split by village we see that this holds only for Montagna — for Collina there is no correlation, and for Marina it is inconsistent. Hence, we cannot base anything on the tendency in the total sample and will rather conclude, as for Table 3.5.1, that there is no meaningful correlation with standard of living.

Again, this does not mean that standard of living is irrelevant, only that it plays a much more subtle role. Let us therefore control for both social stratum and economic sector and try to predict what we might find. According to the 'vested interests' idea we should expect that a high standard of living would accentuate the ideational attitude in the top of the primary sector. As to the top of the tertiary sector, we might expect, from the 'differential access' theory, that a high standard of living would accentuate the sensate inclination because it provides more opportunities for new experiences. But it could also make for more vested interests in this heterogeneous category, so it is difficult to tell.

149

Hence, a theoretical basis for predictions as to the combined effect of social and economic rank is needed, and the theory of rank-equilibration is probably the best available. We shall use the theory in the form it is given by Jackson.[1] According to him people in disequilibrated positions, with a large rank discrepancy between their ranks in different systems, react either extra-punitively by adapting a radical ideology, with a desire for a change of the power distribution, or intra-punitively by developing symptoms of stress. He also gives a structural basis for predicting who will react how: if the respondent is high on a dimension achievement but low on ascription, he will blame the society for dragging him down by tying him forever to his ascribed dimension; if he is high on an ascribed dimension but low on achievement, he has achieved less than he could and will develop self-blame. Although the whole theory seems culture bound to a society heavily bent on mobility and achievement it is a very interesting specification of the simpler theory by Lenski and Goffman, who predicted radicalism and desire for change of power distribution regardless of whether the person was an overachiever or an underachiever.[2]

To apply these ideas we collapse the four social positions to a uni-dimensional rank dimension, using the data in Table 3.6.3. Clearly, the tertiary high have the highest standard of living, and the primary low the lowest. The remaining two have very similar profiles, and to the extent that standard of living is an expression of the institutionalized reward given to the positions by society, it does not seem unreasonable to collapse them to a kind of middle class. We then get the combinations shown in Table 3.6.5.

Table 3.6.5. *Degrees of disequilibrium between social and economic rank*

		Social rank			
		High	Medium	Low	
	High	E	WD	SD	E: *equilibrium*
Economic rank	Medium	WD	E	WD	WD: *weak disequilibrium*
	Low	SD	WD	E	SD: *strong disequilibrium*

Since the sensates are the ones who want a change of power distribution, by the questions in the items forming the index we would predict a preponderance of sensates in the strongly disequilibrated combinations (Table 3.6.6).

150

Table 3.6.6. *Ideological orientation and degree of rank disequilibrium, percentage*

	Equilibrium	Weak disequilibrium	Strong disequilibrium
Ideationals	25	23	23
Medium	38	43	26
Sensates	37	34	51
Total	100	100	100
(N)	(203)	(166)	(39)

The tendency is not very strong but it is present. The interesting thing about this is that we get exactly the same trend as Jackson found in his sample of North Americans:[3] the effect is only noticeable for strong disequilibrium, not for weak. At the same time it is evident that the combination of individual motivation and structural forces in these villages reduces the number of people in disequilibrium. As can be seen from the bottom line of Table 3.6.6, only less than 10% have status sets in strong disequilibrium. Thus, the society is relatively uni-dimensional; it exhibits the rank concordance characteristic of feudal societies.

So far we have shown that there is an effect as predicted in the sense that strong disequilibrium in general leads to a more sensate orientation. We now turn to the specification of this theory, which involves the distinction between achieved and ascribed status; but we shall turn Jackson's theory upside down. Instead of predicting, we shall assume his hypothesis to be correct and use it as an instrument to try to discover differences in location on the continuum from pure ascription to pure achievement of the two rank dimensions, i.e. social rank and economic rank. Thus, we have to make a distinction between the 'social high— economic low' and 'social low—economic high' among the strongly disequilibrated and compare them with the rest (Table 3.6.7).

Again, the general theory is confirmed although the differences are

Table 3.6.7. *Ideological orientation and different kinds of disequilibrium, percentage of sensates*

Living standard	Tertiary high	Tertiary low	Primary high	Primary low
High	34	25	26	54
Low	50	29	21	43
Percentage difference	—16	— 4	+ 5	+11

not overwhelming: we find the expressions of disequilibrium in the highest and lowest social positions because this is where the differences between social and economic rank are most strongly felt. Further, the high percentages of sensates are located where they should be, in the 'social high—economic low' and in the 'social low—economic high'. But, if one of these dimensions had been more ascribed than the other, we should not have encountered this symmetry. Thus, if the social position were considered as given, as ascribed, and the economic position as something one may not achieve on top of this, then we should have encountered the same difference for the *braccianti* (who in this case would have achieved more than their ascribed status would predict) *but not with the tertiary high*. In their case one should have a feeling of guilt for having achieved less than the ascribed status entitles one to. But there is no such effect, and consequently no reason to assume any such qualitative difference between the dimensions. Probably both dimensions can be regarded as relatively ascribed — as will be borne out in the next section. Thus, the conclusion is simply this: economic position alone has little or no effect on ideology. But jointly with social position it has an effect that can be predicted from the general theory of rank disequilibration.[4]

3.7. *Who the sensates are: social perspective*

So far our presentation of the social structure of the villages has been completely static — frozen, as it was, at a point late in the summer of 1960. In this section social structure will be treated dynamically, as a function of actual and desired social mobility. And the discussion of desired social mobility will lead to an exploration of the first fundamental hypothesis about ideological orientation: that a sensate orientation predisposes for high desired mobility.

The empirical basis for the discussion in this section is the answers given to three simple questions: 'What is your occupation?' 'What did your father do?' and 'What would you like your son to be?' — the three standard questions in any mobility investigation. The NA rates were 3%, 4% and 12%, respectively. The first two present us with few difficulties since they are people who do something of everything. Hence, we are more right than wrong, and at any rate make no major error by classifying them as 'tertiary low'. The third rate, however, which is a mixture of 'don't know' and other evasive answers, will be treated as a response category in its own right. In most cases the total sample will be used since the villages were remarkably similar.

1. *Actual father-self mobility.* Let us start looking at the gross features of the horizontal and vertical mobility (Table 3.7.1) that have taken place according to the information given by the respondents.

Table 3.7.1. *Actual horizontal and vertical father-self mobility, percentage*

	Horizontal					Vertical		
	Self primary	Self tertiary	Total (N)			Self high	Self low	Total (N)
Father primary	74	26	100 (261)	Father high		77	23	100 (180)
Father tertiary	16	84	100 (124)	Father low		15	85	100 (228)
(N)	(215)	(193)	(408)	(N)		(174)	(234)	(408)

The Table tells three stories: the high and very similar correlation between father and son, horizontally as well as vertically, is indicative of a relatively closed society — the change of the economic composition of the society toward the tertiary sector (47 % for 'self' as against 30 % for 'father') *and the stability of the class structure of the villages* (43 % lower class for 'self' as against 44 % for 'father').[1]

To study this closer we need the interaction between horizontal and vertical intergenerational mobility (Table 3.7.2).

We have emphasized the self-recruitment rates. They are relatively similar, but indicate nevertheless how primogeniture and other factors

Table 3.7.2. *Actual total father-self mobility, percentage*

Father	Self								Total	(N)
	Primary high		Primary low		Tertiary high		Tertiary low			
Primary high	60	(61)	10	(10)	19	(19)	11	(11)	100	(101)
Primary low	5	(8)	70	(113)	11	(17)	14	(22)	100	(160)
Tertiary high	4	(3)	13	(10)	70	(56)	13	(10)	100	(79)
Tertiary low	3	(2)	12	(8)	12	(8)	73	(50)	100	(68)
Total sample	18	(74)	35	(141)	24	(100)	23	(93)	100	(408)

make for a relatively low rate of self-recruitment for the *contadini*, and how the low tertiary sector may be a deadend street to many.

If we now study the *vertical* mobilty as a function of the four possible patterns of horizontal mobility, the general dynamics of the social structure of these villages becomes clear. We calculated the correlations (Yule's Q) between father's rank and son's rank for each of the four father-self combinations where sector is concerned, as well as the average mobility, m (0 for constant, −1 for downward and +1 for upward mobility), and got the results shown in Table 3.7.3.

Table 3.7.3. *A survey of father-self mobility coefficients*

	Q	m
1. Within primary sector mobility:	0.98	− 0.01
2. Within tertiary sector mobility:	0.94	− 0.02
3. From primary to tertiary mobility:	0.38	+ 0.09
4. From tertiary to primary mobility:	0.09	− 0.35

Evidently, if one *stays* in one's sector, chances are one will remain where one's father was where rank is concerned, with a slight chance of suffering a dropback. If one *leaves* one's sector, the ties to the rank of one's father loosen up considerably, but the possibilities of entering the primary sector at the high level are negligible. The only possibility seems to consist in a change from primary to tertiary, for the *braccianti*. But the 17 who managed did not get far. Nine of them became 'workers', and the rest artisans and clerks.

To summarize: almost 70% stay in the sectors *and* positions of their fathers, 78% in the sectors of their fathers. As to vertical mobility, the primary sector is almost closed, with 84% of the farmers having fathers who were farmers. The tertiary sector has only 56% with fathers in the same 'high' positions, and all the other three compete to fill the gap. However slight, this the only possibility for the *braccianti*, since only 5% of them become *contadini* — assuming the rates are constant.

Thus, the general picture is relatively simple and clear. A total of 22% have experienced horizontal mobility, and 19% vertical mobility. How is this related to their general ideological orientation? Some of them must have been fighting to obtain social positions different from those of their fathers, some of them may have slid back from their fathers' positions and others may have followed some social current more or less willingly and found themselves on a new shelf in their

154

small society. The pattern of actual experience is undoubtedly complex, and its relation to ideology theoretically unclear. One may argue, as we do in general, that a sensate orientation will predispose for a wish to be upwardly mobile, but once one has arrived, there would be strong reasons to adopt an ideational ideology compatible with the satisfaction of the recently arrived — or else to keep one's ideology. Thus, we may just as well argue that people with no mobility experience are ideational since they have not succeeded, as one may argue that they are sensate since they have no reasons for complacency. Just as in 3.5 we have no single basis for a predication about covariation, and just as in 3.5 we get no correlation either when we look at combined horizontal and vertical mobility experience (Table 3.7.4).

Table 3.7.4. *Ideological orientation and combined mobility experience, percentage*

	Occupation items				Allegiance items			
	Ideational	Medium	Sensate	Total	Ideational	Medium	Sensate	Total
No mobility	23	40	37	100	34	26	40	100
Horizontal *or* vertical mobility	26	35	39	100	28	28	44	100
Horizontal *and* vertical mobility	21	42	37	100	32	31	37	100
Percentage difference	2	−2	0	0	2	−5	3	0

The percentage differences could not have been much lower, so it seems safe to conclude that if mobility *experience* is related to ideology, it must be in a more complex way. The relationship was tested for a number of factors that might introduce masking effects, but the result was always the same: no connection for horizontal mobility, vertical mobility or both, for the total sample or for the sample split on economic sector, rank, village or otherwise.

We then turn to the attitudinal question involving what the respondent would like a son to become.

2. *Desired self-son mobility*. Again, it is useful to start looking at horizontal and vertical mobility at one a time (Table 3.7.5).

It is instructive to compare the bottom row with the corresponding rows for 'father' and 'self'. The poor primary sector, already shrunk

Table 3.7.5. *Desired horizontal and vertical self-son mobility, percentage*

	Son primary	Son tertiary	No answer	Total (N)		Son high	Son low	No answer	Total (N)
Self primary	12	77	11	100 (215)	Self high	82	6	12	100 (174)
Self tertiary	0.5	85	14	100 (193)	Self low	73	14	13	100 (234)
Total (N)	(28)	(330)	(50)	(408)	Total (N)	(315)	(43)	(50)	(408)

from 70% to 53% is now down to 7% — and of the 28 who could imagine their sons in that sector only one is himself in the tertiary sector. Such is the effect of urbanization in these three villages in Western Sicily, and if everybody got his will there would not be sufficient manpower even for the highly inefficient Sicilian agriculture with its heavy under-employment. But they are not going to get their will — so the Table gives an indication of future frustration and potential agression rather than of future mobility.

That only 11% want 'low' social positions for their sons is less remarkable; 11 respondents are actually recorded as wanting downward mobility for their sons. Some of these may be artifacts due to the categorization, but seven of them are farmers with very low standard of living who evidently do not want for their sons the toil and sweat that are their burden.

The full scope of this desire to get into the high tertiary sector can be judged from Table 3.7.6.

To increase comparability we have corrected for differential tendency to give no answers by omitting them and calculate the percentages on the basis of the clear answers. With 86% wanting to get into the tertiary

Table 3.7.6. *Desired total self-son mobility, percentage*

	Son									
Self	Primary high		Primary low		Tertiary high		Tertiary low		Total	(N)
Primary high	9	(6)	5	(3)	80	(52)	6	(4)	100	(65)
Primary low	1	(1)	13	(17)	78	(99)	8	(10)	100	(127)
Tertiary high	0	(0)	0	(0)	95	(85)	5	(4)	100	(89)
Tertiary low	0	(0)	1	(1)	95	(72)	5	(4)	100	(77)
Total sample	2	(7)	6	(21)	86	(308)	6	(22)	100	(358)

high sector, there are obviously very strong pressures and competition for the scarce positions of this kind these villages offer.[2] At the same time, this is where the villagers want to get, realistic or unrealistic, and these wishes are consequential in ways that will be indicated later.

The desire to become white-collar, or relatively so, is of course more pronounced in the tertiary sector itself than in the primary sector — probably not so much because of desire in the latter to remain on the farm tilling the soil as for lack of knowledge, experience and insight into what the tertiary sector has to offer. This is clearly seen (Table 3.7.7), if we split the rather comprehensive 'tertiary high' category into 'professionals' and 'others' and measure the fraction the wishes for 'professional' sons make of the total for the various categories.

Table 3.7.7. *Percentage wanting their sons to become professionals*

Primary high	71
Primary low	51
Tertiary high	67
Tertiary low	71

The percentages are actually quite similar, the only exception being the sector most remote from the high tertiary sector: the *braccianti*. Again, we feel this is more because of social myopia than any other factor that they turn their wishes less often to the university educated. Does this mean that there is any opening for a secondary sector — that there is some expression of a desire to become a 'worker'? A total of only 9% of the respondents (10% of the *braccianti*) with clear answers express themselves in this direction, which does not mean that they would not be more than receptive if job opportunities in this sector existed. It is difficult to say whether this is little or much — but it is hardly enough to constitute a pressure.

To summarize: 86% of the total want their sons to get into high tertiary occupations, and only one respondent wants his son to cross the magic line between *braccianti* and *contadini*. Both tendencies may be a natural expression of experiences with father-self mobility: only extremely few cross the line mentioned anyhow; the only realistic opening for mobility is into the tertiary sector. But over and above this comes the reaction of the farmers themselves: only 9% of the farmers want their sons to take up pick and shovel.

Let us then compare Tables 3.7.2 and 3.7.6, and make two assumptions: 1) that the actual mobility rates will remain fairly constant so that we can use father-self mobility as an estimate of self-son mobility and 2) that the son's mobility wishes will be about the same as his father's wishes for him. In other words, we make the assumptions necessary to pool the two sources of information so as to get some measure of the amount of frustration awaiting the coming generation of villagers. The first assumption is probably not too unreasonable, since the tertiary sector will probably continue to grow, and about in the same way, unless some measure of industrialization is introduced. The second assumption is more dubious, but as a baseline it may be worthwhile to see what will happen if the sons inherit their fathers' expectations. For the total sample, then, compare these two distributions shown in Table 3.7.8.

Table 3.7.8. *A comparison of desired and possible mobility, percentage*

	Primary high	Primary low	Tertiary high	Tertiary low	Total
Would like to get into the sector (assuming son's wishes to be the same as respondent's)	2	6	86	6	100
Will be able to get into the sector (assuming mobility rates to be constant)	18	35	24	23	100
Difference between the desired and the possible	−16	−29	62	−17	0

Since the differences will have to add up to zero we shall use the sum of their numerical values divided by 200 — the maximum possible — as an index of mobility frustration, and get .62. One interpretation of this figure is that a maximum of 38% will have their wishes fulfilled within sector — but the real figure will be smaller since this presupposes that those who get into a certain sector also are those who want to get there. The four sectors we get as indices of mobility frustration are shown in Table 3.7.9.

Table 3.7.9. *Indices of mobility frustration by sector*

Primary high	0.61
Primary low	0.67
Tertiary high	0.15
Tertiary low	0.83

In a sense these figures summarize the whole pattern. Lucky are those already in the tertiary high sector — although we shall see in the next chapter that their mobility problem is just as great, only it has to do with geographical as well as with social mobility: they want to leave the whole system. Most miserable are the people in tertiary low, not because their possibilities of moving into tertiary high are lower than, for instance, for the *braccianti*, but because their aspirations are higher — they are already in the blessed sector and want to move up, 95% of them. But as pointed out earlier: when there is less potential frustration among the *braccianti* it is not so much for lack of possibility of moving as for a somewhat lower level of desire to become 'professional'. In some years, when urban culture has penetrated into the villages, into the most humble *bracciante* shack, e.g. because of experience as migrant workers abroad, this desire will be even higher, and the frustration consequently greater.

We then move to the test of the fundamental hypothesis that a sensate life perspective tends to favor a desire for social mobility. A distinction should perhaps be made here between 'social perspective' and 'wish for social mobility'. The former has to do with a number of dimensions, to be discussed more extensively in connection with time perspective, such as the mere cognitive awareness of the entire social range, horizontally and vertically; its division into equidistant ranges; evaluation of different layers, etc. But we decided to simplify by asking the question about desired mobility — and precisely about the son — so as to avoid rigidity and lack of imagination linked to one's own person. To desire mobility for one's son presupposes both a cognition of the social structure as well as a differential evaluation — it presupposes that the structure is endowed some glittering points where one would like one's son to be. Hence, we take it as an indicator of social perspective as well.

Thus, it would be contrary to our fundamental hypothesis if there were no relation between ideology and *desire* for mobility — and the data give no reason for anxiety (Table 3.7.10).

If we look at the percentage differences between ideationals and sensates, they are in perfect agreement with the theory for the allegiance index, and almost in agreement for the occupation index. Thus, ideationals are more unclear (less cognition) than the sensates — in spite of the fact that they are educationally as good or better. And the sensates want both kinds of mobility more often than the ideationals — as they should. The only exception is when it comes to wanting only one kind of mobility; here we would have preferred a percentage differ-

159

Table 3.7.10. *Ideological orientation and desired mobility, percentage*

	Occupation items				Allegiance items			
	Idea-tional	Med-ium	Sen-sate	Differ-ence	Idea-tional	Med-ium	Sen-sate	Differ-ence
Unclear	16	13	9	+ 7	15	18	7	+8
No mobility wanted	27	28	27	0	31	26	25	+6
Horizontal *or* vertical mobility	43	37	31	+12	33	37	38	—5
Horizontal *and* vertical mobility	14	22	33	—19	21	19	30	—9
Total	100	100	100	0	100	100	100	0
N)	(98)	(159)	(151)		(132)	(108)	(168)	

ence of —12%, not +12%! Nevertheless, with six to eight percentage differences (with six degrees of freedom) as predicted, and only one contrary to the theory, the hypothesis is well confirmed — particularly since it also holds for the villages separately.

What, then, is the significance of the results in Tables 3.7.4 and 3.7.10? Briefly summarized: experience in mobility does not contribute to ideology, nor does it look as if ideology conduces to actual mobility, although it is difficult to say this for certain with our data. On the other hand, ideology contributes to desire for mobility, and in the way predicted. Is this simply the old story that ideologies are related — attitudes are correlated — but only with each other, not with the structural variables?

We cannot make any such generalization; for even though ideology was not correlated with education, it was correlated with age, and even though it was not correlated with horizontal *or* vertical position, it was correlated with horizontal *and* vertical position. Hence, we have to look for an interpretation that is specific for mobility. One such interpretation is as follows.

The individual has his wishes and his desires linked to his general ideological orientation. The more sensate he is, the more cognition he has (the lower the probability that he has no desire), and the more he evaluates differentially (the higher the probability that he wants mobility, one or two steps). But the society in which he lives is relatively closed internally. It does not ask for his ideology, for his need for achievement. It probably asks for his connections, his relations, his kinship ties — and by and large asks him to follow in his father's footsteps. Hence, mobility *experience* is determined by extra-ideological or even extra-motivational forces — and the result is the absence of correlation in Table 3.7.3.

This means added frustration for the villagers. In line with our general theory: to be sensate in an ideational culture is frustrating; to want mobility in a closed society is frustrating — *and to be both sensate and want mobilty is at least twice as bad*. This is a perspective that will be used later.[3]

3.8. *Who the sensates are: space perspective*

We then embark on the second major field of exploration: the relation between ideology and how the respondent relates himself to geographical space. Even the most illiterate villager knows that the world unfolds itself around him in all directions, and however closed his channels of communication with the outside world, something will always penetrate, filter through — although it may be very insignificant indeed. An image of the outside world is bound to be formed, if for no other reason than because he has eyes, because he may search the horizon and wonder what is behind, on the other side of those scorched, brown, barren mountains or on the other side of that glittering, undulating sea.

Of the many community studies, the most systematic treatment we have found of space perspective is in Bernot and Blancard's *Nouville: Un village français*.[1] The authors make a distinction between four zones in the life of the villagers:

> Il y a d'abord le *au-loin* (IV) qu'ils connaissent mal mais que le 'je ne suis pas allé bien loin' met cependant en place. Puis viennent *les environs* (III) enfin le *près-de-chez-moi* (II) et le *chez-moi* (I).[2]

The last two zones (numbers I and II) are actually within the village, and the *au loin* starts right after the *environs*.[3] The authors have interesting discussions of the cognition of these four zones, but their discussion is marred by a complete absence of systematic data that could relate these cognitions to such structural variables as age, sex, education and social and economic position. The presentation is ideal typical rather than differential, although there is an interesting distinction between the village's two occupational groups, the peasant and the worker. The worker seems to be even more limited in his spatial perception[4] than the farmer, since his work does not force him outside the limits of the factory and the *quartier* where he lives. But no statistical data are given.

Basic to *our* thinking about space perspective is the idea that for the sensate, with his motivation for change and control of the external world, space takes on significance as a frame of reference for comparisons. It provides him with a scale on which to compare himself or the place where he is with what it could be. Since development is the transformation of the potential into the actual, there must be an idea of what the potential is, and space is one place where the potential or models for the potential can be found. And this is not only potential in the sense of the *desirable*, but in the sense of the *possible*.

This implies, however, that the basic factor in space perspective is not knowledge. We would not get at space perspective by asking the types of questions asked in geography lessons: Where is Agrigento? Where is France? It is the evaluative, not the cognitive aspect of space which is of interest here. Whether this genetically precedes or comes after the cognitive aspect we do not know — but there must be *some* cognition, however rudimentary, before evaluation starts. In principle we get four possibilities, but exclude one of them.

Table 3.8.1. *The relation between cognition and evaluation in indicators of space perspective*

| | | Evaluation | |
		None	Some
Cognition	None	0	impossible
	Some	1	2

The figures are put there to indicate, roughly, three degrees of space perspective. On the one hand we have the person to whom other points in space have no meaning, neither cognitive nor evaluation. On the other hand we have the person who endows space with evaluative structure: he not only sees it and knows it, but evaluates it differentially, relative to his own situation. In between we have the person to whom space exists, but is *flat;* there is no differential evaluation. Thus, we have three levels: the person to whom space is as in a *mist*, the person to whom space is *flat* and the person to whom space has *curvature*. The last person is the one who, in our sense, has space perspective.

To develop an index of this we asked the villagers: 'How would you say this village compares with other regions as far as living conditions are concerned?' And we gave seven such 'regions' — near Palermo, near Agrigento, near Catania, in Calabria, in Africa, in France and in

162

India — seven places on a scale of increasing physical distance ('Africa' i.e. Tunis, is only 160 km. away). The respondent had four possible answers: 'worse', 'about the same', 'better' and 'don't know'. Obviously 'don't know' should be given the value zero, 'about the same' the value one and 'worse' or 'better' the value two according to the thinking above, and that is what we did. Thus, an index ranging from zero to 14 was developed by simple addition, and we got a U-shaped distribution (because of high inter-item correlation): 112 had a score of zero (DK on all seven), and 51 had a score of 14 (evaluation for all seven). For analytical work the index was trichotomized fairly uniformly in 'low' (129), 'medium' (149) and 'high' (130).

According to the thinking above, this is what we mean by space perspective, although we certainly do not claim that there cannot be other interpretations. Hence, we see no immediate necessity for validation over and above the validation that lies in the general impression that the interviewing worked fairly well.

Let us then turn to the test of the fundamental hypothesis about correlation between ideology and space perspective. According to the general line of thinking, we assume both variables to be fairly stable characteristics of the person once they have crystallized, so there is no clear basis for saying that one is more 'independent' than the other. However, we shall treat ideology as genetically prior to space perspective; we shall rather think in terms of sensate man using space for comparisons than vice versa, although both may obviously be the case. Methodologically, the only consequence of this has to do with the direction of percentaging, and we present the data in Table 3.8.2.

The percentage differences are all in the *right* direction, three or four of a magnitude sufficient to conclude that the general hypothesis has

Table 3.8.2. *Ideological orientation and space perspective (total sample percentage)*

Space perspective	Occupation items				Allegiance items			
	Idea-tional	Med-ium	Sen-sate	S–I	Idea-tional	Med-ium	Sen-sate	S–I
Low	39	38	20	−19	30	45	24	− 6
Medium	41	33	38	− 3	45	32	33	−12
High	20	29	42	+22	25	23	43	+18
Total	100	100	100		100	100	100	
(N)	(100)	(157)	(151)		(132)	(108)	(168)	

Table 3.8.3. *Ideological orientation and space perspective (villages, percentage differences between sensates and ideationals)*

Space perspective	Occupation items		Allegiance items	
	High	*Low*	*High*	*Low*
MONTAGNA	+ 9	−10	+ 4	+ 6
COLLINA	+34	− 8	+23	−10
MARINA	+36	−42	+31	−19

been verified. However, we want to test this for both indices and all three villages separately and give the results in concentrated form (Table 3.8.3).

Since we predict '+' for high space perspective and '−' for low, the hypothesis is confirmed in 11 out of 12 cases. The exception is in line with what we have found earlier: the ideationals in Montagna seem more 'forward' than in other places.

However, could it not be that the summary nature of the index conceals important differences? Or more precisely, would it not be reasonable to assume that the locally-oriented ideational has just as 'curved' a space perspective as the sensate, only it does not reach as far — so that he may have a more developed space perspective close to his own village but care less about such distant places as France and India? There is nothing in the theory that qualifies the relationship between ideology and space perspective with regard to how far the individual has a conception of space at all, so we have no real basis for prediction, but did want to look into the matter.

The percentage difference between sensates and ideationals for the three categories of answers was computed for all seven items in the index, and the items were then divided into 'Sicily' (near Palermo, Agrigento or Catania) and 'outside Sicily' (Calabria, Africa, France, India) on the assumption that this would be the classification that would give the ideationals most chance to assert themselves. But when the average difference was computed for these two classes of regions in geographical space there was no difference (Diagram 3.8.1). As far as we can tell from our data, the relationship between space perspective and ideological orientation does not depend on the geographical distance to the point of comparison — the superiority of the sensates starts right outside the village itself, so to speak. Thus, our data give no basis for qualification of the hypothesis in this direction.

So far we have explored the relation between ideology and the ten-

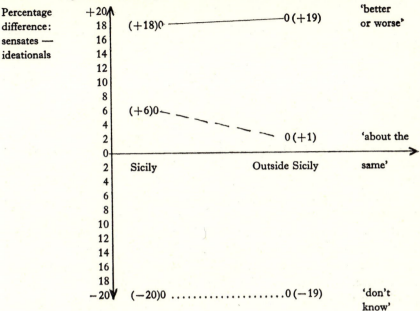

Diagram 3.8.1. *Ideological orientation, space perspective and space*

dency to evaluate. But there should be more to this relation than we have found so far. Thus, one would expect the sensate not only to evaluate more than the ideational but also to evaluate his own village more *negatively*, to *reject*. A closer inspection of the data brings this out very clearly. For all seven items in the index the difference between ideationals and sensates consists in the much higher percentage of 'don't know' for the ideationals and much higher percentage of 'better somewhere else' for the sensates (Table 3.8.4).

The last two rows in the Table tell us precisely what the difference

Table 3.8.4. *Ideological orientation and space perspective items*

Percentage difference, sensates — ideationals	Close to Palermo	Close to Agrigento	Close to Catania	In Calabria	In Africa	In France	In India
Worse	— 4	4	— 2	4	2	0	— 3
About the same	9	3	6	3	— 2	1	1
Better	23	17	14	23	19	15	17
Don't know	—28	—24	—18	—30	—19	—16	—15
Total	0	0	0	0	0	0	0

165

between the sensates and the ideationals consists of. For the ideationals there is the strong tendency to disregard the world outside. The sensates not only perceive that world but also perceive it as better. But does not this mean that they are simply the discontented? It does in a sense, as it should according to theory. They should watch the horizon for bases of comparison, and their conclusion is given by their ideology: *this place should be changed*. With their conclusion given, it would have produced intolerable cognitive dissonance to have perceived the other places of reference as 'worse' — for what would then have happened to the incentive? The remarkable thing, as already pointed out, is how invariant these attitudes are of the places of reference. This is also as it should be according to theory: the perception of the environment is less based on fact than it is a projection of deeper attachments. The world is essentially dichotomous; it is 'here' as opposed to 'elsewhere'.

At this point one may start wondering what else could be conducive to a high space perspective than a sensate ideology, for it would obviously be incorrect to claim that this is the only factor, although it may be decisive. We first tested for the possible effect of *age*, but there was absolutely no correlation: of the younger, 34% had a well-developed space perspective; of the older, 36%. For *education* we got quite similar results. This does not mean that age and education as such have no effect, but that there are counterbalancing consequences arising from these factors. Thus, we know from 3.4 that there are more ideationals among the older, and this may cancel the effect of learning and experience with higher age. Correspondingly, we know there is a slight tendency for the 'well' educated to be more ideational, and this may cancel the effect of having learned more at school. And as to the effect of *social position* on space perspective, the exploration will be made in 4.5, where all four indicators of psychic mobility will be located in the social structure.

In conclusion, let us look at this problem of space and ideology from a different angle. In 3.7 there was noticeable correlation between ideology and *desired* mobility, but not between ideology and *actual* mobility — and our interpretation was that the local structure was made in such a way that it did not ask for ideology when mobility was to be granted. Mobility in a traditional structure is traditional mobility, fully compatible with traditional thinking in general. For the same reason we would expect little or no correlation between ideology and geographical mobility — in the sense of actual mobility already experienced in physical space.

166

There are two kinds of experiences that are relevant here. First of all, not all of the villagers were born in the village where they lived at the time of interviewing, nor were their wives (or spouses) born there. In other words, some of them had important experiences of mobility because they or their wives came from the outside, although only extremely few had their roots outside the province. Secondly, there is the important experience referred to as 'travel'. We asked them about six points of reference: Palermo, Agrigento, Catania, continental Italy and 'abroad'. These points were chosen so as to be as symmetrically located as possible relative to the three villages. We then constructed two indices, based on differences between where they lived and their points of origin, and on travel experience (Table 3.8.5).

Table 3.8.5. *Geographical mobility experience and ideological orientation, percentage*

Ideology	Mobility from birth			Total travel experiences		
	Low	Medium	High	Low	Medium	High
Ideationals	34	23	19	26	23	24
Medium	28	38	50	42	41	32
Sensates	38	39	31	32	36	44
Total	100	100	100	100	100	100
(N)	(74)	(254)	(80)	(109)	(171)	(128)

The results are interesting. The 74 'born in this house' and having a spouse from the same village are both more sensate and more ideational than the 80 having more mobility experience (at least one of the spouses from another village). Two possible interpretations here would be as follows: on the one hand, ideology does not really enter, but rather such factors as primogeniture (inheriting the house) and kinship ties in general do. On the other hand, there may be a negative selection from the sensate point of view. It may be that the person who moved, although into these basically ideational and stagnant villages, is also the person who is moved by some external factor, not himself, and is driven by an internalized ideology with a longing for change and new experience. In other words, to the extent that ideology determines geographical mobility, it is probably conducive to mobility much farther away, to Northern Italy, etc.

But 'travel experience' is related to ideology (although the differences decrease when we control for social position) in the sense that much travel experience seems to lead to a sensate orientation. But the difference is considerably less than for space perspective (and this holds even if we vary the cutting points). Seventy-six per cent of the total had been to the regional capital, to Palermo, more than once: two-thirds had been to continental Italy, and 29% abroad — so the combined experience where travel is concerned is considerable. But among the travelers to continental Italy close to 80% had been there in connection with their military service; the army is also the great provider for travel abroad: 61% had been abroad for that reason — during the war (some of them also to Ethiopia and Libya). This gives a chance to test the *ad hoc* hypothesis that what might be called 'institutionalized mobility' leads less to ideological difference than to voluntary mobility — for, whereas the latter may be both caused by and cause sensateness, the former will at most cause sensateness.

Thus, to go once to Palermo is something almost all of the villagers have to do sooner or later for administrative reasons (the famous 'practiche amministrative'). And this shows up in the percentage difference between sensates and ideationals: it is much less for those who have traveled once than for those who have traveled more than once (1% as against 7%). Similarly, institutionalized travel as a part of the military service should be less conducive to differences than to travel in general — and this was also confirmed (for travel to continental Italy the percentage difference between sensates and ideationals was 4% for travel in general, 1% when it was due to military service; for travel abroad it was 9% for travel in general, 4% when it was due to military service). The differences are small, but they are entirely consistent, so we permit ourselves to regard the hypothesis about the differential impact of structural vs. voluntary travel as to some extent confirmed.[5]

3.9. *Who the sensates are : time perspective*

We have dealt with social perspective and space perspective and now turn to the third of these indicators of psychic mobility: the perspective on time, on how the respondent relates to time. Our reasoning is very much like the reasoning in the preceding sections, but let us start with two illustrations.

On a wall in a house in Madurai, Madras state, Southern India, was found the following inscription:

Yesterday is dead. Forget it.
Tomorrow does not exist. Don't worry.
Today is here. Use it.
Eternity is ahead. Think of it.[1]

And on a wall of the University of Coimbra, Portugal, is this inscription:

Quando tanta coisa que parecia sagrada ou eterna se dispersa è dissolve no mar revolto que e o mondo de hoje, faz bem atentar no valor de uma instituição que não atraiçoa o seu espiritu nem se afasta da missão que lhe foi confiada.[2]

Both were found in countries where at least important sub-systems have a degree of ideationalism unequaled in more industrialized countries. Of course, such inscriptions prove nothing unless one has a statistical sample of them, they are analyzed for content, degree of visibility and internalization and then compared cross-nationally and cross-culturally. But both inscriptions strike a tone remarkably similar to what one would expect according to Sorokin's ideas about ideational systems. Time is a flow, an eternal flow, although it may have its whirls and eddies. It can be relied upon to flow on, into eternity.

But then comes the remarkable thing about the Indian quotation. Time is divided into non-contiguous regions: on the one side are 'yesterday' and 'tomorrow', on the other 'today' and 'eternity'. The former are somehow rejected; the latter are accepted. Ideational man seems to stand planted in his 'now' (and 'here', according to the last section). But unlike his *space* perspective which stops at that very local point, he looks ahead in *time*, over and above the turbulences of the tomorrows and days after tomorrow, and far into eternity. He makes eternity his, amalgamates it with his present — because in his world of essentially external stability he can do so. In a stable world, the present is a guide for eternity, and why then care so much about the middle-range perspectives reaching only yesterday and tomorrow? Even though these are the perspectives that matter for social change, the perspectives in which sensate man specializes? And from this follows the role of the major university in Portugal: to preserve, to stick to the spirit and mission once given to it — not to take a lead in the change and control of the future.

On the other hand, even the most illiterate villager is bound to know something about the past and to have some ideas about the future. An image, at least of the past, is bound to from if for no other reason than because he has memory, eyes to watch with and ears to listen with, for instance to absorb what older relatives hand down to him. And even if

169

he may not intersperse much between present and eternity, with its transcendental overtones, he will probably include tomorrow somewhat more than is done in the saying from Madurai, in fact, even if he lives in that house in Madurai. The problem is how to measure this.

The literature, especially the tradition initiated by Kurt Lewin, is much less of a guide here than one might believe — and the numerous community studies do not contain much more than speculations concerning time perspective. Bernot and Blancard make a distinction between *temps historique ou chronologique, temps passé et temps futur, temps calendaire* and *temps écologique*[3] and give an account of how time is punctuated by these different aspects. According to them the farmer has what might be called a longer time perspective than the worker:

> Pour l'ouvrier, le travail se mesure à l'heure et est compté par journée pour être payé à la quinzaine. Pour le fermier, surtout, mais aussi pour tout rural, le travail se mesure à l'année.[4]

Apart from the fact that no data are given to support this interesting, thesis, there are two assumptions involved, both dubious. First of all, the idea is that the rhythm of work really molds the conception of time in such a simple way that the farmer or worker thinks in terms of one cycle only. Secondly, there is the idea that work alone is decisive. Thus, it is hard to believe that the worker is not forced into more universalistic concepts of time by virtue of his status and his institutionalized links to other positions in the social structure.

At the end of their chapter on space and time a heavily polarized scheme is presented:[5]

	zone	*limite*	*cycle*	*terme*
l'ouvrier	courte	proche	court	court
le fermier	large	eloignée	large	long

Although it is futile to discuss this without more systematic data, it is at least highly improbable that this finding is generalizable. Although there are no workers in our sample, we shall at least show how limited the time perspective of the rural section is — at least as judged by one aspect of this volatile concept — so that if the time perspective of the worker were to be even more limited, there would hardly be enough left to carry out any work.

Basic to *our* thinking about time perspective is the idea that for the sensate, with his motivation for change and control of the external world, time takes on significance as a frame of reference for comparisons and as the medium in which change and control will have to take place. It provides him with a scale on which he can compare himself, or the place where he is, with what it could be. Even more than for space perspective, time is the dimension on which change will have to take place, where the potential may become the actual. Time is also a dimension on which the potential or models for the potential can be located; the conservative finds them in the present or in the past, the radical in the future, but both locate their models on the time dimension and compare them with the present.

We can now distinguish between a number of interpretations of the widely used term 'time perspective'. The corresponding distinctions could also be made with regard to space, but we shall discuss them here since time perspective seems to deserve more attention. More precisely one may distinguish between time perspective in the senses of:

1) *How far* the subjective dimension of time reaches into the past and the future.
2) *The structure* of subjective time; what constitutes
   a) 'short' and 'long' intervals of time,
   b) 'equal intervals' of time, and
   c) the dividing points in time.
3) *Curvature vs. flatness* of subjective time, i.e. the extent to which time is used for comparisons.
4) *Optimism vs. pessimism* with regard to the future, or with regard to the present relative to the past.
5) *Ability to predict and plan.*
6) *Ability to postpone gratification.*

The first two of these interpretations are cognitive; the next two are evaluative, and the last two have to do with action. All six are logically independent of each other and shed different kinds of light on the general problem of how people relate to time. Thus, the first one can be compared to a light at night: *How far does it reach?* The second is defined within the first: it is a question of properties of subjective scales, as defined in measurement theory. People differ not only with regard to how far they see into physical time, but also with regard to what they consider short and long spans of time. Thus, 'short' time perspective may mean that they see only what is immediately ahead or behind, but it may also mean that what they consider 'long' time spans are short relative to what other people feel.

The evaluative dimensions of time perspective do not lend themselves so readily to expressions like 'short' and 'long', so we shall rather talk about 'curved' vs. 'flat', and 'optimistic' vs. 'pessimistic'. The former has to do with the extent to which time is used as a basis for differential evaluation at all, and the latter with the result of this differential evaluation. Obviously, an optimistic or pessimistic time perspective pre-supposes some degree of curvature in the sense discussed in connection with space perspective in 3.8.

As to the action dimensions, the expressions 'short' and 'long' are very applicable, and very often used. The person with the short time perspective is also the person who is unable to plan and unable to post-pone gratification. Obviously, long-term planning presupposes a long cognitive time perspective (the first interpretation); and long-term post-ponement of gratification presupposes not only a curved time perspective, but also long-term optimism, otherwise postponement of gratification would be a rather morbid kind of masochism (interpretations 3 and 4 above).

It would be extremely worthwhile to investigate the interrelations among all these dimensions of the more global concept of time per-spective, but that is far beyond the scope of this work. Our guess is that they are relatively strongly intercorrelated, so that for relatively gross purposes one can study how one of them relates to other variables and still with some justification say one has studied 'time perspective' in a more general sense. For this purpose we exclude the last two because they are not purely attitudinal and the first two because they are too purely cognitive. We want to know how the person relates himself to time and that leaves us with the choice between a measure of optimism/ pessimism, and a measure of curvature of subjective time.

It is the latter we are most interested in, for it is a direct expression of the general problem of using time as a dimension for carrying out compari-sons. This implies, however, that the basic factor in time perspective is not knowledge, nor optimism vs. pessimism. We are not interested in whether the respondent can evaluate his own situation relative to different points in the past and in the future correctly, or whether he is generally optimistic or generally pessimistic in the senses defined above. The question is whether time is endowed with an evaluative structure or not. But for this to take place there must probably be some cognition,

Table 3.9.1. *The relation between cognition and evaluation in indicators of time perspective*

		Evaluation	
		None	Some
	None	0	impossible
Cognition			
	Some	1	2

however rudimentary, before evaluation starts. Thus, we get in principle four possibilities, but exclude one of them (Table 3.9.1).

Again, the figures indicate three levels of time perspective in our sense. The respondents were asked, 'As compared with today, how would you say the economic situation of this village was', followed by six points in time: 'when your father was young', 'before the last war', 'ten years ago', 'in ten years', 'when the children of today are grown up' and 'a hundred years from now'. According to the Table above the answers were coded '0' for 'don't know', '1' for 'about the same' and '2' for 'worse' or 'better'. Thus we got an index ranging from 0 to 12.

The distribution differed interestingly from the distribution on space perspective. The distribution was less U-shaped and more W-shaped, indicating less polarization into either having a well-developed perspective or else having no perspective at all, as was almost the case for space perspective. Moreover, the arithmetic mean was much higher for time perspective than for space perspective (7.2 as against 4.8, even though the range was two points wider for the latter). Thus, with the higher mean and lower dispersion for time perspective *there is good evidence that these people live even less in space than they do in time*. Or rather: they can 'move' their village in their imagination through time much more than they can move it through space, probably because they are mainly involved in only one village, their own, and because life *forces* them to live in time; it does not *force* them to extend their physical life space.

The distribution was then trichotomized into 'low' (123) 'medium' (142) and 'high' (143). As with space perspective, we see no immediate necessity for validation, especially since we have no external criterion. To us this *is* time perspective as we are interested in it; it is a measure of the extent to which the respondent uses time for differential evaluation. Hence, we proceed immediately to the test of the fundamental hypothesis, in the same way as we did for space perspective, with ideology playing the role of the independent variable (Table 3.9.2).

Table 3.9.2. *Ideological orientation and time perspective (total sample, percentage)*

Time perspective	Occupation items				Allegiance items			
	Ideational	Medium	Sensate	S–I	Ideational	Medium	Sensate	S–I
Low	33	31	28	— 5	34	38	22	—12
Medium	40	33	33	— 7	37	37	32	— 5
High	27	36	39	+12	29	25	46	+17
Total	100	100	100	0	100	100	100	0
(N)	(100)	(157)	(151)		(132)	(108)	(168)	

The percentage differences are all in the expected direction and three of them of a magnitude sufficient to conclude that the general hypothesis has been verified.

However, this is not sufficient; we want to test the hypothesis for both indices and all three villages separately (Table 3.9.3).

Table 3.9.3. *Ideological orientation and time perspective (villages, percentage differences between sensates and ideationals)*

Time perspective	Occupation items		Allegiance items	
	High	Low	High	Low
MONTAGNA	+ 1	+ 6	+ 7	— 7
COLLINA	+16	— 9	+13	—16
MARINA	+23	—20	+32	—18

In this Table the hypothesis is confirmed in 11 out of 12 cases. The disconfirmation is located at the same place as for space perspective, among the ideationals in Montagna, the only difference being that in this case it shows up for the occupation items, and not for the allegiance items. The reason for the latter is obvious if one compares Tables 3.8.2 and 3.9.2: the occupation index discriminates best for space perspective, whereas the allegiance index discriminates best for time perspective. However, the magnitude of the deviant case is not too high. And since the deviance is consistent, we feel the general hypothesis is confirmed and that a satisfactory explanation for the deviant case can be found.

There is one major problem, however. The index is composed of six items, three referring to the past and three to the future. Could there be a systematic difference here? Intuitively it seems quite reasonable that the sensates — with their 'worldliness' and their feel for external reality, change and control as relevant and important — would be more space and time conscious. But does that mean that they are more time conscious in both directions — or could it be that the sensate specializes in the future whereas the more locally-oriented ideational is more tempted to explore the past? Everybody has met the *local historian* in small, isolated places; he who knows the past so much better than the future that he sometimes confuses them — and his own place so infinitely much better than the world outside. His vision extends far back in time, but he is certainly no cosmopolitan.

To test this idea we calculated for each item in the index the percentage difference between sensates and ideationals for the three answer categories 'better or worse', 'about the same' and 'don't know', and then plotted the differences along a time axis. For simplicity and to get the general tendency, we then computed the average of the differences referring to the past and of the differences referring to the future, so that we got three straight lines for the answer categories (Diagram 3.9.1).

As the Diagram shows (and as opposed to the corresponding and comparable Diagram 3.8.1 for space perspective), there was something

Diagram 3.9.1. *Ideological orientation, time perspective and time (average percentage differences between senates and idetionals, for past and for future)*

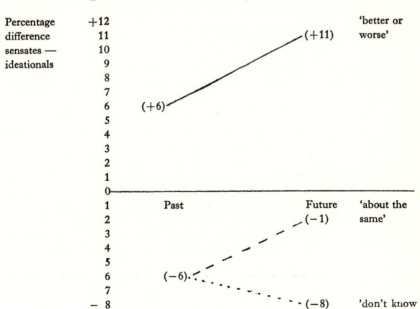

175

to the hypothesis. The sensates are always ahead of the ideationals in having 'curvature' in their time dimension, past or future — *but the tendency is much more pronounced for the future than for the past.* This is as it should be, since change orientation and a desire for control related future to present more than present to past. But instead of disconfirming or changing our general finding this Diagram rather confirms and elaborates it, since it gives no lead in time perspective to the ideationals, only a diminution of the difference. Thus, an important specification is brought into the picture.

This specification refers to time: the difference in time perspective between the sensates and the ideationals decreases with 'decreasing time', i.e. when the reference is to the past. But would it not be reasonable to expect a similar decrease with 'decreasing space', when the reference is not to a relatively gross unit as the village, but to a smaller unit that comprises the respondent, such as the family? Or in general: since the sensates are higher on space perspective should one not expect differences in time perspective to increase the farther out in space one goes? Thus, when asked about the future of Italy or the world, we would expect extreme differences; and when asked about his own future, the difference would be considerably smaller because the effect of differences in space perspective would be much smaller.

Unfortunately we have only time perspective data relating to *two* points on the scale in space starting with the individual and then moving in concentric circles (with the individual at the center) until it comprises the whole universe. But these two are perhaps the most meaningful ones in this culture: *village* and *family*. We have presented the data for the former and Table 3.9.4 shows the corresponding data on time perspective for the latter.

Table 3.9.4. *Ideological orientation and time perspective relative to one's own family, percentage*

Time perspective	Occupation items				Allegiance items			
	Ideational	Medium	Sensate	S–I	Ideational	Medium	Sensate	S–I
Low	50	45	42	−8	49	52	39	−10
Medium	25	26	30	+5	27	27	27	0
High	25	29	28	+3	24	21	34	+10
Total	100	100	100	0	100	100	100	0
(N)	(100)	(157)	(151)		(132)	(108)	(168)	

First of all, it should be noticed that the Table gives an independent confirmation of the general hypothesis about the relation between ideology and time perspective. The second problem is whether we also can say that there is less correlation here than in Table 3.9.2. A comparison of percentage differences bears this out in five out of six cases. But the indices are not strictly comparable since this family index is based on only three items (relative to the family of origin, relative to five years ago, relative to the situation in five years), and not quite on the same items. However, a comparison item by item also gives support to the hypothesis that ideology has less impact on time perspective with increasing proximity, so we regard the hypothesis as confirmed.

Let us then proceed as we did in connection with space perspective and study in more detail how sensates and ideationals differ on the *items* in the index. Although we would expect, according to the hypothesis, that the ideationals were consistently higher on 'don't know', we cannot make the same inference as we did for space perspective, i.e. at they would consistently see 'here' as worse. It does not follow from the sensate premise that 'now' will be seen as worse, that the evaluation of past or present will be consistently in terms of 'better' (or consistently in terms of 'worse' for that matter) — all that follows is that differences will be perceived. A sensate respondent can be motivated into action by a future he sees as 'worse' or as 'better' — in short, all four combinations are possible (Table 3.9.5).

Table 3.9.5. *Combinations of perceptions of past and future*

		Perception of future	
		Worse than present	Better than present
Perception of past	Worse than present	1	2
	Better than present	3	4

Number 2 is a consistently optimistic pattern, number 3 very pessimistic and numbers 1 and 4 more sophisticated in a sense, since they imply a non-linear perspective on social change. Number 1 is highly unlikely, given sensate man's general discontent with here and now and his concern for change — and in fact was empirically almost not apparent. Number 4 is the expression of utter discontent and pessimism.

But all four are possible, although not equally likely. Hence our

Table 3.9.6. *Ideological orientation and time perspective: items*

Percentage difference sensates — ideationals	When father was young	Before the last war	10 years ago	In 10 years	When children are grown up	100 years from now
Worse	10	13	−1	9	4	3
About the same	−5	−6	5	0	−3	−1
Better	1	−2	3	3	3	7
Don't know	−6	−5	−7	−12	−4	−9
Total	0	0	0	0	0	0

prediction can only be that the sensates will be above the ideationals on both, and below on 'about the same' and 'don't know' (Table 3.9.6).

Of the 24 percentage differences, 20 (or 84%) are in the predicted direction, and even though many of the predicted differences are small, *all* of the four deviant differences are also small. Again we arrive at some of the same conclusions as we did for space perspective: the exact zero point of reference in time does not matter so much — it could be put farther back or farther into the future. The sensate respondent would nevertheless see differences in one direction or the other; he would see dynamics where the ideational respondent would tend to see nothing or no difference.

As for space perspective, we tested for the possible effect of *age* on time perspective. This is particularly important, since increasing age is the time equivalent of travel in geographical space — we all have to travel through time, and we can all make our comparisons and reflections. But as for space perspective, there was no correlation whatsoever between age and time perspective: of the younger, 33% had a well-developed time perspective; of the older, 36% (for the time perspective relative to the family the corresponding figures were 29% and 28%). Hence, just as for space perspective, the relation between ideology and perspective holds for all age groups. For *education* we got quite similar results. As to interpretation in terms of counterbalancing factors, we refer to the preceding section. And as to the effect of *social position* on time perspective, we refer to section 4.5.[6]

3.10. *A portrait of the sensates*

We have now been pursuing the sensates for some time, using many of the tricks of social science methodology to get at their characteristics.

178

And we feel we know them better than we did before we started. They are not only defined, but we know something about what else they mean and think in addition to being sensate. And above all: we know something about where in the social structure we have to look to find them. Let us briefly summarize our findings so that we better perceive the implications.

To start with, consider the other attitudes or orientations that seem to come together with a sensate orientation.

First of all, the sensates are fundamentally more change oriented than the ideationals; they want *changes of the system* in which they live, not only *changes for themselves* within the system as it is defined today. Hence, even though we would certainly admit that there are difficulties in connection with the validity of the measures of sensate orientation, this basic finding stands out exactly as was to be predicted.

Secondly, a sensate orientation comes together with a highly developed social perspective, space perspective and time perspective. The sensates see more points in social, geographical and temporal space, and they have a much more pronounced tendency to equip these points with evaluations. These spaces are endowed with much more intense meaning for sensate man; he is able to move mentally around in them, and he knows what he means and feels in connection with them. In the social structure he wants to get to higher positions, at least for his son; in geographical *space* he feels that other places are better although his attitude does not depend much on where these places are located, and in *time* he is particularly future conscious whether it is because he fears the future or feels it will bring better conditions to the village or to his family.

But this means that the sensate orientation is embedded in a highly significant and well-integrated syndrome of orientations. To be sensate is to be change oriented, and changes have to take place in social, geographical and temporal space. But such changes can only take place if these three spaces are cognitively perceived and equipped with evaluations — otherwise the changes will only be hanging in the air. In other words, the way these orientations cluster together, the sensates get their mental tools for forming and even formulating the images of *what could be*, of what could be for themselves and for their families and for the villages.

All this sounds promising in the sense that one may derive from it the impression that the sensate orientation has, by and large, been adequately embedded in psychological syndromes of cognition and evaluation. Undoubtedly, if the sensates had been particularly low on all three perspectives, then their change orientation would have been rather meaningless. But, as promising as these attitudinal correlations may look, from the point of view of what constitutes adequate motivation for development, just as disillusioning is the perspective when one turns to the problem of how the sensates are located in the social structure. At this point we also have a number of findings, some negative and some positive.

First of all: ideological orientation in the sense discussed here is by and large not related to social participation, not related to experienced social mobility and not related to experienced geographical mobility, including travel experience. In other words, it does not seem to be related to more incidental aspects of the social structure, to singular phenomena or more temporary aspects of social life.

Second, ideological orientation does, indeed, depend on more permanent and pervasive aspects of the social structure surrounding the individual. Thus, sensate man tends to be young, particularly if he belongs to the *braccianti*, and he tends to be uneducated. Education in these villages seems to predispose the pupils for an ideational orientation and it takes time, apparently, to overcome the impact of this ideational conditioning. On the other hand, the churches seem to be colored by the ideological ethos in the villages they serve, and to cater to ideationals in predominantly ideational villages and to sensates in predominantly sensate villages.

Third, in the occupational structure there is a curious and interesting distribution. Sensate man is found in the primary as well as in the tertiary sector, in high as well as in low positions, and almost exactly in the same proportions. But if one combines these two dimensions of social structure, then it become obvious that primary low and tertiary high are the combinations with a sensate ethos *par excellence*. Correspondingly, sensate people are found among rich and among poor, but when economic position is combined with social position, then it becomes clear that the disequilibrated combinations are the ones that predispose most strongly for a sensate orientation. Particularly important in this connection are the combinations of *poor* economy with *high* position in the tertiary sector, and *rich* economy with *low* position in the primary sector. In general, the sensates are more disequilibrated and the ideationals more equilibrated.

Thus, the immediate conclusion to be drawn from this is that sensate men are found at very different places in the social structure. Somehow the *periphery* seems to have an overrepresentation of sensateness, if one accepts that being primary low with little education, and at the same time young, sounds peripheral. One would not in general expect these people to have very much influence in society, and since they are surrounded by ideationals one might also expect that with increasing age they would be easily absorbed into society and molded into the general ethos. With time one would also expect more people to have schooling, and if the schools do not change one would expect the result to be highly erosive on the sensate potential in the villages.

But then there are variations in this image, which does not at all reflect all the findings, only some of them. First of all, the highest values for sensate orientations are found not in the extreme periphery but in the more affluent sectors of the periphery, which means that the holders of the sensate orientation are motivated by the disequilibrium they feel between social and economic position. This may also lead to absorption if they are permitted to equilibrate themselves, and we would expect them to change to more ideational colors if through mobility they get a social position more commensurate with their economic situation. On the other hand, our data on social mobility seem to indicate that chances of mobility are slim, which means that the disequilibrium is not very likely to be expended and more likely to be preserved as a generator of sensate ideology, unless there are other outlets for the forces created by the disequilibrium.

But then: another major fraction of the sensates is located in the *center*, in the tertiary high, but also with a built-in disequilibrium, since they tend to be particularly sensate, if in addition they are poor. In other words, the sensates are particularly frequent among the discontented in the periphery and in the center. And these people in the center should, in principle, have some power; if they would dedicate all their energy to the transformation of their societies according to their own blueprints, then one would expect this to be consequential.

But do they? And can they cooperate with the people in the periphery, presumably with the same orientation as they have themselves? To answer this we need more data, and more perspectives, on the villages.[1]

4. The movers and the stayers

4.1. *How many want to move, and where*

The theoretical focus of this chapter is what Lerner calls 'psychic mobility'[1] or, rather, one special aspect of it. Lerner, as discussed in 1.4, sees modernization to a large extent accompanied by and even determined by 'the great characterological transformation we call psychic mobility'[2], and we shall follow his lead in order to apply his hypothesis systematically to these Sicilian data. We shall try to locate this capacity of empathy in the social structure and to trace its effects in this particular situation of underdevelopment. To do this an instrument is needed, and we have settled on a very simple one.

In broad terms, the capacity of empathy is the capacity to imagine oneself where one is not. More precisely, it is to be able to imagine oneself at other points in the social structure, at other points in space and at other points in time, and to integrate something of what one sees or finds at these points into one's own personality. Thus, empathy has both projective and introjective components, and it is endowed with both evaluative and cognitive components. To empathize is not only to know, it is also to want, or at least to 'cathect', to feel some kind of positive identification.

In one sense, then, the concept of empathy can be approached empirically by means of our three indices of social perspective, space perspective and time perspective, introduced and developed in 3.7., 3.8 and 3.9, where they were related to cultural mentality. Later in this chapter we shall locate these perspectives in the social structure. However, we shall start here with a much simpler approach to the same subject, which ties the Lerner theory directly to a very concrete and very important problem of daily life in these Sicilian villages. We are thinking of the problem of *migration*. All the refined argumentation in connection with development is often overshadowed by one simple consideration: for change to take place it is not enough for physical, social and cultural conditions to be adequate; the right people have to be physically *present*. And for change to be effective, they have to be mentally present as well. To avoid 'brain-drain' is not enough; the brain also has to function locally. If by no means sufficient, physical and psychological presence are at least necessary conditions, and worth looking into.

Thus, we focused our attention on geographic empathy, but not in the abstract sense of the space perspective. We wanted to know, not *how far* the respondent was able to stretch his imagination into social and geographical space and time, but rather *where* his optimal point in space is located. The Lerner question that comes closest to ours is: 'If for some reason you could not live in our country, what other country would you choose to live in?'[3] The other eight empathy questions in his system all touch other aspects of what Lerner calls empathy, although others may feel that it is a strange mixture of many dimensions, as mentioned in 1.4.

Our questions were simply:

Attitudinal: If you could choose, where would you like to live, here or elsewhere?
Behavioral: Have you ever tried to move? Do you think it might be possible?

The questions are about the same as the Lerner question with the difference that we wanted a check on the behavioral consequences of desires to move.

The theoretical importance of these simple questions is now as follows. To have positive empathy with 'somewhere else' is also to have negative or at least decreased empathy with the place where one lives, provided the empathy has been translated into action. Everybody can dream, if he has been sufficiently exposed to education and mass media to get nourishment for his vague fantasies; but not everybody translates the dream into action. We regard this conversion into action as a test of the seriousness involved, of the depth of the internalization of the identification with the other place. Consequently, we expected the two questions to be related cumulatively in the sense that, by and large, there will be three groups: those who want to live where they live and never have tried to move, those who want to live somewhere else but never have translated this idea in action, and people who both want to live somewhere else and have tried to do something about it. Since we expected attitude to precede behavior, we expected the fourth possible group to be relatively small and this was indeed what we found (Table 4.1.1).

Table 4.1.1. *Geographical empathy: relation between attitude and behavior**

		Like to live		
	In	*Sicily*	*Outside Sicily*	*Total*
Tried to move	No	157	123	280
	Yes	25	89	114
	Total	182	212	394

First comes the attitude, then the action according to the best prescription about how rational, Western man should behave. The curvilinear correlation is $Q = 0.62$ and the percentage difference 28% (with only 6% in the non-scale category), so the pattern is relatively clear. The methodological question is now whether one shall base the analysis on the attitudinal question, on the behavioral question or on some simple index based on both and using the almost cumulative nature of the correlation.

We actually tried all three possibilities, and the results were extremely similar when compared, which is not strange since the meaning after all is very close, and there is high intercorrelation. All three have to do with desire to move; all three are relatively simple and intuitive. But we preferred the behavioral indicator as our main instrument because it seems more serious. It requires more of the 'movers', they have to have committed themselves by some minimal action, or at least believe they have done so. And we decided against the index based on both because it mixes attitudinal with behavioral items, which in turn introduces differences in interpretation at the different levels of the 'desire to move' or the 'efforts to move' variable. To explore what these variables actually measure, Table 4.1.2 shows how they relate to the villages.

Of special interest are the 20% who merely display negative empathy; there is nowhere they want to go, but a somewhere where they do not want to stay: *here*. There is something corresponding to this in the

* Fourteen respondents were unclear.

184

Table 4.1.2. *If you had a choice, where would you like to live here, or elsewhere? percentage*

	In this house	In Sicily	In Italy	In Europe	In the United States	Somewhere else no matter where	Total
MONTAGNA	34	9	23	8	8	18	100
COLLINA	33	11	9	1	25	21	100
MARINA	48	6	7	0	20	19	100
Average	37	9	13	4	17	20	100

other Table 4.1.3. Here the percentage reflecting some kind of anomia is even higher: 27% would not try to move 'because it is impossible', and if we add the next two categories we find that about half the population feels frustrated in their efforts to move.

Table 4.1.3. *Have you ever tried to move? Do you think it would be possible? percentage*

	No, because I do not want to	No, because it is impossible	Yes, but in vain	Yes, but will not succeed	Yes, and may succeed	Total
MONTAGNA	36	31	18	4	11	100
COLLINA	43	26	24	1	6	100
MARINA	60	20	17	0	3	100
Average	44	27	20	2	7	100

Let us first see how these Tables square with what we have predicted from the demographic extrapolation in Table 2.2.4. According to the calculation, the ordering of the villages in terms of net migration tendency was Montagna–Collina–Marina, with Collina closer to Montagna than to Marina (the potential expressed by the percentage differences 11%, 8% and −2% respectively). According to Table 4.1.2, the ordering is Marina in last place with Montagna and Collina well ahead, and according to Table 4.1.3, it is exactly as predicted — using the first column in both Tables. Thus the correspondence seems to be satisfactory and particularly for the behavioral variable, which is one more reason for using this rather than the attitudinal variable as our basic indicator in this connection.

One cannot say, on the basis of these figures only, whether the desire to move, and the efforts to move, are 'high' or 'low'. However, in spring 1959 and spring 1960 we happened to ask the same question of a random sample in a city highly involved in racial conflict in one of the Southern United States, and it turned out that 77% in 1959 and 80% in 1960 had never considered moving. In 1961 the question 'where would you like to live' was asked of a random sample in a small Norwegian fishing village comparable to the Sicilian villages both in terms of being predominantly in the primary sector and in terms of isolation. Sixty-four per cent wanted to stay (50% in 'the same house'), and the majority of the movers wanted only to move to the nearest town. We would regard both as relatively integrated, harmonious communities in spite of the racial problems in one and the uncertainties in connection with fishing and the future of fisheries in the other. Thus, the Tables seem to reflect well the combination of dissatisfaction, frustration and desire to get away that dominate these villages. When only between a third and a half of the population really want to stay something basic must be wrong. The amount of dissatisfaction seems much higher than what can be tolerated in a healthy community.

This being said, the attention shifts to the differences between the villages, and not so much in terms of different *potential* for migration as in terms of different *goals* of migration. All three villages have their fraction of people who just want to get away, but then there is a clear difference: people from Montagna want to get to continental Italy, i.e. to the North; and people from Collina and Marina want to get to the United States. With the quota restrictions and the costs of travel this desire is very often doomed to end in frustration (65% of them report frustration in their efforts as against 54% of the villagers with the more modest wish of going to continental Italy), but this is not our focus of interest. Rather, it is the interesting change in geographical perspective: *the closer we come to the coast, the higher the percentage oriented toward the United States.* To be audacious in the interior is to dream of a future in Torino and Milano, to be audacious on the coast is to dream of other coasts, far away, joined to them not by common nationality but by the link of communication they know best, the ocean. As is well known because of their special impact on United States society some of them realize the dream, and leave only house and relatives behind.[4]

Thus, geographical maps are not sociological maps: they illustrate physical proximity, but not psychological or sociological proximity. More concretely, we would expect, as we move toward the coast, the link to 'Sicily' to weaken, to 'Italy' to strengthen first and then to weaken, and the link to 'abroad' to strengthen. All three predictions are simple consequences of a principle of increasing cosmopolitanism

186

as one moves from the isolated interior to the more participant coastal region: wider regions of the world emerge in the minds of men.

As a partial test of this hypothesis we asked the villagers 'Where do your wife's relatives, who do not live with you in the same house, live?' We got a large variety of answers showing the wide distribution of the numerous kinfolk of these people, indicating where former residents of the same villages had chosen to go (Table 4.1.4).

Table 4.1.4. *Relative size of contact potentials (proportions of numbers)*

No. of villagers with relatives in	MONTAGNA	COLLINA	MARINA
Italy/Sicily	0.60	0.73	0.24
Abroad/Sicily	0.47	0.95	1.00
Abroad/Italy	0.79	1.30	4.30

All three trends are as predicted: 'abroad' outdoes both Sicily and Italy as one moves toward the coast, but Italy more quickly because it is no alternative relative to the proximity of 'abroad'. This is of some importance for the following, because it means that however similar the *pushes* away from the villages may be, the places toward which people are *pulled* do at least have very different names, even if they may represent the same in terms of mental opportunities in the images held by the villagers. It should be noticed, however, that 'many relatives in X' does mean a potential for contact with X, a bridgehead in X and a proof that it is possible to go to X, but not necessarily an incentive to move to X. It may also mean a permanent loss of illusions because of some relative's failure, or that one is sustained from X, or that X is so filled with immigrants from Sicily that they want no more. For these reasons, we assume, there is no correlation between efforts to leave and distribution of relatives. Nevertheless, Table 4.1.4 gives some indication of where the contact has been directed so far, and where models for possible imitation are located.

The consistency in all these findings seems to justify our use of the behavioral variable. In other words, our indicator of ability to imagine oneself in other places is not the expression of the general human feeling that 'wo ich nicht bin, dort ist das Glück', but the report about at least some effort to get 'dort'. More precisely, we shall use the following trichotomy based on the answers to the question 'Have you ever tried to move? Do you think it might be possible?', as follows:

Stayers	'No, because I do not want to'	44%
In betweens	'No, because it is not possible'	28%
Movers	'Yes', with additional information	28%

However, we must know more in detail how the 'effort question' relates to the 'desire question'. For that reason, let us look at the relation between the two questions we have studied so far, to see *where* people who want to leave want to go — and to see how much consistency there is in the answers (Table 4.1.5). First of all it should be noticed that the three most conspicuous figures in the Table all tell the same story: that they who *want* to stay above all want to stay exactly where they are — in the very same house. And the respondents who really want to move, want above all to go 'abroad', not to 'continental Italy' (this is less true for Montagna, because of a different space perspective), and certainly not to somewhere else in Sicily.

Further, we see that there is considerable consistency in the sense that the two questions are very heavily correlated for all three villages. On the other hand, there are people who say they have tried to move *and* that they want to live 'in this house'. The simple explanation is probably that they *would* like to live 'in this house' but that they feel the external circumstances are so difficult that they nevertheless consider moving; they would like 'this house' to be somewhere else. And there are people who say they have never tried to move *and* that they would like to live abroad — probably for the simple reason that to dream is one thing, to act upon the dream an entirely different matter. But the

Table 4.1.5. *Have you ever tried to leave, and where would you like to live?*

	MONTAGNA			COLLINA			MARINA		
	Stay-ers	In be-tweens	Mov-ers	Stay-ers	In be-tweens	Mov-ers	Stay-ers	In be-tweens	Mov-ers
In this house	61	16	18	65	10	11	69	33	0
In Sicily, somewhere	8	10	8	13	10	11	7	0	10
In continental Italy	13	27	26	5	12	11	7	0	15
Abroad	8	18	28	11	45	26	10	21	45
Anywhere else	10	29	20	6	23	41	7	46	30
Total	100	100	100	100	100	100	100	100	100
(N)	(53)	(49)	(50)	(63)	(42)	(46)	(61)	(24)	(20)

percentage differences in the top line are all at least 43 percentage points, which to us serves as a justification of the trichotomy we have introduced.

Most interesting, however, is the insight we get into the people we have called 'in betweens', the people who report that they have not tried to move 'because it is not possible'. An answer that would be 'in between' geographically for them would be 'somewhere else in Sicily', but this is not what they report. Nor can they be discarded as pretenders, since they show about the same consistency as the movers; only 17% want to stay 'in this house' as against 12% of the 'movers'. For all three villages a heavy proportion in this group answer 'anywhere else, no matter where' — for Montagna and Marina this is even the largest category. Hence, we seem entitled to say that the in betweens are people with less clear ideas; they may feel the push away from the place they live but no specific pull toward new places. In a sense this makes the category particularly important because it signals a diffuse dissatisfaction of a particularly unconstructive kind. And this is actually the perspective we shall make use of for a deeper understanding of the desire to move: it means a relocation of the human spirit, away from the villages where their bodies are — either to *somewhere* else or just to *anywhere* else. On the other hand, this also means that the in betweens strictly speaking are not really 'between' the other two categories, but rather on a separate dimension, probably more tapping apathy and general despair than some degree of readiness to move.

The task ahead of us now, after knowing *how many* want to move, is to find out *who* these different categories of people are by checking systematically how desire to move correlates with a number of important variables. This will be done, as in the preceding chapter, by analyzing the total sample where the villages are similar enough, and the three villages separately where that is needed.[5]

4.2. *Who the movers are : traditionalists or innovators*

In a sense this section plays the same role here as the section 3.2 in the preceding chapter. We want to try out the variable on basic problems in these villages to see how it fits into the picture we think we know from less systematic data, and to explore new insights. So the first question is: Who are the movers, traditionalists or innovators?

The answer to that question may seem rather obvious. Since to move is an innovation it itself, we might suspect that the desire to move would draw on the same psychological sources as general inventiveness and 'modernization'. This is not obvious, however. In well-integrated and expanding cities, the potential movers are more likely to be among the people who cannot adjust to rapid modernization. If we accept inability to adjust, to put up with the external conditions, as a basic underlying factor, then we should get the opposite conclusion in our case: the three villages we study are *not* undergoing modernization, they are *traditional* to the extreme and their *ethos* is that of preservation rather than innovation. Hence the maladjusted, the leavers, should be higher than average on innovation perspectives. Some of our data in Table 4.2.1 illustrate this point fully.

Table 4.2.1. *Efforts to leave and diagnosis and cure for the villages (total sample, percentage)**

	What is the main problem?			Can conditions be improved?			
	Don't know	To get work	To get industry	Don't know	Improve what is	To get work	To get industry
Stayers	58	36	47	71	51	34	42
In betweens	19	31	18	11	29	40	24
Movers	23	33	35	18	20	26	34
Total	100	100	100	100	100	100	100
(N)	(31)	(168)	(49)	(28)	(55)	(90)	(93)

The Table gives confirmation to our suspicion. Since 'to get work' does not specify how it should be done, it means that an evil is pointed out and a cure of a symptom prescribed — but it does not indicate much in terms of true spirit of innovation. Nor does 'to get industry'; it is an answer that is easily uttered, but we feel nevertheless justified in classifying it as more innovative thinking. For the second half of the Table there is an additional category, 'improve what is' — which we have put between 'don't know' and 'to get work' when it comes to radicalness. It means doing something, but nothing new.

Both parts of the Table now tell the same story: *with increasing radical and innovative responses we also get an increasing desire to move, and a decreasing desire to stay.* Since this holds true for both questions (and also for all three villages when taken separately, with some minor exceptions), we tend to have much confidence in the proposition that *those who try*

* The other answers given do not belong to the traditionalist innovator continuum.

190

to move are overrepresented among the most valuable from the point of view of modernization.

This does not mean that we necessarily agree that industrialization is valuable, only that *if* industrialization is wanted, some basis for it in the local public attitudes is highly desirable — if not absolutely necessary. Probably the movers are quite often people who have ideas, dreams, visions as to the future and who feel immensely frustrated when they confront their dreams not only with the dismal present, but also with the not-very-different future they see emerging from this present in which they live. This does not mean, however, that these people will retain their ideas and remain innovators as immigrants in highly industrialized milieus in, for instance, Northern Italy. It does not take much to appear 'modern' by our criteria and by the standards of the village in Western Sicily — further, the attitude is probably just as much a reaction and reflection of local conflicting groups as an attitude internalized because of some kind of rational reasoning.

Let this be enough now about the relation between efforts to get away, the spirit of innovation and the theme of migration as a drainage of talent. There is another theme at least equally prominent in day-to-day conversations in these villages as the theme of modernization: *power*. Essentially, we are interested more in active forces perceived as pushes away from the villages than in the more or less specialized frustration felt by people who somehow want modernization of the communities. More precisely, we were interested in the eternal theme of illegitimate power, a theme which partly coincides with the theme of *mafia*. Our question looks very simplistic, but has a definite meaning within the Sicilian situation: 'Who has the power in this village, the priest, the mayor, the police, the rich, others?', where 'others', *'certi altri'* — is usually taken to mean *'mafia'*. We shall first present a comparison of the three villages in Table 4.2.2.

As we have seen in the preceding section, Marina is the village with, relatively speaking, the lowest migration potential, and this Table gives us some new insights into *why*. In addition to the frustration variable

Table 4.2.2. *Perception of who has the local power, percentage*

	Priest	Mayor	Police	The rich	'Others'	All of them	DK	Total
MONTAGNA	19	34	4	4	1	32	6	100
COLLINA	7	27	3	5	23	31	4	100
MARINA	5	57	8	5	1	17	7	100

alluded to above, there seems to be some relation between efforts to move and coincidence between major sources of perceived power and the formally legitimate power, i.e. the mayor. Where the mayor is not seen as the main power wielder by the majority, there is obviously a widespread local theory to the effect that 'there are certain others behind'. Regardless of whether such a local theory is true or not — and it is most likely to be true to some extent — the consequence must be a widespread *feeling* of lack of legitimate authority, and hence of less reason to obey. The latter, here mentioned as an effect, may certainly also be the cause: with the alleged basic lack of discipline, a theory that deprives the legitimate authority of power and the power wielder of legitimacy will obviously be conductive to anomic power relations. A consequence of this may be a lack of identification with the community, and hence increased manifestations of a desire to leave.

If Marina presents a picture of integration, in the sense that the majority attribute most power to the mayor, the other two villages do not. The common factor in Montagna and Collina is the attribution of power to 'all of them' — a tautology the interviewers have not been able to break up. Evidently, this also points to a feeling of 'conspiracy at the top' in these two villages, and the feeling may be rather widespread since as many as one third feel this way in both villages. But then the differences become apparent: whereas the priest is singled out in Montagna, the 'others' are in Collina. Both assertions correspond well to what is generally considered to be true for these two villages: in Montagna considerable power was attributed to the *arciprete*, and Collina is generally seen as *mafioso*. The category 'others' was designed exactly to tap this — and the answer 'others' was often given in the appropriate way, whispering and/or smiling: 'certi altri'.

At this point one may ask: but if this information about the priest in Montagna and the mafia in Collina were all known in advance, why ask the question at all? Because it was not known in advance, and hence had to be shown, *how these factors are perceived in the local population*.[1] So far, we have shown that the village where more than 50% see power as *legitimate* is also the village where more than 50% want to stay — and we have similarly shown that the villages where more than 50% see power as *illegitimate* are also the villages where more than 50% want to leave. This is hardly a coincidence, as we have reasoned.

But from what we have said so far there are many ways in which perceived illegitimate power may express itself in a high migration potential. The *direct* way is simply this: the respondent who perceives

192

illegitimacy is also the respondent who wants to leave — and in a sense this is the most immediate and tempting conclusion, but at the risk of committing the ecological fallacy. Before we look at the data, however, one should also remember the more *indirect* way in which these factors may be connected: the people who perceive illegitimacy in the power distribution may also be people close to legitimate or illegitimate centers of power, people who aspire to power and hence have a motivation to remain. At the same time, their definition of the situation may spread to the total community as a general disease, causing a certain amount of anomia and general dissatisfaction. The data, however, command us to accept the simpler rather than the more complex hypothesis (Table 4.2.3).

Table 4.2.3. *Desire to move, and perception of local power, percentage* *

	MONTAGNA			COLLINA			MARINA		
	To the mayor	To 'all of them'	Illegit-imate power	To the mayor	To 'all of them'	Illegit-imate power	To the mayor	To 'all of them'	Illegit-imate power
Stayers	30	28	29	40	32	24	56	15	22
In betweens	41	33	22	14	33	50	67	25	4
Movers	32	34	30	20	26	48	50	15	30
Percentage difference	+2	+6	+1	−20	−6	+24	−6	0	+8
Average	34	32	27	27	31	38	57	17	19

The Table is interesting in showing how the hypothesis has to be modified: it is confirmed, indeed, for Collina with its mafia and also for Marina, but not for Montagna (but neither is it disconfirmed). In other words, it also depends on *what* is seen as the source of illegitimate power. Evidently, the hypothesis holds particularly well when the illegitimacy is due to others (equaling mafia), but not when it is due to the priest. Actually, among the stayers in Collina only 5% attributed power to the mafia, while 37% of the movers did so. For Marina, the police seem to play a similar role (7% vs. 20%), and this also has its solid basis in local facts and thinking. Thus, the data presented in this section have the additional virtue of validating our method: by means of standardized interviews it is not at all impossible to catch local issues that are more idiosyncratic, less structural, more topical.[2]

* The percentages do not add up to 100 horizontally because the DK's have been deleted. The Table should be interpreted vertically.

4.3. *Who the movers are: social participation*

As mentioned, we are interested in knowing what differentiates the movers from the stayers for two reasons: the possible contribution the movers can make to the society outside (the factor emphasized by Lerner), and the loss their departure will entail for the village they sooner or later will leave, the local community. Our basic hypothesis is actually that this loss takes place long before they leave because of the 'psychic mobility'. They cannot at the same time nourish plans of a complete departure and participate fully in social institutions. That is, they will gradually transfer the focus of their social participation from local media to more general media. Thus, our first hypothesis was that a transfer of interest from the local level to the national and international levels would take place, but after some pilot projects we changed the hypothesis to one about a transfer from local participation to participation in generalized media, such as music, TV, cinema, etc. Later, maybe, when they are integrated in a new setting in the big cities in the north comes the phase of integration into national and perhaps even international frameworks. Down in Western Sicily even the most empathic personality does not have sufficient perspective to take roots in a new, and possibly committing, area of identification.

To the these hypotheses we asked of all respondents their degree of participation in six forms of activities: newspapers, weeklies, radio, TV, cinema and church. Of the six we consider the first and the last to be potentially more committing on the local level. Cognitive and evaluative standards for local behavior are expressed in either, whereas the standards expressed in the other four media are more generalized. We would expect of the person who considers moving some kind of anticipatory socialization that may actually have triggered the desire to move, hence more participation in generalized media and less in media with a more local focus.

The data are given in Table 4.3.1. We have simplified somewhat by omitting the in betweens, since our hypotheses are only about the differences between the pure cases, between the movers and the stayers. Further, we have not looked at degrees of participation, but tested the hypotheses in terms of differentials in *not* participating.

According to the hypotheses we should have positive signs for the first and the last items, negative signs for the rest. Out of a total of 18 predictions of signs we make three errors, or four errors if we count the zero difference as a disconfirmation. Fourteen out of 18 is 74%,

Table 4.3.1. *Efforts to move and differential lack of social participation, percentage difference movers vs. stayers*

	MONTAGNA	COLLINA	MARINA	Type
Newspapers	+10	− 1	+ 7	local
Weeklies	0	− 3	− 4	general
Radio	− 1	−12	−24	general
Television	− 2	−11	−19	general
Movies	−11	−13	+14	general
Church	+ 3	− 3	+11	local

which we consider a relatively satisfactory degree of confirmation, especially since three of the four errors are very small in magnitude (three or below).

Thus, there may be something to the hypothesis. A dislocation of one's identity from the local scene to 'somewhere else' is accompanied not only by increasing use of general media of social participation, but also by decreasing use of media with a more local focus. The consequence of this is very little difference between the two groups where total participation is concerned. We also controlled these findings for possible influence of age and social position, and they stood up against that test.[1]

4.4. *Who the movers are : age and education*

Let us begin our effort to locate the movers in the social structure with the most basic facts about any person — *when* he was born, and *where* he was born — and see what effects these variables have on his feeling of 'belonging' in the villages. In this category of variables we

Table 4.4.1. *Efforts to move and age, percentage*

	MONTAGNA			COLLINA			MARINA		
When born :	1871–1900	1901–1920	1921–1950	1871–1900	1901–1920	1921–1950	1871–1900	1901–1920	1921–1950
Stayers	46	38	21	48	46	30	79	58	40
In betweens	26	31	38	19	27	36	17	24	27
Movers	28	31	41	33	27	34	4	18	33
Total	100	100	100	100	100	100	100	100	100
(N)	(39)	(65)	(47)	(27)	(79)	(44)	(24)	(50)	(30)

would also have included a third characteristic of any newborn baby, its sex, but since we always tried to get the *capofamiglia*, our sample consists almost exclusively of males. Of course, we expected the movers above all to be young people (Table 4.4.1).

Uniformly, the efforts to move are seen to depend heavily on age — with the stayers being overrepresented among the *old*. Fifty-six per cent of them want to stay, as against only 29% in the youngest group. This is certainly not strange if we accept the truism that the old movers *have already moved* and hence are not present to answer our questions. But nevertheless, it is interesting to note that something which took place in the past, i.e. an *effort* to move, is more frequently reported among the younger than among the old with their comparatively longer lifespan for such actions.

One simple explanation of this may be that a person who tries actually does get away, so that the chance of finding an old 'mover' is negligible. And another interpretation is that the desire to move catches on among the youth both because of higher pull and higher push forces. Whatever the interpretation may be, however, it is significant to note that the desire to *stay* prevails exactly among those who have already settled in the community and represent the traditional way of life, whereas the desire to *move* is found among those who could be the innovators. If the Table had shown the opposite trend, the young people socialized into positions in the villages might still be willing to concentrate on the village and direct their activities toward it. From the point of view of social change, a movement away from the city emanating from the *top* of the age pyramid might even be beneficial, it might smooth and ease the way for new initiative — but when the drive to get away comes from the bottom and the middle it is correspondingly harmful.

The hypothesis of an increased urge to migrate relative to the period, say, around the first world war — reported by may local residents — is important and needs some independent confirmation. One bit of evidence supplying some confirmation can be obtained from the horizontal line for the in betweens in the Table. Imagine that the effort to get away had been constant. In that case we would expect more movers among the young than among the old, for the simple reason that the old movers have already moved — and this is what we find. But we would also expect more in betweens among the old than among the young because they have had much more time to accumulate the experience that 'it is impossible'. We find the opposite, however, in all three villages, which indicates both that the young people are trying more and that

196

they have had more trials in vain. With only 29% of the young people in the total sample wanting to stay *there are a tremendous unrest and apathy in the coming generation*; and the uniformity of the findings suggests that this can be generalized to much of Western Sicily. Needless to say, the findings are also completely compatible with the migration dents in the population pyramids in Table 2.2.1.

We then move on to the place of birth: To what extent does it predispose for stability to have been born in the same house where one lives later on? We would expect this to make for stability, and if we should try to theorize, we would reason as follows. If a person lives in the house where he was born, then he is probably tied to the village with so many visible and invisible ties that he would most likely be a 'stayer'. If he has moved into the house from somewhere else in the village, then the very fact of moving is no longer unknown to him; he has already had the experience of being uprooted at least once. Further, if he has moved it is probably also because of some factors in the economic structure, for instance that he did not inherit his father's house — factors that make for more incentive to move later on. But on the other hand, if he has moved into the village from the outside, he has probably already made a decisive step — *he has already moved* and may still have his illusions about migration or have lost all of them. Hence, we would expect more stability in this group than among the people who have performed some intra-village moving. The data are shown in Table 4.4.2.

In testing the theory we see that the data from Montagna and Collina confirm it nicely, with more movers among people who are born in the same village, but not in the same house. The data from Marina at least do not contradict the hypothesis — when we exclude the columns for

Table 4.4.2. *Efforts to move and place of birth, percentage**

Where born :	MONTAGNA			COLLINA			MARINA		
	In this house	Same village	Else-where	In this house	Same village	Else-where	In this house	Same village	Else-where
Stayers	42	29	(4)	40	42	(6)	(5)	56	(11)
In betweens	34	33	(4)	40	27	(3)	(1)	25	(4)
Movers	24	38	(3)	20	31	(7)	(1)	19	(4)
Total	100	100	—	100	100	—	—	100	—
(N)	(41)	(95)	(11)	(20)	(113)	(16)	(7)	(77)	(19)

* For four columns the bases are so small that no percentages have been calculated.

which we have not calculated percentages. In other words, it seems that this factor of intra-village moving is of some importance, although it means begging the question: *What makes for intra-village moving?* We also notice in passing that we get a corresponding tendency when we look at where the *wife* (or husband in some few cases) is born: if she is born outside the village, there is a slightly higher tendency to become a mover. Probably, inter-village marriages make for or are caused by a broader space perspective, and hence are conducive to an image of a world with more possibilities. But if the *capofamiglia* is born in the house where he lives and has picked his bride from among the village girls, then he seems to be solidly rooted, although the factor is by no means so decisive as the factor of age.

In conclusion, let us turn to *education*. It is very quickly done since the result is quite simple: neither public education, as such, nor vocational training showed any appreciable correlation with efforts to move (percentage differences 4% and 6%). This was true for the sample as a whole, for the three villages and for all four combinations of social class and social sector — with one exception which we offer for what it may be worth: the farmers. They have an average of 40% who want to stay, but there is a systematic variation with increasing literacy: 54% of the illiterates want to stay, 41% of the medium group do, but only 30% of the farmers with five years or more formal training do. Since education also makes the farmers more conscious of possible social mobility into the tertiary sector, we are probably touching a general phenomenon: *literacy makes the farmer conscious of possibilities he never dreamed of, of getting away within or outside the village; it does not at present give him the arms he needs to improve what he has.* But with this generally negative finding we get one more confirmation of the general theme developed in 3.4: there is no simple relation between education and 'modern' attitudes or behavior: it depends on what is being taught and the position of the educational institution in society — it depends on quality rather than on quantity.[1]

4.5. *Who the movers are: social position*

We then start the search for the socio-economic determinants of the efforts to get away, by trying to locate this drainage of manpower in the *social* structure. Where are the openings, where are the holes in the structure that permit people, if not to escape, at least to think of escaping?

Table 4.5.1. *Efforts to move and social position, by class and sector, percentage*

	Class		Sector	
	Topdogs	Underdogs	Primary sector	Tertiary sector
Stayers	42	44	40	48
In betweens	25	31	34	21
Movers	33	25	26	31
Total	100	100	100	100
(N)	(174)	(234)	(215)	(193)

With section 3.5 in mind we can go straight to the categories known to be fruitful in the description of an individual's social position, and start with class and sector, one at a time (Table 4.5.1).

If we focus the attention on the movers we see immediately that the tendencies are not impressive in magnitude. Typically, the topdogs and the tertiary sector are overrepresented as one might have guessed in advance: those are the stratum and the sector that open most to the outside. The picture is complicated by the fact that the stayers are also overrepresented in the tertiary sector.

What is interesting in the Table is the complementarity between the in betweens. From the left part of the Table it looks as if the amount of satisfaction is about the same in both social classes, whereas the dissatisfaction expresses itself in two different ways: as concrete efforts to move for the higher ones, and diffuse desires to get away for the lower ones. This is also as one might have expected, since dissatisfied people higher up in society have more opportunity to realize their desires to get away.

Let us then immediately combine the two variables to see if there are interaction effects between class and sector (Table 4.5.2). Although the tertiary high category is higher than the others (and the primary low category lower than the others), in migration potential there is little interaction effect, and the differences are actually rather insignificant. What emerges from the Table is only a validation of the finding that there is more migration potential among the high than among the low, sector kept constant, and more among the tertiary than among the primary, class kept constant. However, the differences are so small compared to the effect of, for instance, age that we so far have to conclude that social position *per se* either is not a major determinant of the desire to move, *or its effect is masked by third variables*. On the other hand,

Table 4.5.2. *Efforts to move and social position: class and sector combined, percentage*

	Primary high	*Primary low*	*Tertiary high*	*Tertiary low*
Stayers	40	39	44	52
In betweens	30	37	21	21
Movers	30	24	35	27
Total	100	100	100	100
(N)	(74)	(141)	(100)	(93)

we know that the first interpretation cannot be correct: we know there are hundreds, thousands of poor people who only want to get away, and that there are frustrated people higher up who have run their heads against the wall and see no further possibilities in the villages — they also want to leave. Hence, we have to refine the analysis by introducing more variables. In this analysis we shall stick to class rather than sector as the basic expression of social position, since position in the tertiary sector works both ways; it favors both desire to stay and desire to move away.

In conclusion, let us summarize Table 4.5.1; about class:

The lower the social position,
   the lower the efforts to move (down to one-fourth)
   the higher the apathy and resignation (up to one-third)
   whereas the desire to stay is about constant (above 40%)

But the conclusion is uncertain for two reasons: we have derived it from the total sample (and it does not hold for the tertiary sector, nor does it hold for all the villages separately) and we have only two points on our index of social position, which makes it risky to talk about tendencies. Nevertheless, in very gross terms this is the tendency we found.

But even if this indicator of psychic mobility did not produce heavy correlations with social structure the more pure indicators developed in 3.8 and 3.9 — space perspective and time perspective — may. They are based less on experience and behavior than on general exposure; a part of our theory in 3.5 (Table 3.5.3) was based on the idea that the tertiary sector, and particularly its higher levels, should have easy access to new values. If this is true, one would expect it to show up in a much higher *space perspective*, since this is an expression of how the respondent relates himself to the external, physical world. Our findings are shown in Table 4.5.3.

Table 4.5.3. *Space perspective and social position, percentage*

Space perspective	Social position			
	Primary high	*Primary low*	*Tertiary high*	*Tertiary low*
Low	28	39	18	38
Medium	50	38	33	27
High	22	23	49	35
Total	100	100	100	100
(N)	(74)	(141)	(100)	(93)

The difference between the tertiary and the primary sectors is considerable, as predicted. But the differences within the sectors are also interesting. The tertiary high stand out with their well-developed space perspective — well in accordance with their sensate orientation and their structurally endowed possibilies. The tertiary low are lower in space perspective, but not as low as the primary high. And still lower we find the primary low, which calls our attention to a point to be developed later: *they share a sensate orientation with the tertiary high, but certainly not a well-developed space perspective.* Hence, we have one more reason to believe that their sensate ideologies are not of the same kind, a point already made in connection with Table 3.5.3.

As to the relation between *time perspective* and social position, we have no reason to expect results different from what we found for space perspective. In other words, our obvious prediction is a well-developed time perspective in the tertiary sector, particularly in the high strata, and a poor time perspective in the primary sector, particularly in the lower strata (Table 4.5.4.)

The pattern is actually very similar to what we found for space perspective. The tertiary sector is brought into a contact with the external

Table 4.5.4. *Time perspective and social position, percentage*

Time perspective	Social position			
	Primary high	*Primary low*	*Tertiary high*	*Tertiary low*
Low	23	37	25	31
Medium	46	34	33	29
High	31	29	42	40
Total	100	100	100	100
(N)	(74)	(141)	(100)	(93)

world that forces it to think in more dynamic terms both in space and time. And again we see how the *braccianti* have a kind of sensateness different from the tertiary high: the distribution for time perspective is just the opposite one.[1]

4.6. *Who the movers are: economic position*

With the failure to explain efforts to move in terms of social position alone, we turn to economic position, which should give more impressive results according to local opinion. As a measure of economic position we use the measure developed in 3.6, the index of standard of living, with the warning that the measure is not 'sector free'; it is biased toward making people working in the primary sector more poor. This, however, is intentional: part of the general upheaval of our century is precisely the effort to equalize patterns of living in the city and in the country-side, partly changing the countryside, but mainly by leaving it.

We expected the percentage of stayers to decrease uniformly with standard of living, and this is precisely what we get (Table 4.6.1).

Table 4.6.1. *Efforts to leave and standard of living (total sample, percentage)*

	Standard of living			
	High	*Medium*	*Low*	*Average*
Stayers	52	48	37	44
In betweens	17	26	35	28
Movers	31	26	28	28
Total	100	100	100	100
(N)	(108)	(99)	(201)	(408)

This is indeed rather trivial. What is not trivial is that the increasing tendency with decreasing standard of living is found not in the category of movers, but in the category of in betweens. The immediate inter-pretation is that what increases with decreasing standard of living is not the concrete efforts to move, but the desire not to stay, together with low-class apathy, justified or not. The tendency toward diffuse dissatis-faction increases with decreasing standard of living. Actually, this tendency is even more pronounced if we do not collapse the index values for standard of living but take the whole range of standard of living

202

from zero to six into account (from 16% to 39%). This sounds reasonable from the point of view of increasing diffuseness and lack of clarity and mastery of one's own situation with decreasing standard of living. To summarize the Table:

The lower the standard of living,
  the lower the desire to stay (down to one-third)
  the higher the apathy and resignation (up to one-third)
  whereas the efforts to move are about constant (about one-third)

This is actually so important for the analysis to come that we present data for the villages separately, but only as percentage differences in Table 4.6.2.

Table 4.6.2. *Efforts to leave and standard of living (village, percentage)*

| | Standard of living Percentage differences high — low | | | |
	MONTAGNA	COLLINA	MARINA	Total
Stayers	+16	+10	+13	+15
In betweens	−21	−14	−20	−18
Movers	+ 5	+ 4	+ 7	+ 3
Total	0	0	0	0

In other words, the finding holds for all villages. It should be noticed that this is no tautology; the total correlation might well have arisen without similar correlations for all the villages that make up the total sample.

Logically, the next step might now have been to break down the original table (4.6.1) not only by villages, but also by constituent items. We have done this, but there is no reason to report the results in detail: all correlations are as expected except for some aberrances in the Table for animals in the house — probably for the reasons already advanced in connection with that item. The highest correlation had to do with the number of residents per room, so this seems to be tapping the major cluster of factors causing an incentive not to want to stay. The apathy among the people who are packed very densely together is among the highest encountered.

203

So far, so good. We have demonstrated that social position and particularly economic position do play a role, but the total picture is confusing. First of all, we know that occupation and standard of living are very strongly correlated, so it would not be unreasonable to expect these two variables to yield the same kinds of results when run against degree of belongingness. In one sense they do: the lower the social and economic position, the higher the tendency to see migration as impossible, just as we might expect. But, apart from this, the findings diverge. With decreasing *social* position there is less tendency to *move* (with the tendency to stay relatively constant), whereas with decreasing *economic* position there is less tendency to *stay* (with the tendency to move relatively constant). Although these findings are not at all contradictory — since high correlation does not mean that social and economic position are the same — they ask for a deeper understanding of the interplay between social and economic position. In other words, what is the role of the total socioeconomic position of the inhabitants in these villages?

Since we have worked with two levels of social position (topdogs and underdogs) and three levels of economic position (high, medium and low standard of living), we get the six possible combinations shown in Diagram 4.6.1.

Diagram 4.6.1. *The socio-economic space, with distribution of the sample, percentage*

Social position			
Topdogs	a: 15	b: 11	c: 17
Underdogs	d: 34	e: 13	f: 10
	Low	Medium	High → Economic position

We would expect the probability of being a mover or stayer to depend on the combination of the two variables and, more particularly, on the degree of balance between them. Actually, we have three classes of combinations:

1) *Balanced combinations:* c and d (topdogs with high standard, underdogs with low standard)

2) *Medium combinations:* b and e (topdogs and underdogs, both with medium standard)

3) *Unbalanced combinations:* a and f (topdogs with low standard, underdogs with high standard)

204

The last group is most interesting since it contains the deviant cases — and the percentages in Diagram 4.6.1 clearly indicate a tendency in the total structure toward the balanced and away from the unbalanced combinations. This can be seen as an expression of *rank equilibration* at work: the poor topdog will try to improve his standard and the well-to-do underdog his position; they will try to convert resources in their high position into mobility away from the low position. As extreme types we might also expect them to be extreme in terms of migration potential — but to which side? To be able to make more than just an educated guess, an effort to really understand the situation of these two extreme types is indispensable.

Social position carries social prestige, and economic position carries the means of subsistence — the first is good, the latter a necessity. With low *economic* standing, *staying* becomes difficult because the necessities of life are not met — with low social standing, *moving* becomes difficult because of the decrease in perspective, the lack of initiative and connections, etc. among people in the lower classes in society. Besides, we have good reasons to believe (4.7) that an unsatisfied desire for social mobility predisposes for a desire to *stay*. This is only what we have already said and demonstrated in the preceding sections — but reformulated so as to facilitate the deduction of some predictions about the unbalanced combinations.

The topdog has the advantage of his class when it comes to such factors as perspectives and connections, and if in addition he is poor he will have the incentive of all poor not to stay and the added incentive of the topdog poor to find some means of rank equilibration. He is already on the top of the local social pyramid, and if he cannot add to his income in the village, there are no more possibilities for him. In other words, the village makes it impossible for him to *have* as much as he should relative to what he *is* — and if he does not think this can be rectified *inside* the village it is only natural if he thinks a more equitable solution (to him) might be the result of mobility outside the village. In other words, *he has all good reasons to move*, and we would expect a heavy potential migration in this category.

For the well-to-do underdog everything we have just said can be reversed. He has the disadvantages of his class which will tend to tie him to the place; besides, he does not have the incentive of the poor not to stay. Like the poor topdog he may feel the need for rank equilibration. But his need for upward social mobility is most likely to be projected on to the local village. Actually he may even feel grateful to the village since it has made it possible for him to *have* more than he *is*. In other words, *he has all good reasons to stay*, so we would expect a very low potential migration in this category.

Since these are the two combinations leading to extreme predictions in either direction, we would expect all the other four to be in between. The question is only whether there is anything in what we have said that can give us some basis for ranking the balanced and medium combinations in terms of potential migration. The *balanced* combinations, according to our theory, are exposed to cross-pressures and since we have no basis for deciding *a priori* which force is stronger, we have to content ourselves by saying that the relation between stayers and movers will be close to what is found in the total sample, i.e. 'normal'. And we cannot say much more about the *medium* combinations either. The cutting points are too arbitrary, the sample too small, so it seems that the best hypothesis we can end up with, reconciling the fragments we have presented so far, is:

Highest potential migration: a, the poor topdog
Lowest potential migration: f, the well-to-do underdog
Medium or average potential migration: b, c, d, e, all the others

The only problem that remains is the measurement of what we have called 'potential migration'. The difficulty is that our hypotheses are formulated partly in terms of stayers and partly in terms of movers, so they have to be dealt with symmetrically. At the same time, the effect of the problematic (but in this case not so interesting) in betweens should be eliminated. One simple way of achieving all of this is as follows: in the total sample there are 44% stayers and 28% movers which means a surplus of 44% − 28% = 16% of stayers over the movers. Any category which has more than a sixteen point percentage difference has a surplus of stayers; any category which has less has a surplus of movers. We shall make use of this measure, and thus neutralize the differentials in 'in betweens' – frequencies, but also use the uncorrected percentages of stayers and movers so as to avoid the danger of *ad hoc* table reading (Table 4.6.3, page 207).

We can then compare the hypothesis with the outcomes, using all three ways of reading Table 4.6.3: Table 4.6.4, page 207.

In other words, out of the $3 \times 6 = 18$ predictions made, 15 or 83% turned out as expected; with two of the indicators the fit between predictions and outcomes is perfect. In addition, it should be noticed

Table 4.6.3. *Efforts to leave and the six socio-economic categories, percentage*

Social position :	Topdogs			Underdogs			Total sample
Economic position :	Low	Medium	High	Low	Medium	High	
Combination :	a	b	c	d	e	f	
Stayers	32	47	47	38	48	58	44
In betweens	30	29	17	38	24	15	28
Movers	38	24	36	24	28	27	28
Total	100	100	100	100	100	100	100
(N)	(60)	(45)	(69)	(141)	(54)	(39)	(408)
Percentage differences :							
Stayers vs. movers	− 6	+23	+11	+14	+20	+31	+16
For total sample	+16	+16	+16	+16	+16	+16	+16
Difference between the differences	−22	+7	− 5	− 2	+ 4	+15	0

that Table 4.6.3 also constitutes a very good confirmation of the basic hypothesis in section 4.5. Hence, we feel that the problem raised has been answered within the limits of our data.

Thus, the key to the interpretations of the findings in the last two sections lies in the *interplay* between the two kinds of positions. It should be pointed out that neither the hypothesis nor the data are trivial in the sense that 'this was only what was to be expected'. Imagine that we know nothing about the villages except that there was a high migration potential and that the factors of social and economic position were important. A number of alternative hypotheses might be suggested on this meager basis.

For instance; the social position is what a person *is*; the economic position is what he *has*. The case of the poor topdog is the case of the person 'who has less than he is' (his economic standing detracts from

Table 4.6.4. *The socio-economic hypothesis : predictions and outcomes*

Potential migration :	Highest	Medium	Lowest
Prediction	a	b, c, d, e	f
Percentage of stayers	a	b, c, d, e	f
Percentage of movers	a	c, e, f	b, d
Difference of percentage differences	a	b, c, d, e	f

207

his social status) and the well-to-do underdog 'has more than he is' (he has something added to his social status). The first of them has *less*, the second *more* than he may feel entitled to on the basis of what he *is*. But from this alone follows nothing about migration except, perhaps, a tendency toward equilibration. Hence, based on the evidence we already possessed, the hypothesis was introduced that *the topdog will try his rank equilibration outside, the underdog inside the village*. But imagine that the villages were economically expansive so that the respondents felt that there were more chances of *economic* mobility inside the village than outside. In that case the topdogs would be able to add to their income and achieve balances, whereas the underdogs could only achieve even more discrepancy. Even if this might not trouble the latter — after all, money is money; they might like it — it should at least lead to a lower tendency among the topdogs to leave. Hence, with a different assumption about economic growth in the villages we would have been led to very different predictions.

There is also another possibility that could yield the opposite result: we have reasoned as if the topdogs were *troubled by what the low economic standing detracted* from their social standing — why could they not just as well be *pleased by what their high social standing added* to their miserable standard of living? And correspondingly for the underdogs? We feel the key lies in the words 'is' and 'has' above, and that the social position somehow is more salient so that 'less' in economic position gives a motivation to move, and 'more' in economic position a motivation to stay. Even if the findings from sections 3.6 and 3.7 do not warrant the use of the stronger terms 'ascribed' and 'achieved' in connection with the two dimensions, there is clearly some asymmetry present with the villages offering more opportunity for economic than for social mobility. Thus, our data also give a basis for ruling out two additional hypotheses: the obviously unreasonable idea that in a highly improverished village there should not be the dream of better economic opportunities elsewhere, and the less unreasonable idea that economic position should be more salient than social position.

And this gives us an occasion to return to the problem discussed in 3.6: Which dimension is more ascribed, social position or economic position? The general theory is that aggressive responses should be forthcoming when the individual is much higher on the achieved dimension than on the ascribed dimension. Since efforts to move can be interpreted as an aggressive move against the local system ('you do not deserve me'), the conclusion from these data seems to be that social position is the achieved position, economic position the ascribed one; 'social high, economic low' leads to a high desire to move, whereas 'social low, economic high' leads to a particularly low desire to move. In a sense this is reasonable since economic position is so determined by inheritance in these societies: one inherits a house, but since the societies are not based on caste one does not inherit the social position, one makes the social position. But this does not explain the finding from Table 3.6.8, that relatively well-to-do people in low social positions nevertheless have radical inclinations in the sense of being sensate. Hence, the conclusion above can only be seen as tentative, but nevertheless sheds some additional light on the total structure.[1]

4.7. *Who the movers are : social perspective*

We have now located the maximum and minimum of motivation to leave the villages in the socio-economic matrix and turn next to the dynamic dimension of socio-economic position: mobility. By and large we shall use the categories developed in 3.7 with the difference that our focus will be more on class than on sector — just as in the preceding section. Essentially we have two kinds of mobility in our data, actual and desired, and we relate both of them to the efforts to leave (Table 4.7.1).

Table 4.7.1. *Efforts to leave, actual mobility and desired mobility (class, percentage)*

	Actual father-self mobility			Desired self-son mobility		
	Downward	*Stable*	*Upward*	*Unclear*	*Stable*	*Upward*
Stayers	54	41	33	52	41	42
In betweens	31	30	22	30	24	32
Movers	15	29	45	18	35	26
Total	100	100	100	100	100	100

The Tables are based on the crude division of the social positions in 'topdog' and 'underdog'. Nevertheless, the pattern is quite clear: more *upward* mobility *experienced*, more desire to *move*; more *downward* mobility *experienced*, more desire to *stay*. As to the *desired* mobility, the pattern is less clear. The Table should be compared with Table 4.5.1, first part, to which it is very similar. This is no coincidence. To desire upward mobility one has to be an underdog. But there are many underdogs who desire horizontal mobility only (see Table 3.7.4), so the similarity of the two Tables is not entirely trivial. It reflects the complementarity between apathy and action for low vs. high in social structure when confronted with the migration issue. But the inescapable conclusion seems to be: *it is experienced mobility, not desired mobility, that enters as a determinant of efforts to leave the village.* Thus, one is reminded of the finding in 4.4, of how experienced geographical mobility predisposes for a desire to move.

Let us now concentrate on the experienced mobility as a function of the respondent's own position, and see how the efforts to move vary as a function of both position and mobility experience. For simplicity we shall concentrate on the number of stayers, since the in betweens and the movers always seem to have a complementary relation to each other (Table 4.7.2).

Table 4.7.2. *Efforts to leave, social position and experienced mobility*

Mobility	Percentage of stayers		
	Downward	*Stable*	*Upward*
Topdogs, high	impossible	45	33
Underdogs, low	54	38	impossible

The two percentages that are underlined in the Table are, of course, identical with the corresponding percentages in Table 4.7.1. What the Table shows is only this: people with no mobility have 41% stayers, and when split on social position we get 45% stayers for the topdogs and 38% for the underdogs. But these percentages fall between the two extremes, which shows that:

The highest desire to stay has the underdog who has experienced downward mobility

The lowest desire to stay has the topdog who has experienced upward mobility

It should be pointed out how contrary this is to what many would expect. *The desire to move, or rather, not to stay, is not a consequence of failure, but a consequence of success.* The general theory behind this seems to be about as follows. For the underdog who wants to get up, the village is still spacious enough socially, in the sense that there are still positions

210

for him and his sons to fill. He is at the bottom, or close to the bottom, of the village social system — and he may see the top. As we have seen in 3.7, he wants to get up, except for a minority, but it is reasonable to assume that he does not see much of the world outside (compare the findings in Table 3.8.4). Hence, he experiences the pull from the top of the village, but not so much from the outside. *This makes the village his battleground, both for him and for his sons, the village is the place where he is going to assert and affirm himself*. Evidently, if he has a reasonable standard of living he may even look forward to the battle to regain the social positions lost — and that squares well with the findings in the preceding section.

Quite the contrary for the topdog. He has reached the top of the ladder, he has succeeded within the possibilities of the system. He has exhausted the real and imagined possibilities of the village, and the world outside may open up and exercise its pull on him — of course particularly if he is in the tertiary sector. And if in addition he has a low standard of living — he may have inherited the standard of his underdog father but may have been able to climb socially — there is nothing in his social position to tie him to the village.

The assumption behind this way of reasoning is the desire to *move* and to improve the conditions of oneself and one's family, substantiated by findings in 3.7. But in addition to that comes the idea of the desire to *move on*, to change and control new environments. And then there is the third theme, the theme of limited opportunity, of exhausted possibility. For the underdog there is something left to achieve, and if he has been defeated he has to vindicate himself for the same audience. For the topdog there is nothing left, all permutations have been tried — either the village has to open up and offer more possibilities, or the poor topdog on his way up has to look for the possibilities somewhere else. In other words: *first step up the social ladder inside the village, second step outside*.[1]

4.8. *Who the movers are: space perspective*

The finding of the preceding section was that efforts to move were determined by actual experience, not by desires and wishes for mobility. We shall see that this applies to space perspective too: efforts to move are not linked to an abstract space perspective of the type discussed in 3.8 as much as to space perspective in the sense of travel experiences (Table 4.8.1).

4.8.1. *Efforts to move, space perspective and travel experience, percentage*

	Space perspective				Travel experience			
	High	Medium	Low	Difference	High	Medium	Low	Difference
Stayers	58	33	41	+17	39	39	52	−13
In betweens	15	31	38	−23	25	28	31	− 6
Movers	27	36	21	+ 6	36	33	17	+19
Total	100	100	100	0	100	100	100	0
(N)	(130)	(149)	(129)		(133)	(141)	(134)	

The second Table shows the pattern that anybody would have predicted: travel causes and is caused by a desire to move. But the first Table shows no consistent trend: people high in space perspective are overrepresented among the stayers as well as among the movers. This is an indication of something which will be developed later. On one hand we have an *ideological* cluster where to be sensate in orientation is linked to high social, space and time perspectives. On the other hand we have a *behavioral* cluster of the type we are touching here, where the idea of moving is tied to previous travel experience.

Of course, travel experience is neither necessary nor sufficient, and may enter both as a cause and as an effect of the efforts to move. Travel experience, we have argued in 3.8, develops space perspective if it is accompanied by some kind of motivation and if the travel is not a matter of routine only. Thus, the percentage of movers is lower among those who have been to continental Italy or abroad in connection with military service than among those who have been there for other reasons — as was to be expected. But also military service seems to serve as a kind of eye-opener: the magic of the village as the only conceivable place to live once broken is hard to regain.[1]

4.9. *Who the movers are : time perspective*

According to what we have seen in the two preceding sections we would expect no correlation of any importance between the two kinds of time perspective and efforts to move. The hypothesis is about non-correlation, and is so important for what follows that it has to be shown (Table 4.9.1).

In the first case there are percentage differences, but they are between the stayers and the in betweens and disappear when we control for social

Table 4.9.1. *Efforts to move and time perspectives I and II, percentage*

	Time perspective, village				Time perspective, family			
	High	*Medium*	*Low*	*Difference*	*High*	*Medium*	*Low*	*Difference*
Stayers	55	36	38	+17	50	34	45	+5
In betweens	19	31	36	−17	25	31	28	−3
Movers	26	33	26	0	25	35	27	−2
Total	100	100	100	0	100	100	100	0
(N)	(143)	(142)	(123)		(113)	(110)	(185)	

position. In the second case the percentage differences are too low to merit any attention. Thus, whatever motivates efforts to move, time perspective does not seem to be among the decisive forces. As a matter of fact, since moving takes place in social and geographical space and only to a minor extent in time we did not expect time perspective to be decisive at all, although it may be argued that a condition for moving is the ability to space future events in time so as to do the necessary planning.

However, there is another dimension of the general concept of time perspective, barely touched upon in 3.9 which should enter here, viz. optimism-pessimism. Let us first look at it from a collective point of view, taking the villages as groups. We calculated for all three villages the average assessment of the past and of the future, giving a weight of '−1' to 'worse than today', '0' to 'about the same' and of '+1' to 'better than today'. The evaluation of today, then, was taken as point of reference and given the value 0. We got the results shown in Diagram 4.9.1.

The first thing to be noticed is that we again get the same ordering: the order of optimism about the future is Marina — Collina — Montagna. This is precisely the opposite of the ordering of the migration potential from Table 4.1.3 and actual migration from Tables 2.2.1 and 2.2.4. Montagna and Collina are very close, however, and it is difficult to know which of the following reasonings is more correct: a black image of the past conduces to local dynamism keeping the image of the future constant (and hence to increased optimism) or casts a spell of pessimism over the future and conduces to efforts to move. Our data about migration potential seem to indicate that the latter is more true the former, although there are no doubt individual differences. Thus, the perceived dynamism in Marina is noticeable, and no doubt a factor of importance in connection with the relative stability of that village. A more detailed

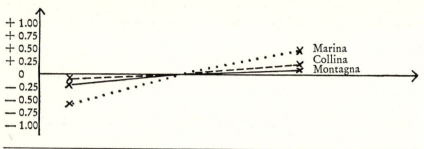

	Past	Present	Future	Difference
MONTAGNA	−0.17	0	+0.10	+0.27
COLLINA	−0.07	0	+0.11	+0.18
MARINA	−0.52	0	+0.34	+0.86

analysis also shows more immediate expectations of improvement in Marina.

But the danger of committing the ecological fallacy is perilously close in this reasoning, so we have to look at the data for the movers, in betweens and stayers themselves, not only at the collectivities from which they are drawn. The results are in general agreement with the findings in Diagram 4.9.1 and also with the second hypothesis put forward (see Table 4.9.2.)

Table 4.9.2. *Efforts to move and evaluation of past and future*

	Past	Present	Future	Difference
Stayers	−0.14	0	0.34	0.48
In betweens	−0.14	0	0.04	0.18
Movers	−0.29	0	0.04	0.33

Thus, there is no doubt that the stayers both are much more optimistic and see more difference between past and present. But on the other hand, the movers have an even more gloomy image of the past and share with the in betweens a feeling that the present harbors nothing new. Hence, there seems to be a tripartite basis for their desire to move where this particular condition is concerned: a gloomy image of the past, a bland image of the future and not too much total span between the images of

214

past and future. In short: we see very little motivation to stay, since the stayers have precisely the opposite image. And the in betweens could not have been more in between: they share the stayers' not-so-gloomy image of the past and the movers' bland image of the future. The net result is a profile showing very little curvature over time — in complete agreement with the finding for in betweens in Table 4.9.1: they are just low on time perspective.[1]

4.10. *A portrait of the movers*

Just as for the sensates, we feel a need to gather together the main lines in the portrait we have tried to draw of the mover, based on the many correlates — some trivial, some less trivial — we have uncovered.

First of all, the desire to move is embedded in a cluster of experiences rather than in a cluster of other attitudes. Thus, the desire to move is not directly correlated with social perspective, space perspective and time perspective, at least not very much. But it is correlated with experiences in social and geographical space: to have experienced upward mobility means a lot, and to have moved already, even if it is only inside the village and even if it is only travel experience, means much. But, since we do not have diachronic data about the inhabitants of the villages, we do not know whether the efforts to move away from the village are due to these factors or can be said to be due a common element also predisposing for social mobility and internal geographical mobility; a certain volatility, lack of rootedness or whatnot. From the point of view of the general atmosphere that prevails in these villages this may not be so important, however — what matters is rather a certain polarization in general terms between stayers and movers, that 'once a mover, always a mover' seems to set people apart from each other. On the other hand, the correlations are not that high, so the polarization is far from perfect. And at one point do we have a correlation with a more attitudinal variable: among the movers there are more innovators, or at least self-professed innovators, than among the stayers. This may be due to the fact that they have been around and seen things, compared with the local scene, and have presented the difference between what they have seen elsewhere and what they see in the villages as proposals — but this is, of course, one of the major mechanisms behind development, the comparison of what is with what could be. The problem is only whether the comparison leads to a desire to change local conditions or a desire to change one's own location, for lack of optimism.

For the movers the answer is clear: they want to move, and a very basic finding relates them to social participation: they show less participation in anything with a local focus and more participation of a generalized kind that does not relate to local affairs at all. Of course, when they listen more to the radio and watch the TV more, then they do so *in* the village, possibly together with villagers outside their own family, but they do not do so *for* the village. They do so for themselves in more or less conscious anticipation of the move they may sooner or later engage in. Meanwhile, they engage in some kind of anticipatory psychological mobility. This, combined with the idea that the village is found wanting, in need of serious change, leads to the guess that their basic attitude toward the villages is not only one of dissatisfaction, but even one of scorn, of contempt — 'the village does not deserve me'. That they see illegitimate power abounding around them belongs to this picture.

Consequently, the movers must be regarded as a liability for the local community. They constitute a volatile mass of dissatisfaction with a highly pessimistic perspective on the future possibilities of the village, with some kind of withdrawal from participation, with their minds off the village and probably generally with loud proclamations of dissatisfaction that their bodies have not yet been able to accompany their souls on their imaginative moves to far-off places. But if this is true, knowledge of where in the social structure the movers are located becomes crucial. Where in the social structure is this erosive force of attrition found, in the center or in the periphery? And in what kinds of center and in what kinds of periphery?

This question can be answered in many terms, and if one chooses to answer in terms of education then the data show no clear correlation, as we would expect from the ambiguous nature of education in these villages. But if one answers in terms of age, then the answer is clearly that the movers are predominantly to be found among the young (partly because the old movers have already left) — in other words, among the people who might potentially renew the society. But what about the location in the social structure, properly speaking?

The answer is simple: the movers are by and large located in the center. They are found particularly in higher echelons of the tertiary sector of economic activity, and much less in all other parts of the social structure. This is also where more pure forms of psychological mobility, space and time perspectives are particularly widespread, as one would expect from the life chances and life perspectives offered and acquired by people in this category. The lower sections of society want less to move — and particularly not if they have experienced downward mobility and if they are relatively well-to-do. And conversely for the higher echelons: if in addition to being located in the tertiary high category they also have themselves experienced upward mobility, but not enough to become well-to-do, then the rate of potential movers is very high. In other words, the simplistic hypothesis that the movers are poor people in the periphery is directly wrong, but the opposite hypothesis, that they are rich people in the center of society, is also wrong. The location is more complicated, and this leads to two conclusions.

First, the social structure is being tapped, through efforts to leave, for people — whether in the form of psychological or actual mobility — at a point where the society is highly vulnerable: the skilled occupations in the tertiary category. These are the people who could potentially give the villages new directives and new directions, but their orientation seems not to lead them in that direction but rather out of the village. As mentioned in 4.7: *the first step up the social ladder is inside the village; the second step leads outside.* The first step gives the appetite for the second step, but if the first step has not been taken, then the village is still seen as the major scene of social mobility. From the point of view of the villages, this is most unfortunate: it means that the villages can only benefit from the social energies expended by individuals when they are making the more traditional moves on the social ladder, on the lower rungs so to speak. When they have come higher up and have acquired social potential and experience, even education and skill, then — if they are motivated to move further on — their energy is devoted to other social arenas, outside the villages, and their constructive energy will be to the benefit of those other places. In their own villages they merely occupy positions to which they are no longer devoted (blocking the access to these positions for people who might be more devoted), and usually show the villages the negative sides of their own personalities, exploiting possibilities for leaving. The consequence of their local local success is the desire to move out and further up, to switch to another ladder rather than to change the local ladder.

Second, and this actually reinforces what has already been said: the potential movers are people who are in disequilibrium. They are in possession of less than they should according to their position. But disequilibrium is a general factor predisposing for radicalism, unless one is very much higher on the ascribed than on the achieved dimension. Thus, disequilibrim becomes a reservoir of social energy that may be converted into mobility, into efforts to change the existing social structure or what not. But as our data show, disequilibrium may also be converted into a desire to move, which means that this reservoir of radical energy dissipates; it is tapped, but for the benefit of others. The forces that derive from disequilibria are not directed toward the village. Of course, this holds only at the top of the system, for the poor topdog. The rich underdog is more content in the sense that he does not want to leave (or his discontent is not so easily translated into that form), and he is at the same time often change directed — according to 3.7. But his position in the total structure reduces his possibilities, unless he could join forces with others in the same position and engage in some kind of revolutionary activity, violent or nonviolent. However, we shall see in the following chapter that there are some structural factors counteracting this possibility. One of them we already know: lower standard of living, in these villages, seems to lead to apathy rather than to precise images of the future of oneself, one's family or the villages.

The significance of these findings can best be appreciated if we imagine that we have found the opposite: that the motivation to leave be particularly developed at the very bottom of the local society, where misery is flourishing, and the desire to stay particularly pronounced at the top society, and even more so in the disequilibrated combinations. In that case, the villages might benefit from some social experiences already gained, and there would be a high motivation for change due to the disequilibrium. At the same time, it is obvious that these villages are overpopulated, that they cannot sustain with the present structure the population they have and that other places can better absorb their surplus manpower and enable them to escape from the misery to which they seem to be chained in these villages.

It may be objected that this is an elitist model of change: one exports the proletariat and leaves the change to the maladjusted among the bourgeoisie, and there is no doubt that this development model can be characterized in that way. For this and other reasons we are not saying that we favor it, only that many things would have been very different if the efforts to move had been differently distributed in the social order. And we shall return to other models when more information about the villages is available to us.[1]

5. The familists and the non-familists

5.1. *A measure of familism*

We now turn to Banfield's variable, the degree of familism, and shall proceed more or less in the same way as in the two preceding chapters, but with a considerably more concentrated treatment of this topic since the general picture has already been made relatively clear. On the other hand, we shall see that the factor of familism adds a very important perspective to the ideas we have developed so far.

We shall, more or less following Banfield, conceive of familism as the tendency to set the family above other spheres of allegiance or identification. In other words, it is not only a question of having a *high* level of identification with the family as such, but of having a *higher* level of identification with family than with other important competitors for the allegiance of the inhabitants of these villages. And which are these competitors? There seem to be three that are really meaningful: the *individual* himself, the *village* as such and *religious life*. To ask about allegiance to Sicily, to Italy or to the world might also have been meaningful, but as has been amply demonstrated in the preceding chapters, space perspective is so limited for many of the inhabitants that we would doubt the validity of the answers in most cases.

Questions contrasting allegiance to the family with allegiance to the other three focuses were asked and have already been utilized in the allegiance index of cultural mentality, developed in 3.1. The way we used these questions to construct the index of familism was very simple: of the *six* paired comparison questions, comparing the *four* spheres of allegiance, the *three* questions involving a comparison of the family with the other three were singled out for closer attention. A value of two was given if the answer was in favor of the family, a value of zero was given if the answer was in favor of the competitor for allegiance, and the value of one was used in all other cases. This produced an index from zero to six, which was then trichotomized in 'low' (106), 'medium' (121) and 'high' (181) categories on familism, as usual. The three categories will be referred to in the text as 'non-familists', 'medium' and 'familists'. This, then, is the instrument — the problem is as usual how valid it is. And here we immediately run into a problem.

For what would one, off hand, expect from familists besides the properties that have already been used in the index? Banfield's theory is actually not very helpful here since he does not develop correlates, he rather elaborates the concept itself. We simply do not have any theory as to where in the social structure they may be located, these supposedly amoral familists; nor do we have any solid knowledge or even hypotheses about other value orientations they might have. In other words, we do not have criteria that can be used for validation. However, since the familists are family oriented it might be worthwhile to look at how they relate to their families, and to get more insight into their family ideology in general, simply to see if the findings look reasonable. Or since we really have no criteria that enable us to conclude anything about how reasonable the findings are, we may at least see whether the index can lead us toward some new insights.

In principle, for the familists more than for others, the family is their society, their social basis. But if this is the case, then we would expect them to compensate by having relatively many parents in their household so that the social surrounding is rich, socially self-sufficient, and so that their own power over their surroundings is multiplied by the number of relatives. This idea is confirmed by the data shown in Table 5.1.1.

This leads to the idea that the familists are simply persons who have

Table 5.1.1. *Familism and number of relatives in the household*

	1–3 relatives	*4–5 relatives*	*6–12 relatives*	*Percentage difference*
Non-familists	30	23	20	+10
Medium	32	27	30	+ 2
Familists	38	50	50	−12
Total	100	100	100	0
(N)	(130)	(133)	(119)	(382)

and/or want to have many relatives around themselves, in other words people whose concept of social life is family life, whose concept of social organization is by kinship and whose concept of welfare lies in the insurance that can be obtained from system of mutual aid among many (and easily accessible) relatives. But if this were all there was to it, then we would also expect these familists to want to have many children, but this is not the case (Table 5.1.2).

Table 5.1.2. *Familism and the number of children a family ought to have*

	0–1	2	3–7	as God likes	DK,NA	Total	(N)
Non-familists	3	25	45	7	20	100	(106)
Medium	5	29	55	2	9	100	(121)
Familists	4	44	36	9	7	100	(181)
Percentage difference	—1	—19	+9	—2	+13	0	(408)

We have given a detailed distribution since there are several interesting factors. First of all, *familists are more opinionated* in this field, as one would expect: after all, this is a rather central aspect of the family. Second, *familists want fewer children;* they want two, not more. In other words, the first image above was too simple. It has at least to be supplemented by an image of consciousness, of knowing and wanting and planning in connection with family life. And thus formulated there is no real inconsistency between the two images: *one can have many relatives and still want few children*; one can be mobile in the nuclear family and still have an extensive network of relatives to fall back upon.

But how do the familists look upon the couple presumably having these children? Do they have a traditional or a more modern outlook on marital relations? Since the family is their social cosmos more than for the non-familists, how do they perceive its structure? Since they are children of a traditional structure, one might expect them to project this structure into their conception of the ideal family, whereas the non-familists would be expected to have a more modern conception of the family, to see the family as one way of transforming society. Unfortunately we do not know whether the respondents would like women to have independent professional careers, but we do know their preferences as to marital age, and that may be just as good as an indicator. Thus, we would expect non-familists to favor a small age span and the familists to favor a larger age span between the spouses, and this is confirmed the data shown in Table 5.1.3.

Table 5.1.3. *Familism and the ideal marriage age for men and women*

	Ideal age for men				Total	Ideal age for women				Total
	16–21	22–27	28+	DK, NA		16–21	22–27	28+	DK, NA	
Non-familists	8	53	24	15	100	64	20	0	16	100
Medium	5	62	29	4	100	81	12	2	5	100
Familists	10	62	23	5	100	80	14	2	4	100

Again, the familists are more clear when it comes to their specialty, family relations. They also want both men and women to marry earlier, in other words to enter that type of familistic existence early. But this predilection for early marriage is particularly pronounced when it comes to women, leading to a larger average age span than for the non-familists — as predicted.

If we now add these bits together we get the following rough features in the portrait of the familist. He comes from a rather extended family which involves him directly in a network that he knows and apperciates. On the other hand, he also somehow realizes that today it is more easy to fight for the welfare of a small than a big family, and consequently he is inclined to have few children. He is a family strategist and is 'modern' where size of family is concerned, even if he is rather 'traditional' when it comes to relations between spouses. But for him this is probably no contradiction: he wants a traditional family, only one that is small, hence more mobile. He probably also wants to use the network of a family that is *big*, and he is not worried by the contradiction in this: his children will not to the same extent be able to fall back upon the support of an extended family. But why should this worry him? He is living now, in a period of transition where family size is reduced drastically — in that sense he is living in the best of all periods with an ample support for a small unit.

But we have now moved somewhat further than our data warrant, so let us look at more aspects of the familists to get to know them better.[1]

5.2. *Who the familists are : traditionalists or innovators*

Our basic assumption was that the familists are narrow in their perspective, somewhat traditional in their orientation, without necessarily being ideational. They will conceive of society as consisting of families and cultivate those perspectives that give possibilities to their families.

In other words, we would expect their general social perspective to be more in terms of what the family can make out of the present situation than to change it. And there are two types of action, above all, that a family as such can try to engage in to make the best out of 'the present situation': to *move upward* in the present socio-economic structure through jobs and work and to *move away* from the whole village to other places. In other words, we would expect the familists to be *ambitious*, since this is a way of taking care of their families, and consequently to be interested both in social mobility inside the village and geographical mobility out of it. For the family can be the unit actor of both types of mobilty, but it is not the unit actor behind, say, industrialization. Hence, we would not expect the familists to be change oriented, for in that case they would have preferred a village orientation to a family orientation and we would have found some of the same correlations as for the sensates in 3.2. Or to be more precise: we would expect them to be oriented toward change of their own families *within* the system, but not toward change *of* the system — in line with Banfield's ideas.

The Table corresponding to Tables 3.2.1 and 4.2.1 comes out as in Table 5.2.1.

Table 5.2.1. *Familism and diagnosis and cure for the villages, percentage*

	What is the main problem?		Can conditions be improved?	
	To get work to get jobs	To develop something	Yes, create more jobs	Yes, by developing something
Non-familists	22	29	29	28
Medium	30	30	28	30
Familists	48	41	43	42
Total	100	100	100	100
(N)	(168)	(172)	(90)	(148)

Thus, the hypothesis is confirmed, but more for the question concerning the diagnosis than for the question concerning the cure. From the first half of the Table the hypothesized difference in perspective emerges clearly: non-familists are more development oriented, familists more oriented toward facilities within the existing system. The differences are small, however — but since, as we shall later see, familists are located low down in society one would expect them to come up with fewer clear answers. In other words, the correlations are probably deflated due to the social distribution of the familists and hence smaller than they would be if we control for social position.[1]

5.3. *Who the familists are: social participation*

Our general hypothesis is very simple, but different from the corresponding hypothesis in 4.3 where a distinction had to be made between media with a *local* focus and more *general* media of social participation. The hypothesis is simply that the *familists will participate less in all other forms of social participation.* Their familism directs their social participation inward, to the family, and although it does not exclude social participation elsewhere, it should tend to reduce it. Thus, we should expect the percentage differences between familists who do *not* participate and non-familists who do *not* participate to be positive, regardless of the medium of participation. The data are shown in Table 5.3.1.

Table 5.3.1. *Familism and differential lack of social participation, percentage differences familists - non-familists*

	Total sample	MONTAGNA	COLLINA	MARINA
Newspapers	+ 8	+ 7	+11	− 2
Weeklies	+13	+14	+14	+ 8
Radio	+ 7	−11	+29	+ 1
Television	+ 3	−13	+13	+ 3
Movies	− 5	+ 2	+ 1	−23
Church	+11	+ 5	+ 6	+15

For the total sample the hypothesis is confirmed in five out of six cases, and for the villages in 14 out of 18 cases, yielding confirmation ratios of 83% and 78%, respectively. Thus, the hypothesis must be said to have received a fairly good confirmation, in particular since the four deviant cases do not show a consistent deviant pattern.

It may be argued that much of this finding is consistent with one simple explanation: the familists are uneducated and poor. However, even if this would explain why they read fewer newspapers and weeklies, it does not explain why they do not go to church — and that they do go more to the (more costly) movies. Rather, the total pattern seems to be

224

explicable simply in terms of the competition from the family, which the familists believe to be a worthwhile competitor. The data go far to demonstrate the claim that they are in fact shielded from other activities by their family allegiance. In other words, just as they have *higher*, not only high, allegiance to the family according to the index, they have *lower*, not only low, participation outside the family — relative to the non-familists. Attitudes, it seems, are in this case translated into behavior.[1]

5.4. *Who the familists are : age and education*

The word 'familism' would have had a connotaion of old age and low education in many ears if it had not been for another image of the familist, particularly prominent in the United States during the Eisenhower period: familism as an ideology of the young and educated, as an expression of low concern for the society as such, of family egoism — so prevalent among the college students of that era according to the interesting study made by Philip Jacob. Familism was as compatible with the conservatism of the Eisenhower years as it was with the conservatism of Sicilian life, but it was also, as mentioned, a factor that permeated life for the young and educated. In other words, there is no reason to assume *a priori* that familism is the privilege of the old and educated. It can just as well be seen as the clever strategy to play for young couples — particularly since they are in a phase in their life cycle where expansion of family as well as concern for its economic survival are predominant features of their daily existence. This idea about age is amply confirmed in Table 5.4.1.

The percentage differences are not overwhelming but convincing: *the oldest are least familist in their orientation.* A closer scrutiny of what the older had as their focuses of identification seems to reveal both

Table 5.4.1. *Familism and age, percentage*

	1871–1900	1901–1920	1921–1950	Percentage difference
Non-familists	34	23	22	+12
Medium	29	30	31	− 2
Familists	37	47	47	−10
Total	100	100	100	0
(N)	(90)	(194)	(121)	(405)

religion and village; in other words, the recent decades have removed people from village identification and religious faith and have let them fall back on the family. The youngest, the new generations, may never have believed in village or religion, and for them family identification may offer itself as the only solid focus in life. This is compatible with the idea of losing (or never developing) faith in the old village, the village that was, hedged around by religious beliefs, norms and hierarchies yet without finding any new village to believe in. For there is no such new village, only the remains of what once was an integrated system without clear contours of new forms of life.

And this is also compatible with the distribution we find for education. We would not expect the most well educated to be familists, for education predisposes them for a more ideational orientation as pointed out in 3.4, which would make them tend to select religious allegiance rather than family allegiance. But we would also expect the respondents without any schooling to be more like the old people in the Table above — since they are, in part, the same people (Table 5.4.2)

Table 5.4.2. *Familism and education, percentage*

	Formal training		
	0 years	*1–4 years*	*5 years and over*
Non-familists	24	25	29
Medium	36	27	29
Familists	40	48	42
Total	100	100	100
(N)	(96)	(192)	(118)

In other words, there is an A-shaped distribution: *familism is most pronounced at the medium level of education.* The image, then, will have to be changed from familists who are predominantly old and predominantly without education to relatively young familists with some education — and this is precisely the type of data we feel Banfield should have made available. For the implication that follows from this is that familism, in all probability, is not a phenomenon of yesterday or of today but above all a phenomenon of growth, tomorrow's pattern of social identification in these villages. Those who favor familism are the young people and people with the minimum of schooling now accorded to almost everybody in the villages. This, together with the general, almost universal change in sex mores (where fears of pregnancy, venerea. disease or lack of privacy are being gradually eliminated by means of contraception, penicillin and the diffusion of used cars acquired by returned migrants) is compatible with a focus on the nuclear rather than on the extended family. All of this would detach the individual even further from the village, its mores and controls. For even if extended families may fight extended, inter-family quarrels, they will nevertheless use the village as their battleground and in that sense be village oriented; the nuclear family may add to family egotism the simple solution of moving away — as we shall see in 5.8. And the findings in Tables 5.1.2 and 5.1.3 indicate that it is precisely the nuclear family rather than the extended family that these familists seem to go in for; they are not familists in the more traditional sense. The old people may perhaps have been forced, almost, to give up familism as they conceived it, the 'new' familism is based nuclear family on the and the old generation is excluded.[1]

5.5. *Who the familists are : social position*

We have conceived of familism in a double perspective: on the one hand it serves to integrate the individual into a social setting, and contributes to a steering of the individual by providing him with a group context that almost all individuals are given and/or acquire. On the other hand, once this protective shield has been created around the individual and has given sense and meaning to many of his activities, the more apparent becomes the negative aspect of familism: the reduction of identification with other levels of organization, as already indicated by our findings about social participation. Family egocentrism or familism brings the individual a part of the way toward social participation, by rooting him in the family, but leaves him solidly there. The problem is: Where in the social structure is this factor particularly operative? We simply do not have any theory that can guide us in selecting hypotheses, so we have to consult the data shown in Table 5.5.1

The percentage differences are not high, but extremely significant. It should be remembered again that the respondents in the primary low category will be handicapped due to the tendency to give evasive answers, which means that their high level of familism probably is an underestimation of the actual situation. At the same time it is clear that the primary *sector* is, on the average, higher on familism than the tertiary

Table 5.5.1. *Familism and social position (class and sector combined, percentage)*

	Primary high	Primary low	Tertiary high	Tertiary low
Non-familists	31	20	28	29
Medium	23	30	30	35
Familists	46	50	42	36
Total	100	100	100	100
(N)	(74)	(141)	(100)	(93)

sector, which in all probability is a reflection of the way agriculture — even at the very modest level of the *braccianti* — is built around the family as a unit not only of consumption, but also of production. But as to *class*, there is no such clear picture. The tertiary low category is true to its nature and expresses its volatility also in a low level of familism, which probably is matched by a certain looseness in family relations in general. *But the primary low category is, as mentioned, highest in familism* — and this serves even more to set the two sensate categories apart from each other. So far we shall only state that to the extent that familism serves to encapsulate people and spin a cocoon around them, this shielding factor — *protecting individuals against a sometimes very cruel society but also protecting society against them* — is most developed in the primary low category, in other words among the people who, objectively speaking, are the most deprived.

For there can be little doubt that familism has a protective function in this society, that individuals feel so exposed that they feel that the family is the only secure place — that they are too exposed if they are completely alone and that neither the village nor religion offers the protection needed. Actually, there are three reasons why we feel that this interpretation of *one* of the factors behind familism is correct, and the first reason is what we have just shown: familism is highest in the most exposed category in the social structure.

But the familism should also be highest in the most exposed village, which is Collina. And this seems to be the case: the percentage of familists in Collina is 49%, as against 42% both in Montagna and Marina, and the difference cannot be explained in terms of occupational distribution alone. Moreover, we should also expect familism to be particularly developed among people who perceive power in the villages as illegitimate, since this is closely connected with a perception of pressure and even danger. And we find in fact that whereas 44% of the total sample has been classified as familists, this applies to 72% of the people in the villages who perceive the local power as being exercised by illegitimate power wielders.[1]

5.6. *Who the familists are: economic position*

With the familists overrepresented in the primary low category, the old index of economic position becomes less useful. In general, there is little new that can be gathered from the dimension of economic position, aside from elaborations of what we already know. The familists tend to be among the poor, as witnessed by the size of their houses, although the differences are not overwhelming (Table 5.6.1).

Table 5.6.1. *Familism and number of rooms in the house, percentage*

	One room	Two rooms	Three rooms	More than three
Non-familists	27	22	29	38
Medium	28	32	27	24
Familists	45	46	44	38
Total	100	100	100	100
(N)	(143)	(149)	(84)	(21)

That they tend to have fewer rooms, less water and more cows in their houses is not surprising, given their location in the social structure. But the correlations are not very high, which means that there are many poor who are not familists by this definition, and many familists who are not poor. Since familism probably has different effect at different levels of economic position this may lead to some speculations about how the two factors interact.

For the poor, familism offers protection, as mentioned several times. But the rich do not need that type of protection so much; they would rather use familism and family relations to exercise influence, would rather use kinship ties as channels for the exchange of favors. But the more well-to-do in this society are less family oriented, which means that they are, in a sense, free to identify with other focuses of social activity. In a society more richly endowed with organizations and associations this would steer the more well-to-do toward that kind of involvement. But with the poverty in this field, the more well-to-do will be more free to fall back on individualism — as data show — and this

229

may in turn be a factor underlying the high desire to move away in higher echelons of the tertiary category. These themes will be developed further in Chapter 6.[1]

5.7. Who the familists are : social perspective

Looking again at the mobility Tables as we have done in 3.7 and 4.7, there is little new that emerges. We shall therefore try a slightly different technique of analysis, playing on our information concerning all three generations — father, self and the desired position for the son. The interesting question is: Knowing that the familists are located in disproportionately high numbers at the bottom of this stratified society, in the primary low category, does familism serve to stimulate ambition upward, or does it serve to narrow the perspective? It is difficult to give any conclusive answer to this because of the many factors that enter the picture, but one approach is shown in Table 5.7.1. We take as a point of departure the simple figures relating the three generations.

Table 5.7.1. *Distributions on the three generations*

	Primary high	Primary low	Tertiary high	Tertiary low
Father's generation	101	160	79	68
Own generation	74	141	100	93
Wanted, son's generation	7	21	310	65
Transition, father-self	0.73	0.88	1.26	1.37
Transition, self-son	0.10	0.15	3.1	0.70

If the transition figure is 1.0, then there is the same number in the two generations; if it is less, then there are fewer in the last generation; if it is more, then there are more in the last generations. Typically, the transition figures are all below 1.0 for the *primary* sector and above 1.0 for the *tertiary high* category, and they are above 1.0 for father to self and below 1.0 for self to son in the *tertiary low* category. The tertiary low category has served to 'modernize' parts of the population but is no longer that attractive. The question is how the corresponding figures for the *familists* relate to these figures for the total sample.

And the familists consistently prove themselves to be more ambitious. They want *less*, but not very much less, to get into the *primary sector* and the

230

tertiary low category, and *more* (transition figure 3.35) to get into the coveted *tertiary high*. In this category, however, they do not quite dare to wish for their sons to become professionals, but are clearly over-represented when it comes to wanting their sons to become merchants, clerks and artisans.

In other words, the familists are, as we predicted, more than willing to play the game offered them by the villages, the mobility game. They know that this is almost a closed game, that the openings are very few — but they also know that the villages have permitted some mobility in the past. This is entirely consistent with what we have already found about people in the primary low category: they are not only familists, they are also likely to have suffered downward mobility, and they want to move up inside, not outside, their own village. This is also entirely compatible with their familism for the simple reason mentionad in 5.2: the family is the unit of mobility, especially provided the orientation is toward the nuclear family.

But that brings us to the second type of activity that combines am-bition with family orientation: geographical mobility. Do the familists want to move geographically, not only socially? This will be discussed in the next section.[1]

5.8. *Who the familists are: space perspective*

There is little sense here in elaborating the correlations between fam-ilism and space perspective in general, so we limit ourselves to the way space perspective is interpreted, in the sense used in Chapter 4, as an inclination to move away from the villages. In other words, are the familists predominantly movers, or predominantly stayers? It is clear what our answer will be: they are movers, because this is the adequate answer for the head of a household concerned about the welfare of his family and being both young and educated enough to have a perspective that leads outside the village itself. And this is confirmed by the data in Table 5.8.1.

The percentage difference is 15, indicating the overrepresentation of movers among the familists. In other words, the familists want to move — but not necessarily with their families. They can also move according to the pattern found all over the Mediterranean basin: the major bread-winner moves to more affluent parts of Europe, sends most of his income home by mail and returns after some time — in some cases to fetch his

Table 5.8.1. *Familism and efforts to move, percentage*

	Stayers	In betweens	Movers	Total	(N)
Non-familists	48	32	20	100	(106)
Medium	47	28	25	100	(121)
Familists	39	26	35	100	(181)
Percentage difference	+9	+6	−15	0	(408)

family, in other cases to convert the funds into mobility in the tertiary sector. But however this is, the major finding here is one of flexibility: the *individual* may be closely attached to his family but the small *family* as such is a mobile unit, hence there is no incompatibility between familism and a desire to more.

But if this is the case, then we would also expect this to show up in where the familists want to live if they could move. We would expect them to show few ties to the villages when asked where they would like to live if they could choose, for due concern is with the family, not with the village (Table 5.8.2).

Table 5.8.2. *Familism and where they would like to live, percentage*

	In the village	Elsewhere in Sicily	Elsewhere in Italy	Abroad	Any-where	Total	(N)
Non-familists	49	3	13	17	18	100	(106)
Medium	47	6	13	17	17	100	(121)
Familists	34	4	13	23	26	100	(181)
Percentage difference	15	−1	0	−6	−8	0	(408)

Clearly, the familists not only want to leave, as we already know, but want to get far away, even 'anywhere', which is the typical expression one would expect when space perspective is not too well developed and is hampered in its development by poor education in general.

But we would actually expect even more from the thesis about the familists' conception of the family as essentially *mobile*. We would expect this to apply not only to the future, but also to their past experiences. In other words, one would expect them, like the movers, to have already experienced mobility, to be used to the idea of having lived 'somewhere else' and to have a wife who has lived 'somewhere else'. By and large this is also what we find (Table 5.8.3).

Table 5.8.3. *Familism and where respondent and spouse are born, percentage*

	Birthplace of respondent				Birthplace of spouse			
	In this house	In this village	In this province	In Sicily	In this house	In this village	In this province	In Sicily
Non-familists	28	26	16	25	42	23	26	17
Medium	34	28	44	25	5	31	38	24
Familists	38	46	40	50	53	46	36	59
Total	100	100	100	100	100	100	100	100
(N)	(68)	(285)	(32)	(12)	(19)	(277)	(42)	(17)

The familists, much more than the non-familists, come from the out-side and bring with them spouses from the outside, although there is also a certain tendency to come from the village or outside the province but to marry into the house of the spouse, or to arrive together with the spouse. At any rate, the basic idea that the familists also have more experiences with mobile families than non-familists has been confirmed. And that of course sheds some additional light on the familist: he may live together with many relatives but he has already had an experience that sets his nuclear family off from the environment. The idea of falling back on the immediate family surroundings is not new; in other words, the protective cocoon has probably already been in operation for some time.[1]

5.9. *Who the familists are: time perspective*

Are the familists high or low on time perspective? Again, the relation to time perspective in general is not so interesting, but, as mentioned in 3.9, we also have at our disposal an index of time perspective that is more appropriate in this connection since it measures time perspective relative to one's own family (see Table 3.9.5). In general, we would expect the respondents high on familism also to be relatively high on time perspective for their families — their familistic concern should bend their thoughts and ideas in this direction, it would seem. On the other hand, we also know that the familists are overrepresented in the primary low category, which, in turn, is known to be low on time per-spective as well as on space perspective.

Hence, it would be less than warranted to expect strong correlations to emerge (Table 5.9.1).

233

Table 5.9.1. *Familism and time perspective relative to one's own family, percentage*

	Time perspective				
	Low	*Medium*	*High*	*Total*	*(N)*
Non-familists	52	24	24	100	(106)
Medium	38	29	33	100	(121)
Familists	47	27	26	100	(181)
Percentage differences	5	—3	—2	0	(408)

The percentage differences are certainly not high enough to talk about any correlation, so the hypothesis is certainly not unconfirmed. It is like the correlations with space perspective and time perspective in general: so low that we have not even bothered to report it. Thus, it is actually only one more case of a general tendency found in data we do not report: *familism is not highly correlated with attitudes*, except when these attitudes concern family matters. It seems to be more correlated with behavior, and this is perhaps not strange since familism is, above all, an attitude strongly related to a particular structural arrangement.[1]

5.10. *A portrait of the familists*

That brings us to the conclusion of this brief chapter. Let us try to combine these features in a more complete portrait of the familist.

First of all: he seems to be a *neo-familist*. He is young, goes in for the nuclear family, the family he creates himself, and is ambitious, which is expressed in concern for social and geographical mobility. This is not the classical familist tied to an extended family both by birth and by procreation; the neo-familist is highly mobile in his thoughts and probably also in his deeds.

Second, this does not necessarily make him a good man for local development, for two reasons. First of all, he is concerned with change, but with change of the life situation of his own family, within the possibilities set by local society. He is not concerned with changes *of* the society, only changes for himself *within* society — and if local society does not offer enough opportunity, then he is quite willing to leave — to move away. In that sense he is *amoral*.

But in addition to this, his family orientation not only serves to protect him but also serves as a filter that makes him less of a participant

234

in other social activities. He serves as a receiver of signals from the outside and transmits them to his family and converts them to the benefit of his family — to the extent the surroundings so permit. But this does not make him a good organization man, he becomes too self-sufficient in terms of social contacts within his own family for that purpose.

Third, by and large it looks as if familism is embedded in a cluster of behavioral elements rather than in a cluster of attitudes, except insofar as the latter concern family relations. More particularly, experience with geographical mobility seems to predispose for familism: the individual is less rooted in the local community and more prone to fall back on the family.

Fourth, and most importantly: this type of familism, with its strong elements of neo-familism, is most developed in the primary low category. Thus, to the extent that it serves to reduce or to decrease the potential for social action, it is significant that it is in the primary low category, among the exploited *braccianti*, that this factor is most operative. It is instructive to imagine that it were the other way around, that the top of society were embedded in these strongly fortified capsules, isolating them from each other, whereas the bottom of society were less structured and hence more open to other offers for social participation, such as associations, radical political parties or other radical movements. It is reasonable to guess that this would tilt the balance less in favor of the top of of the society, but to develop this further we now have to look at the total picture of the villages gathered together in these three chapters.[1]

6. The structure of ultrastability

6.1. *The relations among sensates, movers and familists*

In our effort to unravel the structure of these villages in Western Sicily we have tried to present a tapestry, using three main types of yarn, three major colors so to speak: the themes of cultural mentality, psychic mobility and amoral familism. In addition there are subsidiary colors, such as the perspectives on society, space and time. And there is the background: the basic structure, with its threads of social and economic position, with social participation, age, education, place of birth and all the familiar variables of sociological study. We now want to do what the art historian would do: focus less on detail, on the patterns formed by one color only, on minute description, and focus more on the total picture, on general structure, on the *ideas*, the basic themes, that can be extracted. And this we shall try to do knowing well that with other colors and other materials our picture might have been somewhat different, if not in the final conclusion, at least in emphasis.

The first problem to be solved has to do with the three principal components of our analysis: What are the relations among being sensate, being a mover and being a familist? We know that they correlate differently with many other variables, but could it not be that they are, nevertheless, relatively heavily related so that we have, essentially, been saying the same things over and over again, but under different headings? Obviously, if the correlations are very high, then much of our work would have been wasted, we would have been explaining the same variance over and over again. On the other hand, if the correlations are low or nonexistent, then we would have the advantage of working with independent factors (except for common relations to third variables), and this would make the three approaches much more valuable, since they would complement each other.

And this is, in fact, the situation: with one exception the correlations are surprisingly low (Table 6.1.1) We have presented not only three, but five Tables, since we have used both indices of cultural mentality. And the conclusions are as follows:

sensates vs. movers : no correlation for either index
sensates vs. familists : no correlation for occupation index
correlation for allegiance index: familists are more ideational
movers vs. familists : correlation: familists tend to be movers

Some comments are now in order.

Table 6.1.1. *Relations among cultural mentality, psychic mobility and amoral familism*

	Occupation items			Allegiance items		
	Ideationals	*Medium*	*Sensate*	*Ideationals*	*Medium*	*Sensate*
Stayers	48	42	44	44	38	46
In betweens	25	29	28	27	31	27
Movers	27	29	28	29	31	27
Total	100	100	100	100	100	100
(N)	(98)	(159)	(151)	(132)	(108)	(168)

	Occupation items			Allegiance items		
	Ideationals	*Medium*	*Sensate*	*Ideationals*	*Medium*	*Sensate*
Non-familists	28	28	22	17	37	26
Medium	24	24	28	34	16	35
Familists	48	48	50	49	47	39
Total	100	100	100	100	100	100
(N)	(98)	(119)	(151)	(132)	(108)	(168)

	Stayers	*In betweens*	*Movers*
Non-familists	28	30	19
Medium	32	30	26
Familists	40	40	55
Total	100	100	100
(N)	(177)	(115)	(116)

First, there is no correlation between efforts to move and cultural mentality.

Second, the correlation between cultural mentality and familism, using the allegiance items, should not be taken seriously, especially since it does not hold for the other index. The index of familism is to a large extent based on the same items, so there are intricate patterns of auto-correlation present in the data. At the same time, the direction of the correlation is not unexpected. But what this combined Table tells us is rather that there are two kinds of familists: sensate familists and ideational familists, and further analysis of the data indicate clearly that the former are what we have called the neo-familists, whereas the latter are the classical familists. We shall not develop that theme further, however; we are now heading in another direction.

Third, the correlation between efforts to move and familism is real enough, as elaborated in 5.8 (where Table 5.8.1 is percentaged the other way), but is not very pronounced. There are many familists who want to stay and many non-familists who want to move. But this can also be said about most of the Tables we have presented: correlations are generally low, partly because our indicators are not very high on validity, which again is related to our effort to measure relatively volatile dimensions.[1]

But in this connection the conclusion is clear enough: by and large we are dealing with three themes, three approaches, which can be treated as if they were separate, although they are certainly linked to each other indirectly, and in one case directly. *This means that we cannot apply any simple reductionism to our data.* If we disregard the mediums and in betweens, then all eight possible combinations are found empirically: from sensates who are also movers and familists, to ideationals who are at the same time stayers and non-familists. All eight types have their stories to tell, not all of them equally interesting, though. It would be very simple if the whole system were polarized into two types, two camps — for instance the two groups mentioned above. In that case the sensates would probably pick up their families and move away, leaving the scene, the villages, to less family-oriented ideationals who just want to stay. This is certainly a part of the story, but only a part, for the social structure and its impact are left completely out of this type of picture. And this may also serve as a warning: if one had used only these three variables essentially expressing value orientations, then one might easily have ended with this or a similar conclusion as has been done so many times in development studies focusing on values alone.

238

There is also another conclusion that emerges from these Tables: the sense in which these people are really members of two worlds. We have pointed out before that when index distributions tend to be peaked this is not merely due to weak indicators but is also a reflection of the lack of crystallization of attitudes, the amorphous character of attitude formation in societies in transition. Based on the present data we can now pursue this theme further: the low or even zero correlations between basic dimensions are further signs of lack of crystallization. Many people not only feel and talk in the direction of both/and when presented with a choice between modern and traditional orientation, they also tend to defy any clear rules as to 'appropriate' combinations of basic value orientations.[2] This may be interpreted as a factor preventing or impeding basic conflict because of the potential for contact, because of the many bridges between the extreme categories. But it may also be interpreted as a factor preventing or impeding real change. For change is possible even when there is little polarization and crystallization, but only under the conditions of strong and efficient institutions — conditions that are not fulfilled in these villages. Hence, polarization and cleavage, with clear cuts and divisions, would probably provide a better basis for creative conflict. But these people are *members of two worlds*, set not only against each other but against themselves.[3]

6.2. *Value orientation and social structure: a conspiracy against development*

We now turn to the basic task announced in 1.2 and 1.6: to place all these value orientations in the social structure in order to study the joint effect. Apart from some references to age and education and some geographical variables, we have essentially used two conceptions of *social structure* in this analysis: the *combination of rank and sector*, as it was developed in 1.2 and 3.5, and the *combination of social rank and economic rank*, as it was developed in 3.6. Both perspectives show individuals in cross-pressure, exposed to forces deriving from two social dimensions at the same time — rank with sector, and social rank with economic rank. At the same time the two perspectives give us occasion to draw some conclusions both as to causes and consequences of the value orientations. Let us summarize the basic findings with regard to both perspectives on social structure, starting with the *first structural perspective*, social position (Table 6.2.1).

Comparing all these figures, it should be remembered that, except

Table 6.2.1. *Basic value orientations as a function of social position, percentage*

	Primary high	Primary low	Tertiary high	Tertiary low
Sensates	28	**44**	**46**	23
Movers	30	24	**35**	27
Familists	46	**50**	42	36
High on social perspective	71	**51**	67	71
High on space pespective	22	23	**49**	35
High on time perspective	31	29	**42**	40
High on standard of living	26	**9**	**50**	28

for the effort to move, they are based on indices that have been divided into 'high', 'medium' and 'low' according to a simple grouping used in order to assist analysis, so the absolute figures in and by themselves do not convey much information. The trends read horizontally are important, not the absolute values, and the most important percentages are in heavy type in the Table.

The basic finding is in the distribution of the major value orientation, showing a clear diagonal pattern — model 6 in section 1.6, to the exclusion of models 1 through 5. The percentage differences for rank alone, or for sector alone, were found to be negligible, and the tertiary high and the primary low combinations distinguish themselves as the two carriers of modern values — relatively speaking. This means that reasoning based on polarization in terms of classes, or in terms of sectors, becomes too simplistic: the diagonal pattern impedes group formation along these classic cut lines. More complex analysis is needed.

This is the background as developed is 3.5. *The task now is to show that this particular distribution of value orientations provides these societies with an almost remarkably efficient protection against change, an almost diabolic combination of factors that explains almost too well the absence of endogenous change in the region* (as opposed to exogenous change, coming from the outside). This shall be done in three ways: by pointing to a factor that reduces the efficiency of the tertiary high category as an agent of change, by pointing to a factor that reduces the efficiency of the primary low category and by pointing to three factors that reduce the possibilities of cooperation between the two categories. Correspondingly, it shall be demonstrated how all these factors do not impede the two more tradition-oriented categories from being effective agents of traditional values, or from multiplying their efficiency by working in concert.

Leaving aside social perspective for a moment, the five remaining percentage rows should be inspected with a special view to a comparison of the two categories now being focused upon: the tertiary high and the primary low. It is remarkable how the tertiary high category ranks highest on three variables that all have to do with psychic mobility, with empathy in one form or the other: efforts to move, space perspective and time perspective. But if we focus on familism, then primary low ranks highest. And there seems to be some kind of complementarity at work here: where one ranks high there is a tendency for the other one to rank low, although this is only perfect for time perspective and efforts to move. (Tertiary low is lower than tertiary high on familism, and primary high a little bit lower than primary low on space perspective.) If social perspective is included, based on the percentage of respondents who wish their sons to become tertiary high, the conclusion is almost the same: the primary low down at one end and the tertiary high almost at the top. But this is a very special case. For them to want their sons to become tertiary high involves no desired mobility, thus the measure does not function so well for them. As we have said repeatedly: it is the effort to move *out*, not only *up*, that is the functional equivalent for the tertiary high category.

The conclusion is simple. *The tertiary high are, above all, oriented away from the here and now; they have empathy with other places, with the past and particularly with the future; they not only want to move but have actually tried to do so. In short, for them the village is a prison.* They have reached the top. If they want to reach higher, they have to move, which is reflected in these measures that indicate the ability of their souls, their minds, their thoughts to engage in anticipatory migration even though their bodies are still constrained to remain behind. *On the other hand are the primary low. They are certainly not the victims of excessive empathy but victims of something else, excessive familism.* Mentally they are still in the village, as witnessed by the lower empathy rates, and only half of them want their sons to come to the top. The rest are more inhibited in their desires, more restrained, which means that they still see the village, and even the lower ranks, as a possible stage for social climbing. But this does not mean that they can unleash their modernism at the village level, for precisely at this point does familism interfere and command identification with a collectivity at a lower level, the family. Or better: their experience with the village level has been of such a kind as to make them fall back on the family. Whereas the moderns in the tertiary high are embracing the whole nation in their minds, the moderns in the primary low are thinking in terms of how to advance their own families, if necessary at the expense of other families.

Between the nation and the family stands the village. *Between the excessive openness provided by the Lerner factor and the excessive closure provided by the Banfield factor is an interval that should provide ample identification with the village itself.* Typically, this would be true of categories in Table 6.2.1 that are not extreme on either empathy or familism. These categories are precisely the tertiary low and the primary high, the carriers of the traditional values. They are in a sense combining their traditionalism with the adequate focus of identification, thus *defining themselves as the legitimate owners of the villages, where the tertiary high have grown out of them and the primary low still have to grow into them.*

So much for the differences in value patterns and perspectives using the first structural perspective: *social position.* Let us then turn to the second structural perspective: *interaction,* as it was developed at the end of 1.6. The basic factor is the *possibility of cooperation* within the pairs of groups with similar orientation. This is divided into three parts: first, the possible differences in the nature of the value orientations held by the two groups; second, the social distance factor between them; and third, the general strength of the interaction links in the total system of interaction in this traditional society.

In 3.5 we developed the idea that *the tertiary high have acquired modern values less because of protest than for the simple reason of easy access, whereas the converse probably is true for the primary low.* To some extent this is reflected in Table 6.2.1. For the tertiary high, modernism is part of a general syndrome of modern attitudes and perspectives; for the primary low it stands out as a desire for change but without the rich resonance provided by other cognitive and evaluative dimensions. Thus the tertiary high modern can compare; he can use examples from the outside; he can project into the future. These are all factors that will contribute to a more gradualist frame of mind and to a politically more 'constructive' way of thinking — in other words, to *reformism,* to evolution from the status quo, that is. The primary low will have an image of the present and an image of a better existence. But this is a mental construct to be compared with the present, not a state of affairs they can see emerging before the inner eye and map on a time scale. Social pessimism, alienation and absolutism will probably result from this and lead to such well-known patterns as the *waiting for the revolution,* which will have to come from Rome and not from themselves, for they have no experience for projecting themselves as active agents on the local scene. Contrast this with the modernism of the tertiary high: he could possibly have done it; he could have provoked change, but he is now heading for other hunting grounds.

The second factor, in terms of *social distance*, is implied by the bottom row of Table 6.2.1. It becomes even more pronounced if the category of tertiary high is divided into some of its components. Thus the professionals, tradesmen and clerical workers show a distribution on the standard of living index of 74% (high), 13% (medium) and 13% (low) as against 9%, 18% and 73% for the primary low. In a few numbers this expresses a gulf almost impossible for humans to bridge and particularly difficult in a traditional society of limited size that provides few neutral meeting grounds where status symbols are put aside. Thus, of the villages, the biggest one had only three voluntary associations at the time the data were collected.

But the third factor is perhaps the most fundamental of them all. Looking at the four cells, one may ask: Where is the *institutionalized interaction* located? Where are the *roles* in this social system? If this were painted with a rather crude brush, catching just the essentials, the interaction structure would be as follows — according to consensus of a high number of informants asked about the subject.

Diagram 6.2.1. *The interaction structure of the villages*

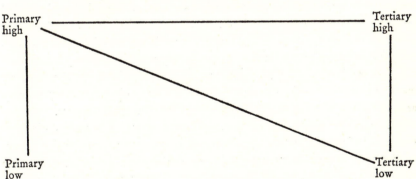

The reader will see that of the 15 possibilities mentioned in 1.6, with two weak links, we feel that the pattern of Table 1.6.2 is the best model of this empirical reality. Of the six possible interaction lines, only four have been drawn, indicating that the other two are weak or missing. One of the two missing links is precisely the link between the tertiary high and the primary low, which would indicate that there is little experience

243

in the structure with this kind of interaction. There are several reasons for this. The structure in Diagram 6.2.1 is in one sense only a reflection of what is customary in social affairs. The topdogs interact with each other and with underdogs (but to a lesser extent) but not (or much, much less) the underdogs with the underdogs.[1] The primary low and tertiary low do not need each other; they do not have complementary goods or services to offer. As usual, societies are organized in such a way that interaction is above all vertical, and to the advantage of the topdogs. Underdogs have only labor to offer, but cannot buy it from each other in institutionalized economic life.

But why the lack of interaction between tertiary high and primary low? It is not because the primary low do not need the tertiary high, for anyone in the village could use the services of the professionals, the tradesmen, the clerks, the artisans, etc. It is rather because the tertiary high do not need the services of the primary low, because their services (those of the tertiary high) are of a kind that are mainly demanded by other tertiary high and by the primary high, with whom they certainly interact. Thus there is no basis for symbiotic interaction. If the primary low want the values offered by the tertiary high, they must be prepared to give something different than their labor in return (whereas the tertiary low can do this, the lawyer can help his servant in a difficult situation). They can give allegiance but will run against competition from the tertiary low who, by nature of their status, have institutionalized interaction with the tertiary high. Since the tertiary low cannot coerce the tertiary high by means of money from their low social position, practically speaking, the only remaining possibility would be to buy interaction with the tertiary high by means of money. And this is precisely what they were not able to do in the past (although this is changing very quickly and they will be able to do so increasingly more in the future.

There are two reasons for this. The first reason is simple — lack of money.[2] It is difficult to restrain oneself in efforts to describe the misery of the farm-hands in some villages of this region, but it has been so well documented by others that another attempt will not be made here. The second reason is just as important — the institution of the *compa-natico*. The institution is probably known in most corners of the world. The farmer pays in kind rather than in cash and may also eat bread together with the workers. The net result may be a highly familistic, warm and meaningful relationship within the primary sector. But it breaks down the possible direct link to the tertiary high position, for this interaction will be via the primary high, as seen from the figures. Thus the primary

low is not only deprived of his chance to use institutionalized interaction in political cooperation with the tertiary high (which would be
difficult anyway because of the social distance) *but is also deprived of the
chance to establish a cyclical pattern of interaction so as to possess two
channels of communication and two channels of influence, both direct and
indirect, to his boss, the primary high.* He is left at the end of the interaction
structure, as an appendix, unlike all the others who are tied to the system
by more than one link.

Compare this with the link between the primary high and the tertiary
low. It is across a much shorter span in social distance, as seen from
Table 6.2.1, and is meaningful even if no ideological similarity existed,
because it is institutionalized. The farmer needs not only the service
of the farm-hand in the field but also somebody to see to other things,
possibly servants, if he can afford them, etc. And the tertiary low with
work of that kind can stay close to the sources of food. Along the lines
of institutionalized interaction, values will flow more easily; people
will tend to become more like each other, probably also tend to like
each other more — and the net result is a far better basis for cooperation.
This theme will not be developed further here but only indicated with
one word loaded with the meaning of what this pattern may be in practice
— the mafia, the alliance of the landowners (but bigger ones than we
have in the villages of the sample) and a tertiary, more urban proletariat,[3]
often of the *lumpenproletariat* variety. Along the interaction lines of this

Diagram 6.2.2. *Value orientation, social position and interaction structure combined*

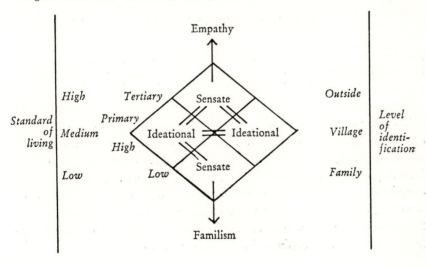

245

alliance, traditional values and anti-modern values flow abundantly and provide the society with a strong backbone that can and evidently has effectively withstood efforts to change the social order. To summarize it all in one, hopefully more suggestive figure, see Diagram 6.2.2.

In this Diagram we see the interplay of factors more clearly, and particularly clearly do we see how all these factors tend to favor the traditionals and disfavor the people with a more modern orientation (Table 6.2.2).

Table 6.2.2. *The structure of traditionalism: arguments reviewed*

	Tertiary high *Primary low*	*Tertiary low* *Primary high*
Cultural mentality	predominantly sensate	predominantly ideational
Efforts to move	directs tertiary high away from village, toward the *outside*	not very pronounced; attention can be focused on the *villages*
Familism	directs primary low away from the village, toward the *family*	not very pronounced; attention can be focused on the *villages*
Empathy in general (social, space and time perspectives)	separates the two groups; indicates differences in basic outlook	facilitates union of these two groups; indicates similarity in basic outlook
Standard of living	separates these two groups	facilitates union of these two groups
Institutionalized interaction structure	does not connect these two groups	connects these two groups

This is the 'diabolic conspiracy' of circumstances, and even if some of the individual differences on which these assertions are based are relatively small, the total picture nevertheless is rather clear. The forces favoring change are *divided* by a weak interaction structure, partly capitalist and partly feudal; and differences in outlook, level of identification and standard of living make it difficult to compensate for this by associations (non-institutionalized interaction). And the forces favoring status quo are *united* by all these factors.

246

Let us then turn briefly to the other presentation we have used several times for social structure, based on the relation between social and economic rank. Again, we have four basic categories but shall only fill in the major findings in qualitative terms, since the approaches used in the various chapters are not always completely comparable (Table 6.2.3).

Table 6.2.3. *Basic value orientations as a function of socio-economic position*

	High social *High economic*	*High social* *Low economic*	*Low social* *High economic*	*Low social* *Low economic*
Sensates	low	high	high	low
Movers	low	high	low	low
Familists	low	low	high	low

The basic point here is, again, how these distributions combine in producing a structure that is particularly unfortunate from the point of view of basic social change. The assumption, then, is that there is a potential for dynamism stemming from people in the two disequilibrated combinations: people who have one foot high and one foot low in the local structure, who consequently are treated differentially and who may be presumed to want to equilibrate upward. These people are sources of ferment in general, but, as Table 6.2.3 indicates, *this ferment seems to be lost.* For, as closer analysis of the figures reveals, the disequilibrated seem to engage *a fortiori* in the type of escapism typical of their groups. We have seen that sensates high up in society have a tendency to be very high on empathy and to translate this into efforts to move away — this is *a fortiori* true for the high level sensates who are disequilibrated. And we have seen how sensates low down in society have a tendency to be very low on empathy (although, certainly, not more than the ideationals — only relative to sensates higher up) and to translate this into familism — and this is also *a fortiori* true for the low level sensates who are disequilibrated. In other words, disequilibrium dissipates — the energy does not disapear but is steered toward a level that is too *macro* for the sensates in the tertiary high category, and too *micro* for the sensates in the primary low category.

But this means that a true revolutionary alliance between the sensates, high and low, is strongly impeded. It would probably have to derive its leadership from the disequilibrated in both groups — and there are, of course, people among them who would be village oriented and would prefer to convert the motivational energy stemming from disequilibrium into changes *of* the system rather than changes for themselves *in* the system by moving up and out of the system, by migrating. But they are few, as the Tables indicate, and they do not easily find each other because of all the factors separating them. Moreover, group atmosphere matters here. If the tendency had been for the disequilibrated to be predominantly village oriented, then one of them, a particularly charismatic individual, would be able to operate in an atmosphere of support — the group ethos would favor him. But as matters stand, such individuals would have to start fighting against tendencies in their own groups, in their closest circles — before they could start tackling antagonists. And the antagonists are village oriented. They do not have any dynamism derived from disequilibrium; nor do they need it. Their task is to preserve, not to change, and their equilibrated positions probably also provide them with the intra-personal stability needed to carry out this task with sufficient efficiency.

It may be objected that this presupposes that the categories we have used in Tables 6.2.2 and 6.2.3 are not only statistically defined groups but also action groups. This would hardly be a valid assumption; as mentioned, the villages are extremely poor in associational structure. But the assumption is not really necessary either. The argument is rather that these categories define people with relatively similar interests in these societies and consequently form a structural basis for action — a basis that may be crystallized into group action if the circumstances so permit. What we have done has only been to indicate some of the many ways in which the structural circumstances do not invite such group formation.

* * *

This concludes our presentation of these villages, in terms of the major themes of our presentation. It remains only to further elaborate some subsidiary themes to round off the picture of how these villages got stuck on a possible road to development.

Let us start with *education*. Many things would have been different if one could have concluded that more education would imply more openness to modern orientations. But we cannot say that: it does not seem to hold when individuals with different lengths of schooling are compared synchronically, and it probably would not hold diachronically when one individual gets more schooling, or when the percentage of the population with completed elementary school increases either. *The school has to be changed, not merely school attendance*; the training of teachers is probably more crucial for development than the training of pupils.

Or to take another factor, *age*, the picture is more complicated. But let us buy the assumption that the young are the key to the future because the old, whatever their orientation and inclination may be or may have been, evidently have got stuck, often have run out of energy and are not able to move the villages much ahead. And the young tend to be sensate. This may be seen as positive from the point of view of modernization, for even if many of them will be absorbed and undergo changes in value orientation as they grow older and change perspectives on life in general and the villages in particular, some of the surplus will survive. But it does not seem to be too helpful in this connection: young sensates also tend to be movers and familists — which means that they have their attention directed either too high or too low — or both at the same time. Hence, young age is not a very helpful factor: it serves as a nucleus of crystallization for several other attitudes, but these attitudes tend to have an erosive effect on the reservoir of sensate orientation.

Still another factor is *mobility*. It would have been so much more positive if the people who had been given rewards by the village, from its very limited reservoir of mobility rewards, were also the people who would devote themselves to the village. But few if any would blame the people on top for trying to make the next step outside: the mobility ladder of the village is so truncated that devotion to it would only rarely lead to more mobility inside. The motivation would have to be found elsewhere, not in individual mobility. And group support is rarely forthcoming in villages so underdeveloped in associational structure as these.

And then there is the basic weakness in the sensate orientation as such; it seems to be embedded in a cluster of attitudes rather than in a behavioral pattern. Of course, we are not saying that one cannot predict sensate behavior from sensate orientation, but the inference would have been safer if the sensate orientation had been supported by a consistent pattern of past and present behavior. On the contrary: the forces that are more negative- the tendency to move out of the village and the tendency to move into the family- are both reinforced because they are embedded in behavioral clusters. Hence we would be more prone to believe that *these* orientations would be enacted. The sensates may keep their ideologies and build them into and around amplified and highly articulate perspectives on society, space and time, but movers and familists are likely to do something much more important: simply to *act* according to their orientation. And what then becomes the gain to the outside (in terms of manpower) or to the family (in terms of devotion) becomes the loss to the village, for it is difficult to be two places at the same time, nor can one devote oneself entirely to two spheres of allegiance at the same time.[4]

Hence, everything works against the people with a more modern orientation, and that makes one ask this question: How important is *number* here? Does it really matter very much whether the proportion of sensates is 30%, 50% or 70% — if the structure is so much against them that their energies are dissipated and they themselves absorbed by, or outside the system? Yes, could it not even be that 10% with a high level of traditional village orientation might be able to absorb 90% with the opposite orientation? Of course, this is where associations in general and political parties in particular enter the picture: they can reduce *pluralistic ignorance* and convert scattered individuals into a force. But what, then, if the associations and parties, in turn, are absorbed by the structure? And what if these traditionals, that small 10% axis in the middle of the system, have the most relevant connections with other levels of the general social structure, with provincial, regional and national power centers so that services can flow in both directions? Is it then very farfetched to believe that *the structure we have tried to unravel is not only the structure of ultrastability within, but also the structure that best renders itself to manipulation from above, precisely because the forces that would favor that manipulation are united, whereas the forces that might oppose it are divided?* We do not have data to explore this further, but we offer it as a basic perspective: for manipulation and domination from above to be effective, a structure of this type is needed, and a structure of this type may also be the result of manipulation and domination from above.

And that concludes the picture. The themes have now been interrelated and they add up to one simple conclusion. It is not so much that each one of them is so strong, so pronounced,[5] but together they combine in an unholy alliance, in a conspiracy against progress. This conspiracy, indeed, has its concrete manifestations in terms of the actions of particular parties, particular groups, particular men. But our method has directed us to a search for the structure underlying what meets the naked eye: the structure of ultrastability. And our search has not been in vain; many factors have been found, so many that it may look as if the phenomenon is over-explained. But the point is exactly the cumulative effect of all these factors: the silent, not necessarily deliberate, conspiracy, the type of conspiracy that is so much more resistant to change than a conspiracy of persons because it is less concrete, less evident, less manifest — because it is truly hidden, not only clandestine; truly evasive, not only secretive. *The conspiracy of value orientation and social structure — against development and progress.*[6]

7. Epilogue: Implications for political action

Let us now take our theory, or perhaps better, image, of these Sicilian villages and expose it to a completely different test. So far our procedure has been the traditional *empirical test* developing theories or images compatible with data collected *a priori* or *a posteriori*. We have done so inductively rather than deductively, *a posteriori* rather than *a priori*, but that is only a difference of empirical time order between data collection and theory formation. The important thing is that theory and data somehow 'hang together' — although sometimes rather loosely, we would be the first to admit. And the pure case with one of these processes being fully completed before the other process even is started is an abstraction; they always interpenetrate into each other to some extent. But all of this only permits us to *explain* that what is most needed in these villages is to *act*.

In this section we shall therefore move forward and expose the theory to an *axiological test,* by which we mean simply this: Does the theory give us some insight into how values can be achieved? This is also a question of compatibility, but this time not between the empirical and the theoretical, but between the theoretical and the axiological, between predictions as to what would happen if one did this or that, and social values. It should be added that in a book this is the maximum one can do. We cannot go still one step further and expose the theory to the *praxiological test* where insights about how values can be realized are put into theoretically guided practice and tested very much like in any other applied science — as when the ultimate test of physical theory is whether the bridge in fact carries the weight, whether the architect's house is in fact convenient, etc. But these belong to the world of action, not to the world of words, although these worlds are certainly not mutually exclusive.

The question is simply: Does this image serve as a basis for deriving a program for political action? Of course, the test would not be whether one could derive ideas already contained in the program of political parties or other interest/pressure groups, or in the programs of executive branches. Some overlap might be an indicator of realism, but complete overlap would make the social scientist superfluous: If there is nothing new the social scientist can contribute, then what is the use? Of course, he can deliver an empirical and theoretically founded basis for a pre-existing program, and this is often done. But the suspicion will remain that he started with the program and worked backward to develop the justification, and although this may be justified if it 'hangs together' he would probably have been able to derive many more insights if he had attacked the data-hypotheses-values triangle in a more symmetrical and more open-ended manner.

Which, then, are the basic values we would like to use as a yardstick to judge our theory? They are *horizontal development, vertical development* and *internal as well as external structural development*. Put in other words: increased averages of socio-economic values, decreased dispersion of them, an internal defeudalization making individuals and groups more autonomous, more masters of their own fates, and an external defeudalization making the villages more autonomous. This depicts a process away from a relation of internal and external dependence and domination leading not only to exploitation but also to stagnation in terms of averages and to increasing or at least not decreasing gaps between rich and poor, between high and low in general terms. However, our analysis will have to be sketchy; it is more an indication of types of analysis that we think social scientists should develop further, rather than a real program of action — which has the additional advantage, however, that it permits us to shed some additional light on the images we have tried to develop.

So, let us accept, for the sake of the argument, that our images reflect the data, at that the data reflect the reality and that the simplifications we have introduced do not distort too much. What then could be done to come closer to the realization of the values mentioned? Let us start by mentioning something that should not be done:

1) *Development initiatives from the outside only.* These villages are at the bottom end of an impressive string of power relations, and they have to develop in a way that also reduces the external structural dependence. However useful and indispensable capital, skills and tools

from the outside, there must be an autonomous, genuine local basis that steers the development. Pumping capital in from the outside will only amplify the domination structure, not change it.

2) *Development initiatives from the dominant inside groups only.* Inside these villages the poor and low are at the bottom end of an equally impressive string of local power relations, which means that the villages also have to develop in a way that reduces the internal structural dependence. However useful and indispensable capital, skills and tools from the dominant group on the inside, there must be mass participation to steer the development.

In other words, we presuppose immediately that the only meaningful actions for development, given these images of the villages, would have to have a grass-roots basis, inside the villages relative to the dominant groups, outside the villages relative to dominant groups at higher levels. If this is not the case, one can never hope to achieve more than classical development in the sense of moving averages only (and in Western Sicily during a long period one did not even achieve that). The goals have to be set from below; the means have to be chosen from below; the total planning process has to be democratic (not handed down by experts in a meritocracy in the same way as orders were handed down by the knights in an aristocracy); the implementation has to be controlled from below. This does not exclude the participation of other layers inside and outside, but their participation has to be in the open, not manipulative, and under mass control.

Given the realities of these villages, all this sounds utopian. The conspiracy of value orientation and social structure is dead against it. Hence, it becomes a question of exploding that conspiracy if it is a real obstacle to the realization of these values. And to do this, again, local action is needed and is unlikely to come from those who benefit from the conspiracy. At this point our abstract values translate into human beings, and the question is: *Who are the possible carriers of these values?* Certainly not the traditional ideationals, but not necessarily the more modern sensates either. The latter are defined in other ways, with an emphasis on change and control. There may not be one person in the villages who identifies completely with the four development values, for that matter. But since the values change, it is of course much more likely that they will be carried on and implemented by sensates rather than by ideationals. Those are the concrete forces one would gamble on, or rather: it is in the sensate groups that the likelihood of concerted grass-roots actions, geared to changing the power relations and to bringing about a growing and more just society, is highest.

Hence, *the problem is how to strengthen the sensates and weaken the ideationals in this society.* This identification of values with concrete human actors may be unwarranted, but it is the best guess we can make on the basis of our data and theory.

This being said, we can now draw upon the insights tentatively expressed in Diagram 6.2.2 and Tables 6.2.2 and 6.2.3 — all about the 'conspiracy'. To put this more in focus, let us start again by mentioning something that should not be done:

1) *The diffusion model: waiting for more sensates to form.* According to this model, the trend is in the direction of more sensates, so all one has to do is to wait for a sufficient number to form and to take over. Mass media and increased exposure in general would be among the mechanisms favoring this development. However, this image is the naive image of society as a set of individuals who are mutually independent carriers of ideas and values; it is an image where structure in general and structural power in particular are left completely out. It is an unrealistic image a) because the content of the modern message is shaped in these media by those who dominate the structure and b) because of the very high absorption capacity of these villages. As developed in the preceding section, it is hardly unrealistic to expect that a village with only 10% ideationals may still be completely traditional. Hence, something of a more structural nature has to be done.

2) *The mobility model: waiting for sensates to occupy ideational positions.* Looking at the structure, with the mobility data from 3.7 in mind, one is struck by how they favor the two groups equally. There are three kinds of mobility: from primary low into tertiary low, from tertiary low into tertiary high and from tertiary high out of the system. The process might transport some sensates into the ideational camp; by the second process some ideationals might get into the senate camp; and by the third process some sensates leave the system. The net result may be status quo, but it may also be a polarization in terms of class: the sensates from the primary low take over the tertiary low, and the latter squeeze out sensates from the tertiary high, leaving a neatly polarized class society. As we shall develop later, this may be good from the point of view of realizing these values. However, the method is hardly realistic a) because mobility is a slow process, b) because there is little mobility anyhow and c) because we have little or no reason to assume that the

255

value orientations are individual rather than structural. If they are individual, they are so deeply internalized that they would be invariant of the structural position occupied by the individual; if they are structural, they are so weakly internalized that they are more invariant of the individual — they belong to the structural position and are left behind when the individual leaves. We feel that the latter is more probable.

3. *The aging model : waiting for the young to become old.* We know there is a surplus of sensates among the young, especially among the *braccianti*, and the idea would to be to wait until they come into positions of power so that they can transform the society according to their blueprints. But this is also a naive model, for the same reasons as pointed out above: a) this is a rather slow process; b) there is no guarantee at all that the sensates among the young will get into power positions — they may have gone elsewhere and/or be denied access to such position — and c) their orientation may be structural, a characteristic of young people rather than of the individual. Radicalism tapers off with age, and in these societies quite quickly according to local hearsay.

4) *The schooling model: waiting for education to play its role.* In this particular case this argument is very weak, since we have shown that schooling is correlated with ideational attitudes, whether this is due to the teaching or to the selection of pupils or to both. But even if it were correlated with sensate attitudes, the arguments from the points above would still be valid: it is not so much a problem of changing attitudes as of changing structures. In addition, it should be emphasized that there is considerable distance between a generalized sensate orientation and a concrete action program and that schools may imbue their pupils with the former without in any sense preparing them for action that might lead to implementation of these attitudes.

We have presented this list of strategies that should *not* be followed because they are strategies that to many, particularly within an individualistic, Christian, liberal tradition, seem absolutely obvious, as obvious as waiting for day to follow night. But there is no basis in our data, or in the theory, for assuming the validity of these strategies. Hence, we turn to other suggestions that come closer to attacking the structure. In so doing we shall start with the logic of our theoretical scheme, as it is presented in Table 6.2.2, but shall invert the order of the factors and start with the structure of institutionalized interaction, since this is absolutely fundamental.

7.1. *Changes in the institutionalized interaction structure*

The interaction network is poor, and if the missing links were added it would strengthen the hands of the sensates and of the lower class. One key here is the transition into the monetary economy of the *braccianti*, and although we are now talking of processes that have already taken place, they would be spelled out, since this scheme has applicability far outside Western Sicily. Strategies:

1) *Demanding payment in cash rather than in kind, using strikes and other means.* The risk is that this increases the price of labor so much that the landowner prefers to invest in labor-saving devices he can run himself (tractors, harvesters, etc.). On the other hand, the threat of losing the advantage of paying in kind may be an incentive to mechanize farming and hence to increase the productivity of the primary sector — precisely because the farmer will, probably rightly, anticipate escalating demands not only for money, but for more money.

2) *Getting money from outside the system.* The most important possibilities are betting and gambling (institutionalized as a compensatory mechanism in the form of lotteries and betting on football games, etc.) and money acquired by working abroad, by the person himself (who returns with the money) or by relatives (who send the money back). Neither method changes the system, but they both bring resources into the system that may be converted into effective levers for changing the system. Thus, these resources may bring the primary low, the group that above all gets salaried work abroad, into more contact with the tertiary high, partly because it is more able to pay for the services of that group and partly because money may be invested in such a way that differences in standard of living diminish.[1]

7.2. *Changes in the non-institutionalized interaction structure*

This is another way of saying association formation, bringing people together for definite purposes other than direct production of economic value. But these voluntary associations should have definite socio-political purposes in mind; they should be geared to development in the way this is defined above. They should not be just any voluntary associations such as hobby clubs, sports clubs, boy scouts, etc. Even though we shall not underestimate the significance of such organizations as training for non-institutional interaction, it is naive as a formula for development a) because there does not seem to be any automatic spill-over effect from association formation in one field to association formation in another and b) because they are too open to ideationals. What is needed here are associations that are focused on the problems of the villages in order to do something in a way that will change not only the villages but also the power structure. Hence, they should be formed in such a way as to exclude ideationals, much as political parties do, for the simple reason that some element of polarization has to be introduced in the structure to be able to do something about it at all.

To be more specific, these associations should unite sensates, thus adding to the interaction structure in a way that would strengthen them. But they should also aim at weakening the ideationals by providing better alternatives for the services offered by the leading traditionalists to their clients. In other words, for these associations to succeed, normative power (conversion, changes in ideology) is not enough; and if coercive power is ruled out for ideological reasons (this would be to fight with the weapons of the enemy, the mafia), only utilitarian power remains. The sensates have to prove that they have alternatives, and in so doing they will also become less dependent, more self-reliant, and thus contribute not only to strengthening themselves but to internal and external structural development. *The means chosen to obtain development have themselves to be part of the development syndrome.*

In more concrete terms, we are of course thinking of *trade unions* (that might possibly even unite the primary low and the tertiary low and thus constitute an important tie), of *political parties*, of *associations* and *meetings* to *discuss* goals, means, planning and implementation, and of associations that *act: cooperatives* (production and/or consumption) and, say, *associations* for running alternative schooling programs. The latter could only be an association uniting sensates from the primary low and the tertiary high and would be a typical case of a fight for structural change with multiple payoffs: one more purpose that can serve as a basis for uniting the two groups, one more occasion for training in concerted action, one more chance to offer a better alternative than the traditional structure has at its disposal, one more chance to invest for the future in the training of young people for autonomy, for change, for development. Many other examples could be mentioned, and they all have one thing in common: practically speaking, they force the participants to enlarge their social, space and time perspectives.[1]

258

7.3. *Changes in the identification level*

This is one of the most important advantages of the traditionals: they have the right level of identification. The moderns have to be taken out of their familism, down from their escapism, and somehow brought to focus on the village as worthwhile. How is that done? It seems that the answer lies in much of what has already been mentioned. For many of them it is not too late. What they have against the villages is not only that they are in the periphery of the nation, but also that they offer no chance for self-realization, and this not merely in monetary terms.

The general key to identification at the village level, is, of course, more utilitarian than normative. Preaching loyalty, diffusing local patriotism, will not do. People have to be convinced that they can have meaningful, symmetrical relations with the villages in the sense that they can give to the villages their working power, talent, initiative and capital and get back in terms of challenge, position, rewards. The familist could expend his energies in the village if he were convinced that it could serve the welfare of his family. The disequilibrated at the top could do likewise if he thought this were a place where he could obtain some equilibration. In short: changes in economic life toward higher levels of productivity in the primary, secondary and tertiary sectors (not necessarily in the classical sense of bringing 'industry' with chimneys into the villages), changes in political life with the broadest possible participation, changes in social life with richer interaction networks, more challenge, changes in cultural life with more possibility of receiving *and* creating. This is a self-reinforcing process: development offers rewards which retain people. But unless this is combined with the more group-oriented perspectives above, the result might still be only a transfer of the same structure to a level of higher productivity, with the same unholy alliance at the top as before.

In this connection some words should be said about migration. It is not an unmitigated evil, partly because it may reduce population pressure in regions that are not only underdeveloped but (perhaps) also undevelopable, partly because it may change the balance of power at the local level by bringing capital back at points in the structure that were formerly (almost) outside the monetary economy. Also, it may rid the structure of people who have expended their best energy already and open mobility possibilities for others. But it is equally obvious that it means a drain of talent and experience that the local level cannot afford to lose.

There are two obvious strategies if one wants to reduce migration: diminish the pull and diminish the push. One can diminish the pull by making it more difficult to enter, by means of quotas, by higher standards of excellence, to get permission to work at the new place (this would have to be coordinated at the national level in a general manpower plan), by means of a crisis that makes the place less attractive, etc. However, even though these strategies, singly or combined, may reduce actual migration considerably, they do not necessarily reduce potential migration. The desire to leave may still be there, which means that more mental efforts will be put into circumventing these obstacles than into contributing to the development of the local scene. Hence, the only realistic way of stopping migration is by diminishing the forces that push people away. And this can only be done, it seems, by means of the strategies mentioned above, for the migration potential is above all among the disequilibrated in the tertiary high group; and to retain them, the structure has to be sufficiently open so that efforts to expend their energy inside the structure seem worthwhile.

However, there is a possible compromise: *to make the regional level more meaningful.* Some of the tertiary high have a very strong feeling of having outgrown the villages, and for them the 'outside' is the only meaningful place to be. But their experience and energy might still be put to use at a local level if the region or district had a sufficiently well-developed structure to permit the absorption and utilization of their talents. If the village is too small, a more ample social space might be made, for instance by organizing villages into a larger, more meaningful economic unit for production and/or consumption, with some new institution building also. For one cannot just admonish people to convert from family egoism to village altruism; there has to be a structural basis. And familists, to use them as an example once more, will soon want employment outside the home for the wife, not only for the husband, as one basic way of catering to their neo-familist needs for consumption together. But the village will often be too small to offer jobs for both, so that they have to leave and go to larger units that can employ a couple. Where both want income, one of them must give up employment (usually the woman), or one has to leave the village (usually the man), which carries obvious implications for his marriage. But these three alternatives are all at the level of the family as strategic choices they have to make. At the level of the communities there are the possibilities of connecting the villages with excellent roads and other means of communication, of making them into parts of a large, territorial, urban structure able to render the services they are looking for as migrants to the big cities in the North. In short: a social space with sufficient security, challenge and expansion offers at one time what these villages cannot offer singly.[1]

7.4. *Polarization in the value distribution*

However valuable the suggestions mentioned above, we nevertheless feel that they will not permit a really new deal, a really new social order. There are very real conflicts of interests in these societies, but without any real confrontation one may risk the opinion that these conflicts will never be resolved in the sense of being transcended in a new social order. The strategies still give too many openings for those with training in exploiting the structure for their own purposes to prevail under the guise of promoting modern values. Also, we doubt that the social structures, as they now are, will acquire sufficient dynamism for a real takeoff into new levels of organization for richer human lives in a more egalitarian society.

One basic reason for this pessimism, which we have pointed to many times during our presentation, is the lack of polarization in these villages. *The entropy of the distribution of value orientations is too high to permit political mobilization.* This is true at all levels of organization we have studied:

Intra-personally :	there are very few people with clear, crystallized ideas; most of them have both worlds inside themselves;
Intra-class :	both classes are split, not only by sector but also within the sectors for each class;
Intra-sector :	both sectors are split, not only by class but also within classes for each sector;
Intra-village :	all villages as such are split and divided; there is no clear crystallization in one or the other direction.

In short, there is a paralyzing lack of crystallization. The villages as such cannot act and demand; the sectors cannot do so; the classes cannot do so; even the individuals cannot do so as forcefully as they could have done with a more clear structure of the value distribution. And we do not think this is an artifact due to our blunt measuring instrument alone; it is too consistent and also too compatible with the general level of inactivity in these villages.

In this there is, of course, a point of considerable significance for the general theory of social systems. What we have described above, sometimes referred to as crisscross or cross-pressure or split loyalties, sometimes as depolarization and sometimes as high entropy, are all extremely significant factors in the general theories of conflict and peace. It is well demonstrated that it has a dampening influence on tendencies toward the use of violence. It is stabilizing and structures masses of people or groups or nations like molecules in a non-magnetized piece of iron: it de-structures them. On top of this, institutions can be built, and mobility patterns can be constructed, lifting people out of this amorphous mass to become leaders, dominators of people set off against themselves, paralyzed by doubt within themselves as well as between groups.

But what is good for peace, in the sense of absence of violence, is not necessarily good for development, and particularly not for what we have referred to as vertical development and internal as well as external structural development. High entropy between actors at the same level becomes an extremely important stabilizing factor between them, but if there is somebody at the top of that stable structure again, then stability below becomes a factor favoring domination from above. It is not the only structural formula behind the *divide et impera* doctrine, but it is certainly one of the more important. High entropy stabilizes, but low entropy is needed to provide the system with sufficient energy to make a real transition from one social form to another.

The implication of all this does not necessarily lead to any battlecry for a bloody revolution according to classical revolutionary formulas. But it does call for more crystallization. Thus, it would probably be a tremendous advantage for these villages if:

Intra-personally:	more persons had a clearcut sensate orientation;
Intra-class:	one class had a clearcut sensate orientation, or
Intra-sector:	one sector had a clearcut sensate orientation, or
Intra-village:	one village had a clearcut sensate orientation.

This would permit persons to be mobilized, without too much ambiguity and ambivalence, and to release their ideas into action; it would permit a real confrontation between classes or between sectors, and it would permit one village to take a lead and set a model or even to demand important structural changes (e.g. of the type suggested) at the inter-village level. Obviously, since class and sector cross-cut each other, we could not have both class and sector polarization, so one has to be chosen. And there is also the problem of which class or sector should be the carrier of the modern values.

As to the latter, we have one simple formula to guide us. If the carriers of the modern values are the topdog sector or topdog class (i.e. the tertiary sector or the upper class), then the probability is very high that they will be able to carry the dominance structure over into a modern or even neo-modern social setting. It is only when there is a polarization with the underdog sector or underdog class (i.e. the primary sector or the lower class), as the reservoirs of the patterns for the new world, that there is any chance of a really new departure; and even in that case chances are that they will take over the dominance patterns of their former masters.

In this particular Sicilian setting we would probably be inclined to believe much more in the possibility of uniting the lower class than of uniting the primary sector, so the best would probably be a polarization along class lines. For that reason, changes in the institutionalized and non-institutional interaction structure should be in that direction, from primary low to tertiary low, using as bridgeheads former primary lows, with a very deliberate attempt to increase the level of class consciousness among the tertiary low. In this process, associations should of course also be open to the tertiary high who would like to join, and to others, but by and large aiming at isolating the primary high who do not see that the old structures are hopelessly inadequate relative to the values of today.

In other words, one should not be afraid of polarization, but rather see it as a necessary condition for progress. There are many ways in which polarization can be translated into very effective non-violent action for social change, and the major key is to provide the village with functional alternatives for structures that are not only inadequate but even highly detrimental. But to do all this, organization is needed; and to organize effectively, people must have something in common; values alone are often too abstract. Social groups are not; poverty is not — it is highly concrete — but for a whole group, defined socially, to join an organization to realize some political aim, a certain polarization is necessary. As it stands now, the whole structure is too complicated, it splits the society too many ways, down to the single individual.[1]

* *
*

263

So, to end with the title of this book: they are *Members of Two Worlds*. But to conquer that new world, so ill defined, that is imprinted on our minds sometimes as a highly concrete program, sometimes as a dream, they have to sever more of their ties with the old world, the world of feudal, capitalistic dominance, of disintegration at the bottom and an unholy alliance at the top, of migration and familism, a world of narrow perspectives. They are not likely to sever those ties equally, all at the same time. They will do it, sooner or later, but, as we have seen, in a way that tends to preserve the system rather than change it. What we argue is that it should be done and must be done more deliberately, with greater strength and with more structure, mobilizing active groups into a political struggle for what is theirs. In trying to jump from the old world to the new, one at a time and in small steps, a change at the social level will never be achieved, often not even at the individual level, for that matter. It is the collective and determined step that matters; for that purpose organization is indispensable, and for that, in turn, polarization is needed.

And then it remains only to hope that in so doing they will be wiser than their predecessors and not believe themselves to be infallible, that they will understand that they will also in turn be superseded by new forces as they did with the old. In short: they must understand that the only meaningful revolution is the permanent revolution.

Notes

1.1.

1. Guiseppe di Lampedusa, *The Leopard* (New York: Signet Books, 1961), p. 108. This is an excellent translation of the original, *Il Gattopardo* (Milano: Feltrinelli, 1958).
2. *Ibid.*, p. 182.
3. *Ibid.*, pp. 184 f.
4. It is interesting to read the *Lettera Pastorale* (*Il vero volto della Sicilia*, Palermo, 1964) by Ernesto Cardinale Ruffini — directed against the three 'sources of defamation of Sicily': the mafia, the *Gattopardo*, and Danilo Dolci. That a high-ranking Church official should react against such images is natural. But his defense o Sicily is limited to a listing of cultural monuments, of famous personalities and natural beauty — all of them indisputable, but of minor relevance as a consolation in a region characterized by misery and exploitation by internal and external forces.

 This letter should be contrasted with the penetrating view given by an insider like Sebastiano Agliano, *Questa Sicilia* (Mondadori, 1959) — not to mention the deep sincerity of Danilo Dolci's books. Suffice it here only to mention two of the first publications about his work: Franco Grasso, *A Montelepre hanno piantato una croce* (Milano, Roma: Avanti, 1956) and Guy Ganachaud, *Les Bandits de Dieu* (Paris, Editions de Seuil, 1957).

1.2. This section was written when the author was a Visiting Professor in the Department of Sociology at Makerere University College, Kampala, Summer 1967. It is a revised version of a lecture held at Radiotelefiss Eireann, Dublin, June 23, 1967, as an introduction to a series of lectures on sociological theory at Makerere. I would like to express my gratitude to Professor Raymond Apthorpe and to Mr. Arnljot Bergh for invitations to give this lecture.

1. The struggle over evolutionism is a typical example of how much scientific debate is a copy of political debate: a doctrine is launched; its protagonists become more and more excessive in their claims to validity for the doctrine until the antagonists are able to catch them and prove some of their claims to be illegitimate, whereupon — as by revolution or parliamentary rule — the whole doctrine is thrown out, water, baby and all, and to mention it becomes a profanity. Thus, to find Spencer's biological analogies too farfetched (although many of his critics would not have had

the imagination or audacity to ever construct anything similar) is one thing, to reject any idea of some kind of unilinear change in the world as a whole quite another. Two relatively balanced accounts of the controversy are found in Gordon Childe, *Social Evolution* (New York: Schuman, 1951), particularly Chapter I, and, by the same author, in *What Happened in History?* (London: Penguin Books, 1965, first published in 1942), also Chapter I.

2. 'Economic *growth* may be defined as increasing output (GNP) per capita. Economic *development* has broader reference to the building of institutions, new lines of production, and the dissemination of attitudes essential for self-sustaining growth ...,' from Karl de Schweinitz, Jr., 'Economics and the Underdeveloped Economies', *The American Behavioral Scientist*, 1965, pp. 3 and 5, quoted from James S. Coleman, 'The Resurrection of Political Economy', *Mawazo*, 1967, pp. 31–40.

3. This is more or less in line with current usage. For an effort to give a systematic treatment of these concepts, see Johan Galtung, *Norm, Role and Status*, forthcoming.

4. Actually, our statements refer to the total world picture over time. One should be much more careful in formulating theses about societies changing from, say, primitive to traditional — for in what sense would it then be the 'same' society that has 'changed'? Because it is located in the same territory, so as to have deposited sufficient sediments, one above the other, for the archeologists to observe? What, then, about migration? What about societies, civilizations, cultures that simply cease to exist, perish, are swallowed up by their neighbors? Thus, the picture of development that we have in mind is not like the organism passing through stages (infancy, childhood, adolescence, maturity, senescence, etc.) where good meaning can be given to talking about the 'same' organism (in spite of the fact that most molecules have been exchanged every thirty years or so); it is, rather, like the image presented in biological theories of evolution where higher species prevail over lower, not because the lower change into the higher, but because the higher have a higher relative survival capacity. But both conceptualizations can be meaningful in this context, as long as it is remembered that when societies often seem to pass through the same stages this is not necessarily for endogenous reasons, but simply due to diffusion and emulation.

5. Thus, like many others, we make the distinction between culture and culture products. Culture is a set of standards — implicit or explicit — defining what is valid (true, right, good, beautiful, holy, etc.) and invalid (false, wrong, bad, ugly, profane, etc.) according to that culture. It is the standard or pattern of evaluation that imputes culture to the cultural product — whether the object is a stone, an act, a painting, a machine, a thought, a word.

6. For an example of a study of this kind, see the series of reports under the direction of Alexander Szalai, published by the European Centre for Documentation and Coordination of Research in the Social Sciences, in Vienna.

7. But the 'democratic assumption' does bring one into some difficulties. Brazil has some of the most urban cities in the world, yet it ranks low in urbanism, because of its size and economic backwardness, when taken as a whole. This, however, leads to the idea that it is not so much the 'democratic bias' as the choice of the wrong unit, that it would often have been better in comparative statistics to treat Brazil as at least two different regions.

8. The basic classical references are to A. G. B. Fisher, *Economic Progress and Social*

Security (London: Macmillan, 1945), Colin Clark, *Conditions of Economic Progress* (London: Macmillan, 1940) and, we would add, two books by Jean Fourastié, *La Civilisation de 1960* (Paris: PUF, 1950) and *Le grand Espoir du XX Siécle* (Paris: PUF, 1952). However, Colin Clark uses the idea in a different way from what we do: 'Low real income per head is always associated with a low proportion of the working population in tertiary production and a high percentage in primary production. High average real income per head compels a large proportion of producers to engage in tertiary production ... as incomes rise the demand for such services increases ...' (*op. cit.*, pp. 5–6). Thus, Clark uses this type of transition on the causal side in a model to explain economic growth, whereas we use it as an independent factor in its own right, as an expression of one of man's desires, whether or not it is associated with economic growth. Thus, there are at least three questions one can ask in connection with the Clark thesis: Is it a feasible classification? Is it a fruitful classification? Is it in fact associated with economic growth, or could it be a case of spurious correlation? We would answer 'yes' to the first two questions and leave the third to the economists. For an example of a discussion, see G. Meier and R. Baldwin, *Economic Development: Theory, History, Policy* (New York: Wiley, 1957), pp. 198 ff. See also the general discussion in section 3.5 of the present work.

9. Many more subdivisions could be imagined, and with the enormous expansion of the tertiary sector, the development of a fruitful classification becomes an urgent matter for all kinds of social scientists. Thus, some Japanese sociologists claim that more than one hundred new professions are created in the tertiary sector every month in Japan.

10. Of course, it was not just by accident that industries tended to be located in cities, or cities around the industries. It was in the interest of the manufacturers to keep expenses down, and to keep transportation of workers, transportation of raw materials and transportation of the finished products at a minimum. The ideal location of an industry would be in a city close to the raw materials (i.e. a suitable port, or close to the mines), because a city could house both labor force and consumers — they could in fact be the same persons if their wages permitted them to enter the market. Since the industrial unit needs more manpower than the farming unit, this logic seems inescapable. But there is a flaw in the reasoning: it presupposes that the social and economic costs of bringing the workers to the enterprise are higher than the costs of bringing the enterprise to the workers, as was done in the watch industry in Switzerland (with parts manufactured on farms or groups of farms and assembled more centrally, thus utilizing the dead winter season of Swiss farmers and at the same time keeping them on the land). But the Swiss system presupposes efficient transportation, good organization and above all a high level of trust in society, in addition to the relevant skills of the individuals concerned. For a basic function of a factory is not only to minimize internal and external transportation costs but also to maximize control by means of proximity and visibility.

11. According to Fourastié, the maximum in the tertiary sector is 80–90% (Fourastié, 1950, pp. 108–109). We disagree; we think the maximum is 100% since it is difficult to see any limit to automation. There will always be people who want to live in the countryside, but who are only able to vacation there not to make a living — their living does not require them to be there.

12. As mentioned, this is Clark's thesis. According to *World Handbook of Social and Political Indicators*, the correlation between GNP/capita and percentage employed in the primary sector is —0.86 (p. 277). But this growth can take place by a pre-dominance of secondary *or* tertiary sector expansion, obviously preferably with the two growth processes in some kind of meaningful balance.

13. Thus, if all industries in the three Scandinavian countries are ranked according to size (as measured by capital invested), then the first Danish enterprise is number thirty-five on the list. But the standard of living in Denmark is not inferior to other countries in the region (*Ekonomon*, 1965).

14. When oil is discovered in a country, the wealth that accrues from it will, of course, accumulate or be distributed and eventually be converted according to the patterns for handling wealth that existed in the society before the oil was discovered. If the rank distance between high and low was considerable, then the distribution would probably at best be proportionate, and if in addition there was the idea of per-sonification, that the leader (sheikh, king) personified the society, then the accu-mulation might be on one side. It is difficult to see how one could expect such persons at the top of traditional structures, with a GNP corresponding to a modern society, to spend the money in other than traditional ways — particularly since these societies would not have structures or occupational distributions adequate for other patterns of dispersion (e.g. physicians, teachers, mass communications people). In the countries that have made their GNP/capita the Clark way, so to speak, the structures for economic growth (expanded secondary and tertiary sectors) have also been the structures for more adequate distribution, the way people in such societies have been accustomed to looking at it. This is, of course, related to the higher potential for organization in the lower ranks of the secondary and tertiary sectors, above all because they work and live in closer proximity to each other.

15. We are using 'ideational' in the sense introduced by Sorokin. The reason why the societies will have to be small is because of the inverse relation between domain and scope: 'extremely ascetic' suggests a high level of value commitment, and that will cut down on the number of candidates for admission; it becomes a sect rather than a church.

16. That the coexistence of segments representing widely different stages of develop-ment within the framework of one nation-state is a potential source of problems is a truism. And the classical way of coping with these problems is also obvious: by means of distance, geographical and/or social. The segments highest on the develop-ment scale are given places in the communications center of the society and the highest position in the stratification system, keeping the lowest segments out in the geographical periphery and/or in the lowest class positions.

17. Margaret Mead in a lecture, University of Oslo 1960.

18. Since any newborn infant can be socialized into any culture regardless of the culture of the parents. If they could only have been socialized a certain distance away from the development stage enjoyed by their parents, this would not have been the case.

19. We are thinking of what are referred to as 'declines and falls' of civilizations, for instance as described by Toynbee in his monumental work, although he is more concerned with the spirit of civilization than with technology. But we would also think of such factors as the hippie revolution on the United States West Coast (for an excellent discussion, see *Time*, July 7, 1967, p. 12–20). Some of the hippies have settled in small agricultural communities, to some extent going back to a

traditional or even neolithic structure in the sense of this paper. Does this disprove our basic thesis? No, for three reasons. First of all, the United States is so quickly entering what is here called the neo-modern society that the whole problem of *what next* becomes urgent — and, in terms of the Clark dimensions, the only possibility would be to step backward. Another answer would be that it still remains to be seen whether the influx of hippies to the primary sector can outweigh the influx of people to the cities from the countryside. And finally, the hippie may be as dependent on the modern and neo-modern societies as the peasant is on the tertiary sector when he exchanges foodstuffs for other commodities; the hippie represents a reaction against most trends in contemporary United States society and will probably need its presence to have something to react against; he exists as a contradiction of his opposite. One test of how genuine his philosophy is would be his ability to exist as a hippie without a non-hippie environment to shock and be shocked by — and it may well be that he will withstand that test. For a discussion, in Norwegian, of some problems of neo-modern society, see Johan Galtung, 'Fremtidssamfunn og fremtidsforskning', *Kontrast*, 1967. For a technical discussion touching the same problems, see Johan Galtung, 'Rank and Social Integration: A Multidimensional Approach II', in Berger, Zelditch and Anderson, *Sociological Theories in Progress*, Vol. II (forthcoming).

20. For a presentation and discussion of the Clark thesis in this form, see Meier and Baldwin, *op. cit.*, pp. 144 ff. As they point out, 'no single sequence fits the history of all countries.' For an early discussion of some diachronic data from a number of countries, see Francisco Sánchez López, 'Movilidad Social en España (1900–1950)', *Revista de Estudios Politicos*, 1962, pp. 29–65; see also Fourastié, 1952, pp. 88 ff.

21. Kindleberger criticizes the unreflected use of census statistics on this basis, in *International Economics* (Homewood: Irwin, 1963): 'Failure to correct for foreign trade would be misleading, as in the case of Britain's 6 per cent and New Zealand's 24. Britain imports half of its food, so that some portion of its food intake is actually secured by men and women working in factories for export. When the figures are corrected for this, the British figure comes out to 8.5 per cent ... the New Zealand figure becomes 6.66 per cent' (pp. 455 ff.). In our view, however, Kindleberger misses one point in his effort to see another: that, nonetheless, the percentage of people in Britain in agriculture is 6 per cent, and this says something about Britain, regardless of *how* they are able to do this. What Kindleberger says is only that Britain (or New Zealand or most other countries, for that matter) is not a closed economic system. Some countries have their primary sector located outside, and that is, of course, usually associated with a pattern of dominance.

22. For a discussion of agricultural productivity in such terms, see Kenneth Boulding, *The Meaning of the Twentieth Century*. (New York: Harper & Row, 1965).

23. Our point is essentially that there is no limit to how many steps man can put between himself and nature, first by introducing tools or hardware, second by non-biological forces of power, third by programmation and fourth — how? Surely, there will be a revolution after the tool revolution, the power revolution and the computer revolution, but which one remains to be seen.

24. Gordon Childe, *What Happened in History* (London: Peuguin Books, 1965).

25. *Loc. cit.*

26. *Loc. cit.*

27. Thus, we lean upon the distinction made by Robert Redfield when he writes: 'There were no peasants before the first cities. And those surviving primitive peoples who do not live in terms of the city are not peasants. The peasant is a rural native whose long-established order of life takes important account of the city', *The Primitive World and Its Transformations* (Ithaca, N.Y.: Cornell University Press, 1953), p. 31. Eric Wolf uses this as a point of departure in his important article 'Types of Latin American Peasantry: A Preliminary Discussion', in *American Anthropologist*, 1955, pp. 452–471, reprinted in George Dalton, ed., *Tribal and Peasant Economies* (Garden City, N.Y.: The Natural History Press, 1967), pp. 501–523. We mention this article because it is a good example of how our crude type 'traditional' can be subdivided by means of crucial distinctions as to *how* peasants enter into exchange with non-peasants.

28. Childe gives the following information on pottery: 'No doubt the size of the productive unit was increased. For example, the ceramic industry of Arretium (Arezzo in Tuscany) was organized on a larger scale than the same industry in Athens five centuries earlier. Out of maybe 25 potteries operating there between 25 B.C. and A.D. 25 two employed more than 30 artists who 'signed' their products, 10 had from 10 to 14 artists, and only 6 as few as 7 to 10. . . . So in the ceramic industry of Lezoux in Southern France, which after A.D. 70 took the place of Arretium in supplying the western market, 8 distinct firms are known by their trade marks' (Childe, 1965, pp. 280, 281). Thus: it seems that by far too much emphasis is put on the power revolution at the end of the eighteenth century, so that one loses track of the continuity in the growth of the secondary sector.

29. See footnote 23.

30. In Table 1.2.2, some indications are given for the two kinds of communication, the speeds being too well known to merit any repetition here.

31. A quick count indicates that this would hold for about 80% of the world's capitals, but a real study would involve complicated geographical indicators. A typically deviant case is Vienna — which proves the point since it once was a non-deviant case in a country with a quite different extension. The westward move of Polish and German borders after the Second World War has also dislocated Warszawa and Berlin relative to their central prewar positions. We would count Lisboa and Stockholm as conforming to the rule — but not Washington, D.C. The 'war capital' of the United States, Omaha, Nebraska, would be a better case.

32. We are using the terms 'extensive' and 'intensive' in much the same sense as they are used in thermodynamics.

33. But see footnote 10 for some remarks on the location of the secondary sector. Today this seems to be the trend: to locate industry in the countryside so as to keep people there (electronic industry in the United States' South, North Carolina being a typical example).

34. For an excellent discussion of manumission in different slave societies, see Frank Tannenbaum, *Slave and Citizen* (New York: Alfred A. Knopf, 1946).

35. 'People tend to marry people who are in various social ways like themselves, rather than to marry people with differing characteristics,' say Berelson and Steiner in *Human Behavior* (New York: Harcourt, Brace and World, 1964), p. 305, and continue with four pages of evidence.

36. *Op. cit.*, p. 309, but the correlation is only 0.47.

37. *Op. cit.*, p. 217.

38. If a society has both of these groups, then a bitter conflict is bound to arise if both allocation systems are in operation simultaneously (labor leaders against 'degenerate' landed gentry). If only one of them is present, the conflict will be milder. Data from the United States suggest that only very few people have too high positions for their low IQs, whereas many are in the other group (Berelson and Steiner, *op. cit.*, reporting on a study by Harrell and Harrell, pp. 223–224). Ultimately, with more adequate placement according to what we have called allocation model II, this group will also be 'engineered away'. For an analysis of the consequences of this, see the article by the present author referred to at the end of footnote 19.

39. We are thinking of the 'picture phone' currently being developed by The Bell Telephone Company and a corresponding system to some extent being installed in Moscow.

40. For a discussion of the problems involved in creating world currencies, see pamphlets published by the International Finance Section at Princeton University.

41. He who reads Dante's *Divina Commedia* will readily agree with the saying 'lasciate ogni speranza, voi ch'entrate', although Dante's inferno also has very human, and indeed humorous, characteristics.

42. For an impressionistic comparison of some marxist and Christian utopias, see Johan Galtung, 'Rapport fra fremtidssamfunnet', in *Byen og samfunnet* (Oslo: PAX, 1966). As many have pointed out, Marx's own ideas about the final stage of development, the communist stage, are not too clear. But his conception of justice is very clear: it is based on the idea that achievement is no basis for allocating rewards, since people are different, 'one man is superior to another physically or mentally and so supplies more labour in the same time, or can labour for a longer time ... Further, one worker is married, another not; one has more children than another, and so on and so forth. Thus, with an equal performance of labour, and hence an equal share in the social consumption fund, one will in fact receive more than another, and so on. To avoid all these defects, right instead of being equal would have to be unequal ...' And this quotation from the *Critique of the Gotha Program* ends with the well-known slogan: 'from each according to his ability to each according to his needs,' For, as Marx says in *The German Ideology* (pp. 189–190), 'differences of brain, of intellectual capacity, do not imply any difference whatsoever in the nature of the stomach and of physical needs. ...' This tallies very well with the emerging hippie perspective that man should receive a basic salary simply because he *is*, not because of any work he *does* (a principle almost institutionalized in the unemployment insurance of the welfare state, but the condition is still 'willingness to work'). However, one does not have to interpret principles of proportionality between work and reward as an expression of greedy capitalism or reactionary socialism, but simply as an expression of a society that is not yet rich enough to distribute its income on the basis of 'needs'.

But Marx has another interesting passage in *The German Ideology* about the nature of the final stage (p. 22): 'For as soon as labour is distributed, each man has a particular, exclusive sphere of activity, which is forced upon him and from which he cannot escape. He is a hunter, a fisherman, a shepherd or a civil critic, and must remain so if he does not want to lose his means of livelihood; while in communist society where nobody has one exclusive sphere of activity but each can be accomplished in any branch he wishes, society regulates the general production and thus makes it possible for me to do one thing today and another tomorrow, to hunt in the

271

morning, fish in the afternoon, rear cattle in the evening, criticize after dinner, just as I have a mind, without ever becoming a hunter, fisherman, shepherd or critic.' In order for this to be possible, 'such an ideal society would no doubt require high productivity and practically unlimited abundance' (comment by David Caute, ed., *Essential Writings of Karl Marx* (London: Panther Books, 1967), p. 245). Thus, it would probably have to be a neo-modern society, since only that society would have sufficient productivity as far as we know today. But since everybody can 'do one thing today and other tomorrow', there will be no fixed relation between man and profession. Nor can any population distribution be kept at any level, since it is subject to the whims and desires of the people. Theoretically it could fluctuate all along the scale we have used as the axis of socio-economic development. There is a contradiction in this, and it is sad that Marx did not focus his prolific mind on the task of clarifying this problem. Thus, it looks from the quotation above as if he is in favor of some kind of pluralistic society, but he seems to forget that most statuses ('hunter, fisherman, shepherd or critic') need contra-statuses or role partners to be enacted, and how should this be arranged? By waiting for somebody to do something that one could criticize? Or by having one part of the population fixed in permanent position and the other part rotating so that they can hunt in the morning (who will make the weapons?), fish in the afternoon (who will provide the boats?), rear cattle in the evening (for what purpose? will there be a dairy? a slaughterhouse?) and so on?

43. This was the case with Thomas More's utopia, a kind of agricultural collective, heavily regulated and circumscribed, where everybody worked six hours a day. Thus, it was heavily loaded on the primary sector in terms of work (but then it was written in 1516). But if we apply a time-budget analysis and some hypotheses as to what they would do the rest of the day, there would nevertheless be a bias in favor of the tertiary sector. Gandhi's utopia was very agricultural, however.

44. Just to quote one such study, by the author, from a very modest fishing community on the Malabar coast, in Kerala, 86% wanted their sons in the tertiary sector (unpublished manuscript).

45. A study should be made of the relative costs involved in producing an intellectual and producing a job for an intellectual — since this seems to be crucial. The former is so much more easy, particularly as long as complicated training machinery is not needed. Cheapest to produce are probably jurists (the former specialty of Latin America and Southern Italy) and humanists (the specialty of Southern India, for instance).

46. Last two references in footnote 19.

47. We disagree with those who say that it would be better to talk in terms of poor-rich than in terms of development, since these terms refer to quite different matters (see footnote 2 and corresponding text). But with regard to development, one should distinguish between where on the axis a society is located and whether it is stable or changing. All these four words with 'develop' in them only confuse the issue, since a traditional society may be completely stable and a modern society rapidly changing toward a neo-modern society (and vice versa).

48. For an analysis of this, see Johan Galtung, *Theories of Peace* (forthcoming),

49. Of course, both could happen at the same time. Modern societies, like many European nations around 1800, encroached on traditional societies all along the African coast from Senegal to Zanzibar that in turn had encroached on neighboring and

more primitive societies to obtain slaves. Or, the slaving societies could do it directly by means of raids, with no help from intermediaries. For an excellent account, see Daniel Mannix, *Black Cargoes* (New York: The Viking Press, 1962), particularly Chapters 1 and 2.

50. The ideas here are inspired by Karl Deutsch; see his article in *Conflict and Society* (London: Churchill, 1966).

51. For a discussion of this, see Johan Galtung, 'The Social Sciences: An Essay on Polarization and Integration', in Klaus Knorr and James Rosenau, eds., *Contending Approaches to International Politics* (Princeton, N.J.: Princeton University Press, 1968).

52. This is of course the standard definition of 'society' in sociology textbooks: it is a social structure that is self-maintaining. But this means that it should include the 'significant others', the role partners of the members, otherwise some members will not be able to enact their statuses properly. Thus, it is not only a question of economic basis, adequate procreation and cultural integration — whatever that means.

53. We are thinking of such 'ideologies' as familism, localism, regionalism, nationalism, chauvinism, ethnocentrism, racism, etc. — all of them basically the same in structure, differing from each other only in reference to the magnitude of the group included.

54. And the relation between the social and the technological is, as mentioned, like the realition between the hen and the egg. It is interesting to note that Marx had essentially this vision: '... it is clear that the real intellectual wealth of the individual depends entirely on the wealth of his real connections. Only then will the separate individuals be liberated from the various national and local barriers, be brought into practical connection with the material and intellectual production of the whole world and be put in a position to acquire the capacity to enjoy this all-sided production of the whole earth (the creations of man)' (*The German Ideology*, pp. 27–28). This is further elaborated in Johan Galtung, 'On the Future of the International System', *Journal of Peace Research*, 1967, pp. 305–333.

55. A paradigm for this type of analysis is found in Johan Galtung, *Theories of Peace*.

56. Marx's attempt is probably the most audacious one to date. Essentially, it is based on the idea of some kind of structural imbalance, or tension, and this formula is also found in many contemporary theories of development. A general approach to development theory in terms of imbalance is found in Johan Galtung and Tord Høivik, 'On the Definition and Theory of Development with a View to the Application of Rank Order Indicators in the Elaboration of a Composite Index of Human Resources' (mimeo, 1967), 52 pp.

57. An attempt in this direction is currently in progress at the International Peace Research Institute, Oslo, to be published in a book entitled *Theories of Development*.

58. The whole approach to development used here is in terms of growth and differentiation. We do not apologize for that, since this is the way in which development is most commonly conceived of. But there is another approach to development in terms of equality and justice which has been left out. That approach would put in focus the vertical dimension of society, instead of leaving it untouched and unproblematic as in the present study. For two approaches in this direction by the present author, see 'Structural Pluralism and the Future of Human Society' (paper

273

presented at the Second International Future Research Conference, Kyoto, April 1970) and 'A Structural Theory of Imperialism', *Journal of Peace Research*, 1971.

1.3.

1. Pitirim A. Sorokin, *Social and Cultural Dynamics* (New York: American Book Company, 1937–1941), Vols. I–IV, 2912 pp.; reissued by The Bedminster Press (New York, 1962).

2. Our references are to Pitirim A. Sorokin, *Social and Cultural Dynamics* (Boston: Porter Sargent, 1957). (The reference above is to p. 600.) For a version in Norwegian, see J. R. Gjermoe, *Kultur og Fred. Pitirim A. Sorokins sociale og historiske filosofi* (Oslo: Nordli, 1957).

3. *Ibid.*, pp. 27–29.

4. C. H. Cooley, *Social Organization* (Glencoe, Ill.: The Free Press, 1956), p. 23.

5. Sorokin, *op. cit.*, p. 25.

6. *Ibid.*, p. 37.

7. *Ibid.*, pp. 37–39.

8. 'Get' seems to be a more adequate expression than 'logical deduction', used, for example, on p. 14 (Sorokin).

9. 'The probability is that neither the Ideational nor the Sensate type has ever existed in its pure form; but all integrated cultures have in fact been composed of diverse combinations of these two pure logico-meaningful forms' (*ibid.*, p. 24). This theme of variation is a major concern in the excellent chapter 'Dominant and Variant Value Orientations' in Kluckhohn and Strodtbeck, *Variations in Value Orientation* (Evanston, Ill.: Row, Peterson, 1961), pp. 1–49. Actually, this system could also have been used in our study in lieu of Sorokin's — but the book was not published and there is a certain commanding simplicity in Sorokin's system which is missing in Kluckholm and Strodtbeck. Incidentally, these two authors make almost no reference to Sorokin in their work in spite of the very close similarity in approach.

   There is also another interesting parallel in the literature. Sorokin's distinction is clearly, but not completely, related to Koestler's distinction between *The Yogi and the Commissar* (New York: Macmillan, 1946): 'The Commissar believes in Change from Without. He believes that all the pests of humanity ... can and will be cured by Revolution ... [The Yogi] believes that nothing can be improved by exterior organization and everything by individual effort from within; and that whosoever believes in anything else is an escapist' (pp. 3–4). But Sorokin's categories are more general than Koestler's; there is no assumption that sensate man is a marxist and/or violent or that ideational man is a gandhian and/or nonviolent.

10. Sorokin, *op. cit.*, pp. 7 f., 11. The problem is what 'logico-meaningful integration' is. Sorokin refers to a feeling 'that the two are inconsistent; they do not belong together; they do not make any sense'. Of course, a more objective criterion than this feeling would have been preferable, but as long as it is probably true that 'we' (not only Sorokin) feel this way, it becomes a sociological, if not a logical, truth. But like so many other sociological truths, it may be highly culture bound and hence lead to vicious circles in the conceptualization.

11. This is the theme of Max Weber's *The Protestant Ethic and the Spirit of Capitalism* (London: Allen & Unwin, 1956). Incidentally, when this classic work has not been made use of here, it is largely due to the brilliant and, in our view, devasting criticism

made in Kurt Samuelson's *Religion and Economic Action* (New York: Basic Books, 1961).

12. This, of course, is the theme of Merton's 'Puritanism, Pietism and Science' in *Social Theory and Social Structure* (Glencoe, Ill.: The Free Press, 1957), pp. 574–606.

13. For instance, there is no contradiction between 'being' and 'becoming'. If 'being' means some kind of 'invariance', then there may be a 'being' in a 'becoming', Compare the discussion about 'Funktionsbegriff und Substanzbegriff' (Cassirer); 'Funktion' may be seen as a 'Substanz'.

14. Sorokin, *op. cit.*, p. 35.

15. *Ibid.*, Chap. 26.

16. One way of explicating these modalities lies in contrasting the comments Sorokin himself makes with the description of the pattern variable employed by T. Parsons, *et al.*, *Towards a General Theory of Action* (Glencoe, Ill.: The Free Press, 1951).

The first modality is not found in Parsons' system, but the other five bear striking resemblances with five of Parsons' pattern variables — if we include among them 'long-run vs. short-run focus of valuation' in the oft-cited footnote in his article 'Some Comments on the State of the General Theory of Action', *ASR*, 1953, pp. 618–639.

The *first* modality refers, actually, to the definition of interaction in sociology, as mutual dependence or interdependence. When two individuals interact, 'we may talk of *two-sided* or *mutual*, and one-sided conditioning' (Sorokin, *op. cit.*, p. 438). Of course, the latter are mostly found in very hierarchical forms of social organization — and a number of sociological studies have as their common theme that the interaction is not that one-sided after all, that the underdogs condition the behavior of the topdogs in many and often subtle ways. One may say that this modality is built into Parsons' system by the way he defines interaction (e.g. Parsons, *et al.*, *op. cit.*, pp. 153 ff.). For an analysis of the concept of 'interaction', see Johan Galtung, 'Expectations and Interaction Processes', *Inquiry*, 1959, pp. 213–234.

The *second* modality is closely related to Parsons' distinction specificity vs. diffuseness. Sorokin is concerned with 'the proportion of the activities and psychological experiences involved in interaction out of the total sum of the activities and psychological experiences of which the person's whole life process consists'; Parsons is concerned with 'whether he should respond to many aspects of the object or to a restricted range of them — how broadly is he to allow himself to be involved with the object?' (Parsons, *et al.*, *op. cit.*, p. 83).

Sorokin uses a circle as an illustration of a person's 'whole life process'; the interaction is limited if only one sector is engaged in it; he actually uses the term 'specified' (Sorokin, *op. cit.*, p. 440). The examples he gives coincide very closely with Parsons' examples. However, there is the possible difference that Sorokin refers to Ego's sectorial involvement, whereas Parsons is concerned with how much of Alter Ego is oriented toward it — but if there is reciprocity, interaction relations would be categorized in the same way.

The *third* modality has to do with intensity, and the examples given seem to indicate that this means 'emotional involvement' — which is almost indistinguishable from Parsons' 'affectivity vs. affective neutrality'. Again, we may use the circle model to illustrate what Sorokin is driving at: if the center represents the 'hottest emotions' and the periphery the absence of emotional involvement, the second and third modalities can be combined as follows:

Extensity	low	low	high	high
Intensity	low	high	low	high
Example	grocer-client	politicians	villagers	lovers

As usual, the two 'mixed types' are in a sense the most interesting ones, particularly if the assumption is made that the others are more stable, so that the questions may be asked: What are the strains? What institutional bonds keep the two mixed types from changing in the direction of the more pure types, etc.?

The *fourth* modality is more trivial in a sense. It looks as if Sorokin is more concrete in his perspective; he is thinking of how long the physical interaction lasts, and Parsons is adressing himself more to the problem of 'focus of valuation' — but then Sorokin uses mental terms such as 'forgets', 'perpetuate this memory', 'affect the behavior and experience of the surviving party even after the death of the other' — so the difference between the two authors seems minimal.

The *fifth* modality is more difficult. Sorokin only makes the distinction between solidary and antagonistic and does not mention the important category 'individualistic orientation', which means this may or may not imply any antagonism on Ego's side or clashes with Alter. On the other hand, Parsons' distinction between individualistic and collectivistic orientation is too polite and nice, too much a reflection of his own protected New England living — it does not mention hatred, etc. explicity. Thus, a trichotomy might be better:

Sorokin's modality	solidary		antagonistic	
Ego's orientation to Alter	associative	neutral	dissociative	
Parsons' pattern variable	collectivistic		individualistic	

The scheme is an illustration of the difficulties that may arise when the world shall be expressed in the form of dichotomies. But again, the similarity is striking. Actually, Sorokin also has a third category, 'mixed', but this turns out to mean that 'the parties concur in only part of their aspirations and efforts, while in another part they are antagonistic to each other' (*ibid.*, p. 441). In other words, concrete interaction is either one or the other but may be different for different sectors of the total person.

The *sixth* modality has to do with the degree of organization. By this Sorokin means the extent to which 'the clearcut delineation of the rights, duties, and functions of each member perfectly defines the *social status* or *social position* within the systems of interaction' (*ibid.* p. 442). This may be interpreted to mean simply what most sociologists would call *institutionalization*: that social interaction is 'frozen' into status interaction. In that case, the sixth modality is like the first, a sort of general condition defining the patterned and sociological. But there is also another interpretation. Sorokin has many references to the group in connection with this modality; people are seen as acting according to group standards. In other words, they fulfill their status obligations or exercise their status rights according to group standards, not according to more subjective standards developed in status dyads. Thus interpreted, this modality is very close to the pattern variable called 'universalism' — 'particularism', but Sorokin is not quite clear on this point.

276

There is, however, nothing corresponding to quality vs. performance in Sorokin's scheme — but similarities are nevertheless so striking that sociology might have done with one of these sets of terms. On the other hand, it illustrates how grand theory has a tendency to start from scratch, how little cumulation there is in the field.

17. Since Sorokin does not commit himself to clearcut dichotomies in the sense that a type of interaction is one of the six modalities, his scheme permits 'both' and 'mixed' and a total of 3^6, or 729, types. But only a few of these combinations form systems of interaction, which occur frequently and are met in any human universe. Of these 'combined' types, three appear to be particularly important from many standpoints: 'they are the Familistic, the Contractual, and the Compulsory types' (*ibid.* p. 445). Actually, the two categories given in parentheses in Table 1.3.3 for familism are not mentioned explicitly by Sorokin. But they seem to follow from his use of the Aristotelian definition of friendship: 'one who intends and does what is good (or what he believes to be good) to another for that other's sake, or one who wishes his friend to be and to live for that friend's sake' (*ibid.* p. 496). In other words, the friend is conditioned and conditions the action of the other friend, but he not only does what is expected of him 'by mere contract', he wants to do so himself, and he does so because he expects him to do so. Thus, the interaction pattern becomes highly particularized — *it is the pattern for that pair of friends*. For that reason we have styled it, with some reservations, 'unorganized', in the sense of being neither institutionalized nor universalistic.

Similarly, the contractual relationship is definitely mutual, the two parties condition each other, and it is highly organized in both senses (institutionalized and universalistic). But the compulsory type is no longer mutual; characteristic of it is precisely the asymmetry in the degree of mutual conditioning designed to tame the forces of antagonism. According to Sorokin, 'in the *pure compulsory* relationship, the parties remain to each other total strangers and outsiders' (*ibid.* p. 450) — although one might perhaps conceive of relationships between master and slave where this is not true except by definition of 'pure compulsion'. Thus, the emphasis on specificity for the compulsory type.

Whether or not it is true or fruitful to say that 'these three forms seem to embrace almost all the pure forms of social relationship' (*ibid.* p. 450), they are remarkably useful. The distinction reappears, for instance, in the central distinction made in Etzioni's *A Comparative Analysis of Complex Organizations* (Glencoe, Ill.: The Free Press, 1961), *viz.* the distinction made between organizations that are *coercive* (power used in coercion, in patterns of alienation, etc. — examples are prisons and mental hospitals) (p. 27), *utilitarian* (power is based on differential remuneration; involvement is calculative as in industries) (p. 31) and *normative* (power is normative, symbolic, and the orientation is moral as in voluntary association, convents, etc.) (p. 40). Etzioni's distinctions, in turn, are drawn from many sources (see pp. 4–11); Sorokin is not mentioned among them. But then, Sorokin's intention is more to describe societies than complex organizations.

18. Sorokin, *op. cit.*, Chap. 27.
19. *Ibid.*, p. 469.
20. *Ibid.*, p. 470.
21. *Ibid.*
22. *Ibid.*

23. *Ibid.*, p. 471.

24. *Ibid.*, p. 472.

25. *Ibid.*, p. 621.

26. *Ibid.*, p. 612.

27. *Ibid.*, p. 612.

28. *Ibid.*, p. 621.

29. 'The difference between the 100 per cent of Ideationalism in mentality and the 30, 40, 48 per cent of Ideationalism in personality and conduct is a rough measure of the much looser connection of the type of culture with *behavior*, as compared with the closeness of the connection between the type of culture and *mentality*' (italics ours).

30. For definitions of the ideational, idealistic and sensate styles of art, see *ibid.*, pp. 220–221. For these comments, see pp. 144, 159, 167 f., 173 f., 185.

31. *Ibid.*, p. 222.

32. *Ibid.*, pp. 239 ff.

33. *Ibid.*, p. 697.

34. *Ibid.*, p. 607.

35. *Ibid.*, pp. 697 ff.

36. *Ibid.*, p. 698.

37. For critical comments by the author and one of his collaborators, see P. A. Sorokin and R. K. Merton, 'The course of Arabian intellectual development: a study in method', *Isis*, 1935, pp. 516–526. A typical comment in the more traditional vein is this: Sorokin tries to quantify 'what is qualitative, and this is almost like supposing it is possible to square the circle. A book, or work of art, is all quality because it is spirit. The unity of a culture consists in the stylistic similarities shown by its ingredients, not in their statistical identity'; see Stark and Werner, *The Sociology of Knowledge: An Essay in Aid of a Deeper Understanding of the History of Ideas* (Glencoe, Ill.: The Free Press, 1958), p. 28. Sorokin's work is certainly an expression of idea of 'stylistic similarities' — but it goes beyond this in at least attempting to devise indicators and testing hypotheses about more or less well-integrated periods in history.

38. Sorokin, *op. cit.*, p. 612.

39. *Ibid.*, p. 40.

40. *Ibid.*, p. 570.

41. *Ibid.*, p. 600.

42. The image of ideational as 'high' and sensate as 'low' is reflected all through Sorokin's works, which are pregnant with all kinds of value judgments and even the flattest propaganda. Sorokin, evidently, does not like the sensate periods and especially dislikes its present 'period of decline':

> The sequence — purely religious literature, heroic epic, chavalric romance, pastoral romance, picaresque story, realistic and satirical fiction — is the track along which these landmarks denote the main stages of the long-distance descent of literature from the Ideational heaven to the Sensual sewer (*ibid.*, p. 212).

> It is really an interpretation of man and of all the socio-cultural values on a decidedly low level, and is a general characteristic of the overripe phase of any Sensate culture and mentality. From the heavens and heroic heights it always descends to social gutters and cellars. That is its destiny! (*ibid.*, p. 185).

278

'Sewers' and 'gutters' may be seen as refreshing elements in an academic treatise or as symptoms of fundamental bias; we prefer the former perspective. Expressions like 'The sensate values will sink still deeper into the muck of sociocultural sewers' (*ibid.*, p. 699) remind one of a famous painting by Repin and the common factor: the extremely rich abusive vocabulary provided by the Russian language tradition. But one can also imagine what impression the following statement:

> The political science, or economists, of the Middle Ages has little in common with those of the eighteenth and nineteenth centuries — while these latter are declared outdated by the political science and economics of the twentieth century, especially in the Communistic, Fascistic and Hitlerite countries, and also in the New Deal regimes (*ibid.*, p. 409).

must make on American sociologists, the majority of whom are reportedly of the Democrat persuasion. The younger and the more productive, the higher the probability that a sociologist votes Democrat; see P. F. Lazarsfeld and W. Thieleus, *The Academic Mind* (Glencoe, Ill.: The Free Press, 1958), pp. 14–15. We mention this since it belongs to the list of factors that should be considered in explaining why Sorokin is so underquoted in contemporary social science, in addition to the obvious fact that he was always outside the mainstream. He was after his generation in selecting such a tremendous field of inquiry, ahead of his generation in using quantitative approaches to such topics. But Sorokin will definitely have his renaissance; he will be rediscovered; he will not remain underquoted for long.

43. For a perspective that in a sense combines what we have presented here in sections 1.2–3, see A. Birou, 'The role of sociological and psychological research in the programmes of rural development', UNESCO, Seminar on Social Research and Problems of Rural Life in Southeast Asia.

1.4.

1. Lerner, *The Passing of Traditional Society* (Glencoe, Ill.: The Free Press, 1958), p. 58. 'We subsume industrialization under our index of urbanization.'
2. See the excellent essay by John H. Kautsky, 'The Politics of Underdevelopment and of Industrialization' in Kautsky, ed., *Political Change in Underdeveloped Countries* (New York: Wiley, 1962).
3. Lerner, *op. cit.*, p. 58.
4. *Ibid.*, p. 63.
5. *Ibid.*, p. 58.
6. *Ibid.*, p. 63.
7. *Ibid.*, p. 58.
8. For this method, see Johan Galtung, *Theory and Methods of Social Research* (Oslo: Universitetsforlaget, 1967) (pp. 265 ff.).
9. Lerner, *op. cit.*, pp. 61–62.
10. *Ibid.*, p. 61.
11. *Ibid.*, p. 59.
12. I am particularly indepted to Simon Schwartzman for assistance in connection with this test.
13. Lerner, *op. cit.*, Appendix C.
14. For definitoid statements, see *ibid.*, pp. 49–50.

15. *Ibid.*, p. 439.
16. *Ibid.*, p. 52.
17. *Ibid.*, p. 60.
18. *Ibid.*, pp. 69–70.
19. *Ibid.*, p. 72.
20. Dalton Potter, review in *American Sociological Review*, 1959, pp. 117–119.
21. Lerner, *op. cit.*, p. 70.
22. *Ibid.*, p. 55.
23. It should be pointed out again that Lerner's theory is weak as a basis for empirical prediction. To predict correctly only in two out of three cases (nations) is, as mentioned, in the text, not in itself worse than is often found in social science. But alternative theories predict better. Thus, if we keep 'political' as no. 4 but make predictions for all six possible permutations of the other three variables, Lerner's theory *(first* 'urbanization', *then* 'literacy', *then* 'media participation') comes as no. 5 of the six in predictive power. The best is urbanization, media participation, and then literacy, which predicts correctly in 74% of the cases, or three nations out of four. One natural interpretation is that media participation in fact comes before literacy in much of the world today — a circumstance that could well have been integrated into Lerner's thinking. I am indebted to Manual Mora y Araujo for this comment. It actually all hinges on the contrast between pattern 13 (predicted, but empty) and pattern 11 (not predicted, but quite frequent); and the difference between these two patterns is precisely the relative order of literacy and media participation.

1.5.

1. E. C. Banfield, *The Moral Basis of a Backward Society* (Glencoe, Ill.: The Free Press, 1958).
2. *Ibid.*, pp. 33–35.
3. *Ibid.*, p. 35.
4. *Ibid.*, p. 36.
5. However, Banfield seems to be ambivalent about this. He says: 'In part the peasant's melancholy is caused by worry. Having no savings, he must always dread what is likely to happen' (*ibid.*, p. 64). But he returns to his argument on p. 66: 'this complaint is ridiculous. Except at the busy times of planting and harvesting, there is nothing to prevent the peasants from playing as much as they like. What is to stop them from dancing and singing?' On the importance of poverty, see also p. 168.
6. Personal interview with the author.
7. Banfield, *op. cit.*, p. 36.
8. *Ibid.*, p. 37.
9. *Ibid.*, p. 39.
10. *Ibid.*, p. 125.
11. *Ibid.*, p. 41.
12. *Ibid.*, p. 40.
13. *Ibid.*
14. These rank correlations are based on Banfield's Table 2 (*ibid.*, p. 40), and data for the 1956 votes are from his Table 1 (*ibid.*, p. 27). Since he does not mention when his structural data about the villages were obtained, it is difficult to know which

voting records should be used. If he uses the census data (which are from 1951) the 1953 records are closest; if he uses data from the period he stayed there himself, the 1965 data are closest. We have two reasons for believing that he has used the census data: 1) the extreme difficulty in getting other data and 2) the fact that he has used the 1953 election data in his Table 2. However, we have given both in our Table, with the data relating to the 1956 elections in parentheses, since there may have been some structural changes over the five-year period, however unlikely. The rank correlations have all been corrected for ties, according to the method given in Kendall, *Rank Correlation Methods* (New York: Hafner, 1955) p. 38.

15. This would also be in accordance with the general theory of rank disequilibrium. See Johan Galtung, 'A Structural Theory of Aggression', *Journal of Peace Research*, 1964, pp. 95–119.

16. The correlations, based on 1956 elections (put in parentheses in Table 1.5.1) are different in absolute size, but similar in the sense that the correlation between leftist voting and proportion of laborers is between the other two on the continuum from $+1$ to -1. These data emphasize even further the importance of literacy for leftism.

17. Banfield, *op. cit.*, p. 41. Actually, Banfield is arguing that there are erratic shifts both in space and time. We have seen that the differences in 'space' have important structural bases, with two rank correlations that are both theoretically and statistically significant. But Banfield also gives data for the differences in time (*ibid.*, p. 27), and here we agree that changes look almost random: rank correlations are 0.44 for leftist votes, 0.13 for center votes and 0.19 for right-wing votes. Changes in time can only be explained by other changes in time — but at this point Banfield offers no data.

18. *Ibid.*, p. 85. It should be noted that Banfield's 'familist' is 'familistic' in Sorokin's sense only within the family; outside he is 'contractual'.

19. Only that polarization is referred to as endogamy at the level of marital ties between different human groups.

20. Banfield, *op. cit.*, p. 85.

21. *Ibid.*, p. 100.

22. *Ibid.*, p. 135.

23. *Ibid.*, pp. 119, 150 ff.

24. *Ibid.*, p. 107.

25. *Ibid.*, introduction to Appendix B.

26. *Ibid.*, pp. 10 ff.

27. In a very important methodological article 'Technique for Analyzing the Effects of Group Composition', *American Sociological Roviow*, April 1961, pp. 215–225, Davis, Spaeth and Huson discuss this analytical problem in a more general form. We have simplified greatly 1) by omitting the possibilities of interaction between village level and individual level effects and 2) by omitting all the different degrees of relative importance given to the individual and village levels. Our Case 1 corresponds to their Type III; our Case 2 to their Type I; our Case 3 to their Type II, and our Case 4 to their Type 0. The interaction types (their Type IV) are in a sense the most interesting ones. As the authors say (*ibid.*, p. 222): 'The considerations advanced above suggest that the basic technique for the analysis of compositional effects is standard bivariate regression and covariance analysis.'

28. 'Here, however, the TAT has been used mainly for what it may tell about ethos rather than personality' (Banfield, *op. cit.*, p. 66, footnote). See also pp. 151 f. for the reasons why 'a people who have the extended family' was brought into the analysis (Rovigo).

29. Weber, *op. cit.*, p. 109.

30. W. W. Rostow, *The Stages of Economic Growth* (Cambridge: Cambridge University Press, 1960), p. 51.

31. A major criticism of Banfield's approach, and one which we have not included because it falls outside our scope in the present book, is, of course, its general failure to explain *why* these people have become the way they are. Italian sociologists react sharply at this point, and it is perhaps fair to say that they see Banfield's approach as an effort to psychologize away from stark political realities. Lack of cooperation at the bottom may be engendered by exploitative cooperation from the top. Most vocal is the criticism by G. A. Marselli, 'American Sociologists and Italian Peasant Society', *Sociologia Ruralis*, III, 4, 1965. And Alessandro Pizzorno concludes his very critical remarks in 'Amoral Familism and Historical Marginality', in *International Review of Community Development*, 1966, pp. 3–15, saying that the phenomena 'should have been defined and studied in a wider context'. And Anna Anfossi in her excellent 'Aspetti sociali dell'industrializzazione del Mezzogiorno', *Il Nuovo Osservatore*, 1963, 10, pp. 22–74, concludes that 'i problemi sociali del Sud sono problemi politici'. We agree. Banfield does not explain, he explores static interconnections without really asking for the *cause*. But his description may nevertheless be adequate, and extremely important in terms of its *consequences*. As will be clear from Chapters 5, 6 and 7, particularly 6.2, our focus is on these consequences in terms of structures and value that serve to reinforce underdevelopment and dependency.

1.6.

1. In developing this plan of study we were inspired not only by our empirical impressions and the theoretical explorations given in the three works chosen as guidelines, but also by much of the literature on the Mediterranean village culture. It would lead too far to list all these references, but we would like to mention some that were particularly important. The documentation given by Danilo Dolci and his collaborators of the conditions in villages in this zone is too well known to be repeated here, and we have wanted to draw on our own data as much as possible.

For a description of a community relatively similar to the villages in the present study, see Anfossi, Talamo, Indovina, *Ragusa, Communità in Transizione* (Torino: Taylor, 1959). Particularly important in this connection is Chapter 7 by Anna Anfossi on characteristics of the social structure.

In *Acts of the Mediterranean Sociological Conference* (Athens: Social Sciences Centre, 1963) there is a wealth of interesting observations on most Mediterranean societies, particularly the papers on patron-client relations. For an ample documentation with a rich spectrum of methodological approaches of the life of the workers in another Mediterranean country, see P. Bourdieu et al., *Travail et Travailleurs Algerie* (Paris: Mouton, 1963). The work is particularly good for its analysis and documentation of economic behavior and economic strategies of the poor.

For other famous accounts of Southern Italian reality seen through the temperament of an artist, see not only the famous *Cristo si e fermato a Eboli* by Carlo Levi, but also his less known *Le parole sono pietre* (Einaudi, 1958).

Of other books we would like to mention E. Peggio et al., *Industrializzazione e sottosviluppo* (Torino: Einaudi, 1960), with economic and demographic data from the province of Siracusa; Joseph Loperato and Domenico Lococo, 'Stefanaconi; un villaggio agricolo meridionale in relazione al suo 'mondo'', *Quaderni di sociologia*, 1959, pp. 239–260; F. G. Friedmann, 'Osservazioni sul mondo contadino dell' Italia meridionale', *Quaderni di sociologia*, 1952, pp. 148–161; Guido Vincelli, *Una Communità Meridionale* (Torino: Casa Editrice Taylor, 1958); Gabriele Morello, Petrolio e Sud: *Inchiesta a Ragusa* (Milano: ET/AS Editrice, 1959); L. Wylie, *Village in the Vaucluse* (Cambridge: Harvard University Press, 1957); J. A. Pitt-Rivers, *The People of the Sierra* (Chicago: University of Chicago Press, 1961); Halpern, J. M., *A Serbian Village* (New York: Columbia University Press, 1958); and numerous community studies from Latin America of, perhaps, more remote relevance. Somehow studies from the Middle East and from Africa seem more relevant, e.g. J. L. Boutillier, *Bongouanou, Côte d'Ivoire* (Paris: Berger-Leurault, 1960) and L. E. Sweet, *Tell Toqaan: A Syrian Village* (Ann Arbor: Anthropological Papers no. 4, Museum of Anthropology, University of Michigan, 1960).

2.1.

1. Descriptions of the kind we have given here usually fail to point out the positive characteristics of these villages, among other reasons because the inhabitants themselves rarely volunteer such descriptions. For this purpose the following account for a planned village, constructed in order to bring the farmers closer to their plots, is useful (from R. L. Langworthy, 'Some Problems of Community Development in Italy', *The American Journal of Economics and Sociology*, 1964, pp. 95–109):

'When one first inspects these settlements and is briefed on the tremendous amount of aid given to the new settlers, this resentment seems to be the rankest sort of ingratitude. Landless people were practically given a new, large house, several acres of land, livestock, and provided with many services practically at cost. But as one drives along row after row of stark, antiseptic sameness, the mere physical and aesthetic contrast with the organic quality of the usual Italian villages begins to be felt. Then one visits a few houses, and the harsh, white emptiness o almost barracks-like houses begins to sink in. Then one talks to the people: "Of course we ought to be thankful, but it just isn't like my village." "I miss my mother and sisters, so I can hardly stand it." "These houses look nice, but they are cold, damp and uncomfortable to live in." The women often complain of being unable to go the several miles to Mass in the morning before the day's work'.

Langworthy also notes that no social scientists were consulted in connection with this land-reform project, and that 'many senior land-reform officials were colonial agricultural officials (Fascists) in Africa in the Nineteen Thirties' (p. 106).

2.2.

1. The census figures should be taken with more than a grain of salt — stories about how the census is sometimes carried out do not conduce too much to belief in their

reliability. On the other hand, they are probably reliable enough for the kind of rough comparisons we shall make. For a skeptical note, see Banfield, *op. cit.*, p. 46. I am indepted to ISTAT in Rome for making 'Dati riassuntivi comunali e provinciali per alcune principali caratteristiche della popolazione' available and to the Centro Studi e Iniziative, Partinico and Leon Tabah, the demographer, for helpfulness in connection with interpretation.

2. 'Negl'elenchi dei poveri.'

3. According to the simplistic formula $P_n = P_0(1 + r/100)^n$, where P_0 is the initial population, r the rate of increase in percentage, n the number of years and P_n the population after n years.

4. If, in addition, there is in-migration to the villages, the out-migration must of course be even higher to produce the net rates we have indicated. In the small study from the village of Roccamena, ecologically somewhere between Collina and Montagna, the out-migration in the period 1954–1957 is said to have been 1,097, and the in-migration 745, leaving a total of about 30 persons per year of a population that in 1957 amounted to about 3,400 (Pontara and Adler-Karlsson, *op. cit.*, pp. 696, 698). This indicates a considerable mobility between villages, much of which is probably due to marriage. Nevertheless, it serves as a reminder that the constancy in the population of Marina does not exclude a heavy emigration and out-migration checked by a corresponding influx.

5. Dennis Wrong, *Population* (New York: Random House, 1956), p. 36.

6. *Ibid.*, pp. 21 f.

7. *Ibid.*, p. 55.

8. Birth and death rates for Italy in 1950 were $19.6^o/oo$ and $9.8^o/oo$, respectively (*ibid.*, pp. 37, 54), in 1959 B: $18.4^o/oo$.

9. For Egypt the rates are $42.6^o/oo$ and $20.3^o/oo$ (1948) and for India $26.7^o/oo$ and $16.0^o/oo$. Mexico has $45.7^o/oo$ and $16.4^o/oo$ (*ibid.*, pp. 37, 54).

10. *Ibid.*, Table 2, p. 37, and Table 5, p. 54.

11. When one has no other data, one can always find what one needs in the literature of the region. Thus, one feels it is no mere coincidence that a *Sicilian* author lets his hero, looking at a young couple, have these thoughts: 'For both of them death was purely an intellectual concept, a fact of knowledge as it were and no more, not an experience which pierced the marrow of their bones. Death, oh yes, it existed of course, but it was something that happened to others. The thought occurred to Don Fabrizio that it was inner ignorance of this supreme consolation which makes the young feel sorrows much more sharply than the old; the latter are nearer the safety exit' (Lampedusa, *op. cit.*, p. 234). But then Don Fabrizio did not have to worry about the economic plight of his children. Banfield sees 'fear of premature death and leaving one's children "on the Street"' as a major theme behind the local ethos, explained by death rates as high as 25 and even 40 or 50 per thousand before 'anti-biotics came into common use' (Banfield, *op. cit.*, p. 148).

12. Svimez, *Un Secolo di statistiche italiane: Nord e Sud 1861–1961* (Roma: 1961), p. 345.

13. It may be useful to contrast the information given here about Sicilian villages with that of a Piemontese village, according to the study reported in 'Primi elementi per l'analisi sociologica di un comune piemontese: Castellamonte', *Quaderni di sociologia*, 1951, particularly pp. 84–5. There are 38% workers and 31% farmers (contadini) — but one half of those workers help in working the farms of their

families, in addition to being workers, in the high season. This is important because it gives a clue to one of the many forms of transition between a primary sector and secondary sector oriented society.

We wanted to catch a maximum of variation in order to get at exactly such differences in work composition, but for that purpose Western Sicily was too uniformly underdeveloped — as the data show. Ecological variation was what we could get and obtained. Thus, in another research project by the Centro, in 1962, all municipalities were divided into three groups referred to as 'montagna', 'collina', and 'pianura' — partly generalizing our terms — and 'our' villages came out as quite representative of each group.

2.3.

1. For some comments on this type of research in many developing countries, see Johan Galtung, *Theory and Methods of Social Research*, p. 134 and footnotes.

2. It is interesting to note that the refusal rate in the study reported by Pontara and Adler-Karlsson (*op. cit.*, p. 695) is 15/85, which is about 18% — even higher than Collina, which Roccamena is most similar to, although it is less *mafioso*.

3. Another hypothesis, quite consistent with the mafia hypothesis and perhaps even more reasonable, would explain refusals on the basis of social class. Four factors that may make the lower classes more susceptlible as interviewees do not apply so much to the upper classes: the feeling of being *flattered* because one is 'chosen', the habit of *obeying* or at least not flatly refusing a request from somebody higher up, the feeling that foreigners can do one one *no harm* and a wish for some kind of *new experience*. Pontara and Adler-Karlsson indicate something to this effect: 'è possibile che nelle 15 famiglie che si sono rifiutate all'intervista ci fossero alcuni dei maggiori proprietari' (*ibid.*, p. 696). Banfield also has an indication to this effect: 'The investigators had no difficulty in getting answers from peasants. Upper class people were more reserved. From the standpoint of the peasants there was nothing to be feared from giving information to 'the Americans'; they came from, and would soon return to, a different world. Moreover, many small favors and some large ones were to be had by cooperating. For the upper classes, however, the situation was entirely different. For them America was not so far away; who could tell how their information might be used? And for the upper classes, who could not accept small loans and handouts of food and old clothes, there was no material incentive to cooperate' (*op. cit.*, p. 127, footnote). Though we agree with the interpretation that upper class people feel more like members of the investigator's world and hence are more different, we find Banfield's gift system highly different from what a survey director would make use of — but then his methods are different.

4. This is by no means evident. Such probabilities are usually higher than people believe. Thus, the chance that no two birthdays coincide in a party of forty is, for instance, only about 1/8 (see A. Rapoport, *Fights, Games and Debates* (Ann Arbor: University of Michigan Press, 1960), p. 114, for the reasoning involved). We shall not calculate the exact probability of no neighbors when m houses are picked at random in a city with n houses. Imagine, for the sake of simplicity, that each house has two and only two neighbors and that we pick one house. For the second house *not* to be a neighbor there are three positions it cannot have:

the first house itself, and its two neighbors. The probability of this is (n–3)/n. In principle, each house carries away a set of three neighbors, but some of these sets may overlap without two houses being neighbors. Hence, the probability that the third house will not be a neighbor of either of the former two is actually more than (n–6)/n, only carry away five houses. Thus we get:

$$P(\text{no neighbors}) \quad (n{-}3)/n \quad (n/6)/ \ldots (n{-}3(m{-}1))/n$$

In our case n is about 600, for we see from Table 2.2.7 that there are 2.2 residents per room and 2.3 rooms per house, hence an average of 5 persons per house. With a population of around 3,000 this gives 600 houses. M equals 16 so that we get:

$$p \quad 597/600 \text{ x } \ldots \text{ x } 555/600 \quad (570/600)^{15}$$

which is equal to about 0.46. The assumptions have reduced the probability which is well beyond one-half. On the other hand, in a real city, there are more ways of being neighbors than just two — still, on the other hand again, 5 is not much of a significance level, and we have three pairs, not just 'one or more'. Thus, we feel the event is rare enough to warrant suspicion, but not rare enough to believe in a systematic neighbor effect.

5. These three interviewers accounted for 51% of the interviews, dividing the remaining 49% among the other ten interviewers.

6. Pontara and Adler-Karlsson seem to imply that the six days their interviewing lasted were three too many: 'Negli ultimi giorni però si incominciò a sentire qualche "frizione" nel corso normale spedito dell'inchiesta: tutte e 15 le famiglie che si rifiutarono di rispondere appartengono al gruppo intervistato gli ultimi tre giorni' (*op. cit.*, p. 696). Of course, for any resistance to be built up some time is needed, especially if the interviewing has not been announced beforehand. The authors actually add that it looked as if the reluctance to answer was due to the intervention in some way of another by 'autorità politiche religiose'.

7. A propos of the preceding footnote, a 'difficulty' was experienced on the last day, a Sunday, in Montagna, adding another reason for making Sunday the last day. The *arciprete* had warned his congregation in church against participating in the interviewing, because it was organized by people who were 'not for the Catholic church' (it seems that the most important factor here was the Protestant identity automatically attributed to Norwegians, however unjustified in this individual case). The warning had no effect, however, because not too many people were present in church, because of the random distribution of the interviewees (there was no way of knowing whom to contact, since there was no principle except randomness involved in their selection) and because it was the last day: only a couple of interviews remained to be done. Had Sunday been the first or second day, the interviewing might well have had to be canceled.

8. I am particularly indebted to late Teresio Bonini for his assistance with this section.

9. Pontara and Adler-Karlsson, *op. cit.*, p. 699 (italics ours).

10. The reader is referred to 3.1 for a definition of the indices.

11. The type of data we would most have liked to have, in addition to that we do have, would be data on interaction structure — particularly the type of data needed to answer the problems about structure that were put in section 1.6. However, as so often happens in social research: there was a lot of thinking before the questionnaire was drafted, but the first findings stimulated even more thinking and led to

problems that could not be answered in terms defined by the questionnaire. We do not see that as a weakness; rather, we are sceptical about the social scientist who feels he can think through a problem *a priori* and arrive at a plan for data collection that will leave no question unanswered. This is only possible if he stops asking questions.

Hence, we returned to the villages in 1964 and got much more information about the interaction structure — but admittedly of a more hearsay nature. We should have included anthropological observations in the first run, or at least asked interaction questions in the questionnaire to get a better data basis for selecting a proper interaction model.

The occupational index was also tried on a Danish sample of 311 persons, out of which 271 carried out the six paired comparisons (the question was slightly different, the respondents were asked whose statements they would hold to be of most significance or interest). The sample proved on the average not to be more sensate than our Sicilian sample. But the index related to some dependent variables very much in the same way as the findings in the present chapter will show for our sample (Danmarks Sociale Højskole, October 1965):

	Ideational			Sensate		
Level	3	2	1	1	2	3
% women	80	71	74	62	39	24
% attracted by a radical socialist party	5	10	15	13	10	29
% positive to Christianity	65	71	41	32	24	12
Interest in political participation	8	9	5	8	21	31
Interest in church and religion	24	15	7	3	6	7

The last two are important since they point in the direction of the second index developed.

3.1

1. Sorokin himself has some ideas as to how 'each of the main types of cultures has one class or several classes which are its main bearers, agencies and integrators' (*op. cit.*, pp. 725 and 475). Among others, he contrasts the priest with the engineer, the sacerdotal class with the 'scientific' intelligentsia. But his reasoning is not quite systematic; many important positions are not mentioned.

2. All four are engaged in control. But for the two ideational positions the focus of the control is intrinsic, whereas the two sensate positions engage in extrinsic control. The first two make man conform to his conditions; the latter two adapt the conditions to man's wishes. Thus, we feel we are well in line with our definitions.

3. All this is based on numerous conversations with inhabitants of the area when the project was in its pilot phase. The intersubjectivity of the ordering of the occupations was also checked by a number of our colleagues, and the agreement was very satisfactory.

4. Svalastoga, *Prestige, Class and Mobility* (Copenhagen: Gyldendal, 1959), p. 80.

5. Tiryakian, 'The Prestige Evaluation of Occupations in an Underdeveloped Country: The Philippines', *American Journal of Sociology*, 1958, pp. 390–399.

6. Inkeles and Rossi, 'Cross-national Comparisons of Occupational Ratings', *American Journal of Sociology*, 1956, pp. 329–339, especially pp. 336–337.

7. For a discussion of these problems, see Johan Galtung, *Theory and Methods of Social Research*, I, 5.6 and II, 3.2.

3.2.

1. But could not the 'modern' answers be given by young people mainly? We checked Table 3.2.1 for the influence of age — which is correlated with ideology according to Table 3.4.1 — but the relation was unchanged for all three age categories.

2. This question was considered so difficult those days (this was still in 1960) that we did not even ask how many children they personally wanted, but how many children they thought, in general, it was good for a family to have. Today, after the many open discussions of these matters, such precautions would hardly have been necessary.

3. It is interesting to see that we get the same differences between *family sizes* in the two provinces of Enna and Torino. The averages are 3.95 and 3.04, respectively. Thus, what these Sicilians want, on the average, is precisely to make the jump from Enna to Torino. See A. Anfossi, 'Famiglia e socialità, *Quaderni di Sociologi,* 1960, p. 247, based on ISTAT data.

4. One objection that has been raised against this empirical procedure has to do with the role of the lawyer. As Vilhelm Aubert (and also Torstein Eckhoff) has pointed out (e.g. in *Tidsskrift for samfunnsforskning,* no. 4, 1960) an expansion of lawyers may precede, and be a necessary condition for an economic expansion to follow. However, even of this were the case in Norway it is certainly not a sufficient condition for economic expansion elsewhere. Two possible intervening variables here may be: (1) the nature of the legal system (with Roman law being more authoritarian, more aimed at regulating relations between state and individuals; and Anglo-Saxon law being more horizontal, more aiming at regulating the type of contractual relations highly instrumental for economic development within a system of private capitalism) and (2) the place of the society within an international division of labor (with Norway being more autonomous and Southern Italy being fitted into a vertical system of exchange with Northern Italy).

3.3.

1. It was because of suspicions in this direction that we preferred to use 'participate in religious life' and not church-going in the paired comparisons leading to the index (see 3.1).

2. This negative finding is particularly important in view of the significance we later on (7.2) attribute to social participation.

3.4.

1. Gioacchino Greco ('La Struttura del tradizionalismo, un metodo di studio della Sicilia Occidentale: Estratto ed osservazioni', typewritten), has pointed out, in a critical and very helpful examination of the manuscript, that the school is an equalizer, nevertheless, and that it remains problematic why schooling does not have more impact. The answer is probably to be found in the fact that there is so little schooling anyhow, and that the schooling there is has an ideational bias.

3.5.

1. Only seven of them (27%) had no schooling, as against more than one-third of *braccianti* and *industriosi.*

288

2. A possible explanation is Marina's easier access to media of communication, which may increase relative weight of the factor of differential access to new values.
3. An exception to this is R. T. Morris and R. J. Murphy, 'The Situs Dimension in Occupational Structure', *American Sociological Review*, 1959, pp. 231–239. They attack the unidimensional conception of society, and their categories 5 and 3 are very similar to the primary and secondary sectors; the other eight are specifications of the tertiary sector.
4. According to Colin Clark (*op. cit.*, p. 492). Clark's theory is concentrated in Chapter 9 of his work. The reference to Leibenstein is from his 'Specialization, Income Level, and Occupational Structure' in *Economic Backwardness and Economic Growth* (New York: Wiley, 1960.)
5. Clark, *op. cit.*, pp.490.ff.
6. Leibenstein, *op. cit.*, p. 90.
7. Leibenstein, *loc. cit.*
8. A. G. B. Fisher, 'The Economic Implications of Material Progress', *International Labor Review*, 1953, pp. 5–18.
9. Leibenstein, *op. cit.*, p. 91.
10. *Ibid.*, p. 92.
11. López, *op. cit.*, pp. 29–65. For data from Morocco, see D. E. Ashford, *Political Change in Morocco* (Princeton, N. J.: Princeton University Press, 1961), p. 15.
12. López, *op. cit.*, p. 63.
13. Clark, *op. cit.*, p. 498. Many publications give higher proportions, however. For instance, in *Situação Social da America Latina* (Rio: CLAPCS, 1961), Honduras*/* Haiti are given as 83% (p. 162).
14. Clark, *op. cit.*, p. 491.
15. *Ibid.*, p. 495.
16. This has actually already been anticipated in 1.2, both in Table 1.2.2, under 'traditional society', and in the general reasoning about the relation between horizontal and vertical differentation.
17. Needless to say, there are many unsolved problems in connection with the empirical and theoretical foundation for this key section to the whole book. A basic difficulty has already been pointed out: the classification of the skilled workers. Something of the same can be said about the artisans (a point made by Greco, op.cit.), but they are less dependent in their work situation than the skilled workers, making their classification more justifiable from a more marxist point of view (whereas the classification of the skilled workers must be justified in terms of living standard oriented criteria). But again, the conclusions do not depend on the classification of these groups since they are in-between groups anyhow.

For another attempt see Joseph Lopreato, 'Social Stratification in a South Italian Town', *American Sociological Review*, 1961, pp. 585–596. Lopreato tries, however, to fit the occupations into a one-dimensional scheme, and we doubt the fruitfulness of any such attempt. Occupations should be ranked within economic sectors in order for the social structure to become more apparent.

3.6.

1. E. F. Jackson, 'Status Consistency and Symptoms of Stress', *American Sociological Review*, 1962, pp. 469–480.

2. G. Lenski, 'Status-Crystallization: A Non-vertical Dimension of Social Status', *ASR*, 1954, pp. 405–413, and I. W. Goffman, 'Status Inconsistency and Preference for Change in Power Distribution', *American Sociological Review*, 1957, pp.

3. Jackson, *op. cit.*, p. 473, Table 1.

4. It is perhaps worth pointing out again that this is an example of a finding that, although not contra-intuitive in any sense, would have been rather hard to predict in advance.

3.7.

1. But it should be pointed out that the Table exaggerates the closure of the society since we do not get data about the sons who migrated and probably changed both sector and stratum. On the other hand, it is the situation inside the villages we are concerned with, and this is given by Table 3.7.1.

2. This is, of course, a nearly universal phenomenon. Just to give some examples from our own data: of 2,000 North American highschool students, 49% wanted professional occupations — although only 15% of their fathers had such positions. In two villages in Kerala, South India, the percentages wanting tertiary occupations for their sons were 55% and 57%. But the wishes of these poor fishermen were more humble: they were aiming for positions as government servants (38% and 47%), which often means positions as mailmen.

3. More particularly, the finding will be made use of in the concluding part of the theoretical summary in 6.2.

3.8.

1. L. Bernot and R. Blanchard, *Nouville: Un village français* (Université de Paris. Institut d'éthnologie, 1953. Travaux et mémoirs de l'institut d'éthnologie, LVII),

2. *Ibid.*, p. 332.

3. *Ibid.*, p. 339.

4. *Ibid.*, p. 356.

5. But it might perhaps be added that this is not a very important finding. It is probably more important to emphasize the relatively low level of effect travel seems to have in these villages. It is a part of social life; people are not forced to stay at home always, they travel as a part of their existence — and that is about all.

3.9.

1. I am indebted to J. Meisfjord, formerly of the Indo-Norwegian Project, Kerala, for this quotation.

2. By Oliveira Salazar: 'When so many things that seem sacred or eternal are dispersed or dissolved in the agitated ocean that is the world of today, it is good to attend to the value of an institution which neither betrays its spirit nor runs away from this mission that has been given to it.'

3. Bernot and Blanchard, *op. cit.*, pp. 321–332.

4. *Ibid.*, p. 328.

5. *Ibid.*, pp. 355–358.

6. There is a good, intuitive, and well-written account of some fundamental Western

Sicilian attitudes to their own situation with emphasis on low time perspective in Ilys Booker, *Report on Menfi*, (February 1960–July 1961) (London: Danilo Dolci Trust, 1961).

3.10.

1. It should be emphasized here that there is, of course, no limit to how much data we ideally should have liked to have. Instead of, or in addition to, Sorokin's perspective we could have based ourselves on anybody else's perspective — for instance on McClelland. However much we might disagree with McClelland's single factor theorizing, there is hardly much doubt that there is such a thing as n-achievement and that it plays a role, particularly in a society that is individualistic and vertical: in other words in liberal society. It would have been interesting to do for this variable what we have tried to do here for the ideationalism indices: just find out where in the social structure the various types are overrepresented. But there has to be a limitation, and our explorations will therefore be limited to the three approaches given in chapter 1.

4.1.

1. Lerner, *op. cit.*, p. 51.
2. *Loc. cit.*
3. *Ibid.*, p. 69.
4. Of the literally thousands of sources that might be cited on this theme, we have chosen Gavin Maxwell because his impressions are recent, are from the same region and have an impressionistic stamp we like (*The Ten Pains of Death* (New York: Dutton, 1960)): 'Here and in Castellammare there are houses that have stood empty and untended for half a century or more; their anomaly in this densely populated island where housing is a perennial problem is at first sight striking. They have, however, as great a human significance as any home enclosing a swarming, vociferous Sicilian family, for they are anchors. Their owners, long since emigrated to the United States, to Brazil, to Canada or Australia, would no more think of selling them than of selling their identities. However prosperous these families may be in the countries of their adoption, some *disgrazia* may overtake them and make it necessary to return to Sicily, and then how would they fare without a home?' (p. 36). And then there is this observation (p. 243): 'Perhaps three quarters of all Castellammarese families have relations in America, who emigrated before the quotas were imposed, and to follow them is the unrealisable dream of all who remained behind in Sicily.' Both assertions are somewhat exaggerated but square well with the general impression we have. Castellammare is located not too far from Marina and Collina and is on the coast as the name indicates.
5. It should perhaps be pointed out that this approach to the study of social structure, in terms of migration potential, is rather meaningful in the context of Sicily. According to SVIMEZ: *Un secolo di statistiche italiane, Nord e Sud 1861–1961* (Roma, 1961) emigration from Italy 1876–1930 was 10.9 million from Nord, 6.8 million from Sud, and 1.7 million from Sicily. But whereas the migrants from Nord went to many different parts of Europe and the Americas, with only 9.4% to the US, migrants from Sud went 59.2% to the US, and from Sicily even 69.1%. Thus, emigration was largely synonymous with emigration to the US. (p. 124).

291

In general, this impressive volume contains ample information about why they emigrate. Thus, the percentage difference in degree of illiteracy between Nord and Sud is about constant from 1861 to 1961 (around 20 in both years, with a peak of 30 in 1901 — p. 795); in 1951 it is still high for the age group 10–18 (12%); the birth rate is higher for the entire period (p. 99); they die from more primitive diseases (p. 112); the rate of natural increase (birth minus deaths) has become much higher in Sud than in Nord since the last war because mortality has gone down (p. 79); infant mortality used to be very much higher but has gone down so that the difference is less (p. 86); the income per capita of Sud remains relatively constant at 45% of that of Nord for the period 1951 to 1959 (p. 767); Sud's share of the income in the private sector of the economy decreases from 1928 to 1959 (p. 770); the consumption of meat per capita is only a little more than one half in Sud of what it is in Nord (p. 787); Sud is agricultural and Nord is industrial, *and* Sud has more people in the tertiary sector (p. 673); and so on. In short: the usual picture of internal colonization — only that the picture would have been more complete if the relation, not only the difference between these two parts of Italy were made clear in columns of statistics.

4.2.

1. It is significant that the order of perceived legitimacy among the villages is also the order of standard of living: Marina — Montagna — Collina (Tables 2.2.2 and 3.6.2). With more villages, the hypothesis that very poor conditions also foster illegitimacy could perhaps be confirmed.
2. In the conference organized by the Centro in July 1961 where some of these findings were first presented there was much of the usual, and usually warranted, resentment against statistical description of a reality the participants assume they know much better than the outsider. Usually the participants are right — but at this particular point statistics pointed in exactly the same direction as hearsay evidence.

4.3.

1. Such tests were actually carried out as a routine for many of the findings but are usually only reported when something interesting showed up.

4.4.

1. Thus, single-minded reliance on schooling as a factor that automatically will have to bring about development is over-optimistic and naive. This also throws considerable doubt on all the correlation studies between schooling and other aspects of development: it may well be that development took place in spite of, rather than because of the educational investment.

4.5.

1. For a very sophisticated and innovative critique and elaboration of the general Colin Clark approach (which we have used here in an extremely simple and non-committal way) see Torcuato S. di Tella, *La teoria del Primer Impacto del Crecimiento Economico* (Buenos Aires: Instituto de sociologia, 1961).

292

4.6.

1. One might argue that what we actually should study is not the joint impact of social and economic position, but the impact of a really meaningful attachment to the agriculture. Emile Pin shows in his interesting study 'Effetti psicosociologici della riforma agraria', *Rivista di sociologia*, 1964, pp. 79–102, that those who have benefitted somehow from agrarian reform show less propensity to migrate to the cities than a well-chosen control group (40% as against 70%, p. 89). When the question is asked in terms of a job in local industry, the percentage increases to 55. This may indicate that they do not want to leave, but rather want to change life situation on the spot. Pin also shows that they have much higher ambitions for their children, 'definitely not agriculture', and there are indications in his data that their lack of interest in moving may be due to lack of migratory experience in the family (Table 9, p. 88). But what Pin's findings seem to indicate is the reservoir of people dedicated to stay in the region provided they can have jobs that are more 'modern'. As Alex Inkeles so often has argued, industry tends to create a more modern man (but not necessarily a less dependent man, one might add) and thus have benefits not only of an economic nature. This theme is also touched upon in Gandolfi, D., 'Aspetti del processo di addatamento in un gruppo di ex rurali assunti da una grande industria dell'emilia-Romagna' (Bologna: Centro Studi Sociali e Amministrativi, 1960).

4.7.

1. Amando de Miguel, in 'Social and Geographic Mobility in Spain', *Journal of International Affairs*, 1965, pp. 259–275, shows rather conclusively the same findings as we had in Table 4.7.1.: the more mobility experienced, the more migration. Mobility seems to be contagious through generations; and moreover it escalates.

4.8.

1. But again, as in 3.8, it should be emphasized that the relation is not strong, nor the findings very significant in practical terms.

4.9.

1. In an interesting study of one hundred Italian emigrants in their host country (Brazil and Argentina) by Aldo Durante ('Statistical Psychological Examination of a Group of Italian Workers Expatriated Overseas in the Years 1958–59', Rome, 1961) there are few indications of a well-developed time perspective in the one hundred answers reported to the question 'What motives urged you to migrate?' The answers are typically in terms of improving the standard of living. But there are also future-oriented answers of a more specific kind, and this may indicate that we have here run against the methodological difficulty inherent in this kind of study: we have only interviewed those who want to move, not those who have already moved.

   For an impressive testimony of the fate of immigrants to Milano in this period see Franco Alasia and Danilo Montaldi, *Milano, Corea — Inchiesta sugli immigrati* Milano: Feltrinelli, 1960).

4.10.

1. In a sense, the whole emigration approach is typical of liberal or capitalist society: it gives opportunities to the best, to the strongest and so on, and leaves the weaker and poorer behind. The opposite would be a development model which started with those at the bottom of the present system by giving to them, for instance, the capital they would need to change their own situation radically.

5.1.

1. A significant piece of work has been done by C. S. Gugino in *Coscienza Collettiva e Giudizio individuale nella cultura contadina* (Palermo: Manfredi, 1960). His basic theme is also solidarity, and he shows (although on the basis of a rather small sample) the dominant position of the faith in the family. The family receives an index of 21 in Gugino's calculation, then come schooling with 16 and personal relations with 12 — and at the very bottom — 'da ciascuno violentamente criticata, come la piu viziata, incapace di assicurare un minimo di benessere' (p. 56f) — the economic structure.

5.2.

1. Familism must be intimately connected with the size of the family although our findings seem to point in the direction of two types of familism. The innovator will probably use contraception to keep the size down, the traditionalist abortion. For a study of abortion practices in Sicily, see Vincenzo Borruso, *Pratiche abortive a controlle delle nascite in Sicilia* (Palermo: Libri Siciliani, 1966).

5.3.

1. Obviously, however, we would have needed more and better data to be able to explore this important point in a more satisfactory manner.

5.4.

1. Gugino, op.cit., p. 68, reports a negative relation between education and family orientation. On the other hand, he finds the same relation between education and church orientation as we found in chapter 2, a slight positive correlation.

5.5.

1. Our findings in this key section are replicated in Gugino, op.cit., p. 69, where he reports highest attachment to the family among the 'lavoratori dell'agricoltura' and lowest among the 'lavoratori intelettuali' (23 and 15 points respectively, the average being, as mentioned, 21).

5.6.

1. If, with increasing economic position, there is less familism, this is of course also because there is decreasing reliance on the family as a unit of production (although there may be increasing reliance on it as a unit of consumption, of sharing of material and cultural goods as well as experiences). This theme is developed to some extent, in a setting relevant for Italian development, by Salvatore Cafiero, in *Aspetti e problemi sociali dell sviluppo economico in Italia* (Bari: Laterza, 1959, p. 220), who talks about a crisis in the family institution.

5.7.

1. In the SVIMEZ statistics (see note 5 in section 4.1.) there is also interesting information on the number of children per woman (in 1931) according to the occupation of the husband (p. 101). For all categories Sud shows higher numbers than Nord, as expected. Lowest are the people that with no doubt would belong to tertiary high — *impiegati, ufficiali, professionisti* — which makes them more free to migrate. As one rises through the social structure the burdens of the family become less heavy and the means to carry them more developed — till some kind of take-off point is found.

5.8.

1. And in this, of course, these villagers do not differ much from people in more developed areas, although family disintegration may have proceeded further in more industrial and post-industrial parts of the world. Much of the research by the family specialist W. J. Goode throws some doubt upon that assertion, however.

5.9.

1. It may also be a sign, as will be pointed out in the next chapter, of low level of crystallization of attitudes simply because familism has not yet become an open issue integrated into clear attitudinal syndromes.

5.10.

1. And this is what we shall attempt to do in the following chapter.

6.1.

1. The reader may have been surprised that we have not used standard techniques for testing the statistical significance of our findings. The major reasons for this have been set forth in Johan Galtung, *Theory and Methods of Social Research*, II, 4.4. In general, the methodological orientation underlying the present work is found in that book, since the present project to a great extent stimulated efforts to formulate methodological theory. As to statistical tests, the major reasons why we have not used them are 1) our concern with the total picture, with the type of theory that can be developed by combining a number of scattered findings, not with the single finding, and 2) the generally unfulfilled conditions for testing.

2. The periphery of a society is probably, in general, not steered by the same logic or psycho-logic, socio-logic when it comes to how attitudes shall be combined as the center. See Johan Galtung, 'Foreign Policy Opinion as a Function of Social Position', *Journal of Peace Re earch*, 1964, pp. 206–231, and Nils Halle, 'Social Position and Foreign Policy Attitudes: A Comparative Study between France, Norway and Poland', *Journal of Peace Research*, 1966, pp. 46–74. Since these villages can safely be classified as belonging to the periphery of Italian society, it may well be that the low correlations are a sign of low crystallization in the periphery in general. And the data seem, also, to indicate that the correlations increase somewhat when one moves closer to the center of these local societies.

3. See footnote 1 in 7.4 for a continuation of this particular theme.

6.2.

1. This theme is developed in Johan Galtung. 'International Relations and International Conflicts: A Sociological Approach', *Transactions of the Sixth World Congress of Sociology* (International Sociological Association, 1966), pp. 121–161. If one looks at the idealized and schematized interaction diagram presented in Diagram 6.2.1, one notices that the associated number (the number of links a given status has) is two for tertiary high and for tertiary low — but three for primary high. In other words, the primary high have a more central position in the interaction network than the tertiary high who, are higher in position and standard of living — on the average. The most significant aspect of the Diagram is the relative isolation of the primary low — as an appendix to a triangle where the three higher statuses interact, and above all as an appendix that does not relate directly to their fellows ideologically speaking the tertiary high, only indirectly and via the 'enemy'.

2. Among the many excellent works that give added insight into the Sicilian economy, we would like to mention as particularly significant Renée Rochefort, *Le travial en Sicile* (Paris: Presses Universitaires de France, 1961), Erling Bjøl, *Sol og Sult: Underutviklingens Problem i Italien* (Copenhagen: Institutet for Historie og Samfundsøkonomi, 1961), Danilo Dolci, *Spreco* (Torino: Einaudi, 1960) and his numerous other works and Joseph Lopreato, *Peasants No More: Social Class and Social Change in an Underdeveloped Society* (San Francisco: Chandler Publishing Company 1967). The works by Dolci and Lopreato have perspectives that point far outside economic analysis, but economic factors are nevertheless basic to theiranalyses.,

3. Perhaps the best work on the mafia is still E. J. Hobsbawn, *Primitive Rebels* (Manchester: Manchester University Press, 1959). See also Renato Candida, *Questa mafia* (Roma: Sciascia editore, 1960).

4. Strictly speaking, this is not quite true. Thus, the person who has migrated can still contribute to the village by means of his postal checks. But this type of participation is not likely to lead to innovation. It is the type of vicarious participation that improves the condition of the family left behind, within the existing order, but does not necessarily change that order. But then, one may say that a person devoted to his family can also be devoted to the village, which, of course, is true in general terms. However, if very limited leisure time is taken into consideration, and the limited amount of energy particularly in an underdeveloped society, then one sees more clearly how one type of allegiance may exclude another: the day simply does not have enough hours.

5. Thus, some of the differences encountered would not have been classified as significant by standard statistical reasoning — see 6.1, footnote 1. However, we would like to draw attention to another aspect of the analysis given. When differences have been encountered, we have often asked the question: How did these differences come about? In other words, which are the antecedent factors that can be said to have *caused* these differences? Many answers of that kind have been given, and we have essentially explained the same variance over and over again. But most answers have been given to a different type of question: Given these differences, what do they mean? What are the consequences of this rather than of distribution? In other words, our analysis has often been *functionl* rather than causal, but in general may be said to be both.

6. For another approach to the problem of ultrastability in this area, see the stimu-

lating study by Anton Blok, 'Land Reform in a West Sicilian Village: The Persistence of a Feudal Structure', *Anthropological Quarterly*, 1966, pp. 1–16. Blok, following Sjoberg, places the blame squarely on the elite, 'since it occupies a strategic position in the existing order it is able to veto any proposed change which could pose a threat to the *status quo* with which the privileged position of the elite is so closely linked' (p. 15). We agree, but hope also to have indicated that the elite has an anti-elite in the tertiary sector; but whereas the elite has a bridge-head further down in society, the anti-elite does not. Blok also mentions the mafia explicitly, but it is a very difficult analytical category to handle, since it, understandably, tries to evade empirical investigations of recruitment and leadership patterns, etc. But the mafia as an instrument of status quo is well described in Salvatore Palazzolo, *La Mafia* (Firenze: Parenti editore, 1959), pp. 29–31. Also, see N. Lewis, *The Honoured Society: Mafia Conspiracy Observed* (London: Collins, 1963) and his article on 'The Brotherhood of Violence', *The Sunday Times*, Dec. 18, 1960, p. 21.

The documentation by Danilo Dolci on the mafia is impressive, particularly because it goes much deeper than the usual concern with big crimes and big business, and down to mechanisms built into the social structure at the micro level, effectively impeding counter-action by the small and impoverished. See, for instance, Danilo Dolci and Franco Alasia, *Un fondamentale impedimento allo sviluppo democratico della Sicilia occidentale* (Partinico: Centro, 1965).

7.1.

1. In a sense this is the basic finding reported by Lopreato, op.cit., Chs. VIII and IX. Emigration leads to money in the form of remittances, this dissolves the threat of total *miseria* — and the inhabitants become *peasants no more. But what do they become?* Probably partners in a gigantic tertiarization explosion where they become dependent on the lords of the tertiary sector in the big cities, rather than on a combination of local primary and tertiary sector lords. The *Herr* changes name, but the *Knecht* is still a *Knecht*. We have difficulties sharing Lopreato's optimism in his concluding paragraph: '— — the southern Italian peasant has won a sense of security in relation to the present and the future as well'. The change is growth rather than development; it is difficult to see real autonomy and change of structure in this accumulation of remittances, not too different from their predecessor, the lottery ticket. In a sense this conclusion was unexpected, given Lopreato's excellent account of how the South always has been exploited.

   This general objection is also to some extent, but much less, valid in connection with the apparently excellent suggestions made by Michael Faber (*The Faber Report*, London: Danilo Dolci Trust): too many of them presuppose initiatives from the center, too few of them can be periphery-generated — in the way Danilo Dolci tries to work. But as a part of a periphery-generated demand they may be very meaningful — except the suggestion to let Italian aid to the Third World consist, in part, of 'tinned foodstuffs which have themselves been grown and processed in her own underdeveloped areas' (p. 75). Good for Sicily — but exactly the type of aid of which the even more underdeveloped areas of the world have had enough!

7.2.

1. A study by the late Arnold M. Rose, *Indagine sull'integrazione sociale in due quart- ieri di Roma* (Roma: Instituto di Statistica, Universita di Roma, 1959) has interesting findings from his investigations of the level of lower class associationism. He finds, among other things, that Communists have a wider circle of association contacts, but possibly of a less personal nature. Since Rose's Communists probably are well represented among our sensates, this is an optimistic finding for those who, like us, see lower class associations as an absolute necessity if the social structure is to be changed. See also Pier Paolo Benedetti, 'I circoli culturali in Italia', *Quaderni di Azione Sociale*, 1968, 2, pp. 3–15, and 'La funzione della città nei paesi in via di sviluppo', *Quaderni*, 1968, 3–4, pp. 333–52. I am indebted to Benedetti for stimulating criticism during the seminar organized by the Centro in Trappeto July-August 1968. The difficulty with the associationist perspective is only that this factor also favors the rich and mighty. Thus, Anna Anfossi has found a cor- relation between economic growth and associationism of the mafia type (presented in a seminar on development in Oslo, March 1964) — possibly due to a higher level of interconnectedness in the social structure. Where the state is weak the mafia will find an empty hole, a factor indirectly pointed to by Senator Wiley in connection with the fight against the American mafia: '— — other organizations (may also) think they are bigger than the state' (from F. Sondern, Jr., *Brotherhood of Evil: The Mafia* (New York; Bantom Books, 1959).

7.3.

1. A basic pattern here is, indeed, the dissolution of the village due to the penetration from the nation-state. In his lucid introduction to *Mediterranean Countrymen* (Paris: Mouton, 1963), Julian Pitt-Rivers makes the point that for the nation- state the administrative unit was, ultimately, the individual — not village as a corporation, the parilineal group or other collectives. The administrative structure of a nation-state based on the idea of the individual as a unit is compatible with liberal ideas of individualism and with relatively high mobility — destroying the fine structure of the village and accumulating individuals in the more amorphous collectivities known as cities. Thus, ultimately the nation-state presupposes the drainage of individuals from village to city.

7.4.

1. Since we have found so low correlations it is clear that much of the *conflict* is intra- personal rather than inter-personal and inter-group. Some implications of that will be explored in 7.4. below. But it should be pointed out that there is an im- portant research project hidden in this type of finding: *what are the psychological consequences of having to live with this type of ambivalence*. Of course, some of this may be an artifact brought into our analysis by our method, but not all — and it would constitute an interesting subject for a psychological investigation. In general it may, perhaps, be said that inter-group stability, to the point of the pernicious ultrastability that we have explored, has been bought at the expense of placing the conflict inside individuals instead of between them. What we have argued in this final section has been for the opposite pattern: relieve the individual of his indecision and bring the conflict out in the open.

APPENDIX: *The Questionnaire*

1. *As compared with today, how would you say the economic situation of this village was:*
   When your father was young?   worse   about the same   better   DK*
   Before the last war?   worse   about the same   better   DK
   Ten years ago?   worse   about the same   better   DK
                                              * Don't Know.

2. *And how do you think living conditions will be:*
   In ten years?   worse   about the same   better   DK
   When the children of today are grown up?   worse   about the same   better   DK
   A hundred years from now?   worse   about the same   better   DK

3. *How would you say this village compares with other regions as far as living conditions are concerned?*
   Near Palermo   worse   about the same   better   DK
   Near Agrigento   worse   about the same   better   DK
   Near Catania   worse   about the same   better   DK
   Calabria   worse   about the same   better   DK
   Africa   worse   about the same   better   DK
   France   worse   about the same   better   DK
   India   worse   about the same   better   DK

4. *What is the most important problem in this village?*

5. *Is there much extreme poverty in this village?*   Yes   No

6. *Is it possible to improve living conditions in this village?*   Yes   No
   What has to be done?

7. *Who has the power in this village? The priest, the mayor, the police, the rich, others?*
   The priest   The mayor   The police   The rich   Others   All of them together

8. *In your opinion, who ought to have more to say about things in general in a village?*
   A priest or a lawyer?   A lawyer or an engineer?
   An engineer or a physician?   A physician or a priest?
   A priest or an engineer?   A lawyer or a physician?

9. *What is better in your opinion:*
   To look out for oneself or to improve the life of one's own family?
   To improve the life of one's own family or to participate in religious activities?
   To participate in religious activities or to improve the living conditions of the village?
   To improve living conditions in the village or to look out for oneself?
   To look out for oneself or to participate in religious activities?
   To improve living conditions in the village or to improve the life of one's own family?

10. *How many years of school have you completed?*
    0   1   2   3   4   5   6   7   8   9   10   11   12   more

11. *Have you any vocational training?*   Yes   No

12. *Where have you learnt the most? At school, in the family, at work, in military service, or by yourself?*
At school   In the family   At work   In military service   By yourself
About the same amount from each of them

13. *What is your occupation?*   *What did your father do?*   *What would you like your son to be?*

Professional	Professional	Professional
Tradesman	Tradesman	Tradesman
Clerical worker (white collar)	Clerical worker (white collar)	Clerical worker (white collar)
Craftsman	Craftsman	Craftsman
Salaried craftsman	Salaried craftsman	Salaried craftsman
Industrial worker	Industrial worker	Industrial worker
Farmer	Farmer	Farmer
Farm hand	Farm hand	Farm hand
Day labourer	Day labourer	Day labourer
Retired, with a pension or on relief	Retired, with a pension or on relief	Retired, with a pension or on relief
Other	Other	Other

14. *Do you have regular work?*   Yes   No   *How many months a year?*

15. *How would you say the economic conditions of your own family today compare with the situation of your family:*

When you were born?	worse	about the same	better	DK
Five years ago? (your own family)	worse	about the same	better	DK
In five years? (your own family)	worse	about the same	better	DK

16. *Have you ever travelled?*   *Where?*   *How many times?*

To Palermo?	never	once	more than once	(military service)
To Agrigento?	never	once	more than once	(military service)
To Catania?	never	once	more than once	(military service)
In Italy?	never	once	more than once	(military service)
Abroad?	never	once	more then once	(military service)

17. *If you had a choice, where would you most like to live? Here or elsewhere?*
In this house
In another part of this province
In another house in this village
In another part of Sicily
In Italy   In Europe   In the United States   Elsewhere   No matter where

18. *Have you ever tried to move? Do you think it would be possible?*
No, because I do not want to
No, because it is not possible
Yes, I have tried, but in vain
Yes, I am trying, but do not believe in it
Yes, I am trying, and I believe that I shall succeed

300

19. *During the last week, how often have you:*

Read a newspaper?	never	once	twice	more than twice	do not know how to read
Read a weekly?	never	once	twice	more than twice	do not know how to read
Listened to the radio?	never	once	twice	more than twice	it is not possible
Watched TV?	never	once	twice	more than twice	it is not possible
Gone to a movie?	never	once	twice	more than twice	it is not possible
Been to church?	never	once	twice	more than twice	it is not possible

20. *What do you prefer to read in the papers?*
International news   National news   Local news   Sport figures   I never read

21. *What do you most like to listen to on the radio?*
News   Music   Sport   Shows   I never listen

22. *In what year were you born?*

23. *Where were you born?*

In this house	In this village	In this province
In Sicily	In Italy	Abroad

24. *How old were you when you were married?*   widow   widower

25. *How old was your wife when you were married?*

26. *Where was she born?*

In this house	In this village	In this province
In Sicily	In Italy	Abroad

27. *How many children do you have?* (living and dead)

28. *What is the age of the youngest child?*

29. *At which age do you think a man should marry?   A woman?*

30. *How many children should a family have in your opinion?*

31. *How many relatives are now living with you in the same house?*

32. *Where do the other relatives, both yours and your wife's, live?*
In this village   In this province   In Sicily   In Italy   Abroad

33. *How many rooms are there in your home?* (counting all rooms)

34. *Is there running water?*　　Yes　　　No

35. *Do you have animals in the house?*　　*Which?*
　　No　　Cow　　Mule　　Horse　　Goat　　Sheep　　Hen　　Other

36. *What do you think about this interview?*

　　Village　　　　　　　　　　　Number
　　Interviewer　　　　　　　　　Evaluation of contact:
　　　　　　　　　　　　　　　　insufficient　　medium　　good

Note :　In cases where more than one family live in the same house, indicate which
　　　　family was interviewed; for instance the one downstairs, to the right, etc.